ESSENTIAL ISSUES IN SYMBOLIC INTERACTION

STUDIES IN SYMBOLIC INTERACTION

Series Editors: Norman K. Denzin and Shing-Ling S. Chen

Recent Volumes:

Volume 35	Studies in Symbolic Interaction
Volume 36	Blue Ribbon Papers: Interactionism: The Emerging Landscape
Volume 37	Studies in Symbolic Interaction
Volume 38	Blue Ribbon Papers: Behind the Professional Mask: The Self-Revelations of Leading Symbolic Interactionists
Volume 39	Studies in Symbolic Interaction
Volume 40	40th Anniversary of Studies in Symbolic Interaction
Volume 41	Radical Interactionism on the Rise
Volume 42	Revisiting Symbolic Interaction in Music Studies and New Interpretive Works
Volume 43	Symbolic Interaction and New Social Media
Volume 44	Contributions from European Symbolic Interactionists: Reflections on Methods
Volume 45	Contributions from European Symbolic Interactionists: Conflict and Cooperation
Volume 46	The Astructural Bias Charge
Volume 47	Symbolic Interactionist Takes on Music
Volume 48	Oppression and Resistance: Structure, Agency, and Transformation
Volume 49	Carl J. Couch and the Iowa School: In His Own Words and in Reflection
Volume 50	The Interaction Order
Volume 51	Conflict and Forced Migration
Volume 52	Radical Interactionism and Critiques of Contemporary Culture
Volume 53	Studies in Symbolic Interaction
Volume 54	Subcultures
Volume 55	Festschrift in Honor of Norman K. Denzin: He Knew His Song Well
Volume 56	Festschrift in Honor of Kathy Charmaz
Volume 57	Festschrift in Honor of David R. Maines
Volume 58	Symbolic Interaction and Inequality

STUDIES IN SYMBOLIC INTERACTION VOLUME 59

ESSENTIAL ISSUES IN SYMBOLIC INTERACTION

EDITED BY

NORMAN K. DENZIN (DECEASED)
University of Illinois at Urbana Champaign, USA

AND

SHING-LING S. CHEN
University of Northern Iowa, USA

United Kingdom – North America – Japan
India – Malaysia – China

Emerald Publishing Limited
Emerald Publishing, Floor 5, Northspring, 21-23 Wellington Street, Leeds LS1 4DL

First edition 2024

British Library Cataloguing in Publication Data
A catalogue record for this book is available from the British Library

ISBN: 978-1-83608-377-1 (Print)
ISBN: 978-1-83608-376-4 (Online)
ISBN: 978-1-83608-378-8 (Epub)

ISSN: 0163-2396 (Series)

Printed and bound by CPI Group (UK) Ltd, Croydon, CR0 4YY

CONTENTS

ABOUT THE CONTRIBUTORS

Mehmet Bicakci is an academic and educator, renowned for his works in gifted education, giftedness, and underachievement within the sphere of educational psychology. His research is primarily dedicated to comprehending and augmenting the educational experiences of gifted students. It spans an array of subjects, including the impacts of labeling, individual personality traits, cultural orientations, and intervention strategies tailored to address underachievement among gifted individuals. He is currently working as a PhD researcher at Friedrich-Alexander University in Germany.

Gary Alan Fine is the James E. Johnson Professor of Sociology at Northwestern University. He has been a member of the Society for the Study of Symbolic Interaction since 1975 and has served as the President and as an editor of the journal *Symbolic Interaction*. He is a recipient of the organization's Cooley, Mead, and Lopata awards. He writes frequently about symbolic interaction theory in light of local sociology, as in his recent book *The Hinge: Civil Society, Group Cultures, and the Power of Local Commitments*.

Zeynep Melis Kirgil is an Assistant Professor at the Department of Organization Studies at Tilburg University. Her research focuses on societal transitions and behavior change at different levels of analysis. She investigates how collective intentionality affects cooperation and solidarity on the micro, meso, and macro level. In another line of research, Kirgil studies leadership and governance in times of crisis via computational and qualitative text analysis. Moreover, she is currently interested in gender norms over time and across different social spheres.

Krzysztof T. Konecki is a Professor of Sociology and works at the Institute of Sociology, Faculty of Economics and Sociology, University of Lodz. He is the Editor-in-Chief of *Qualitative Sociology Review*, a member of the Board of the Polish Sociological Association, and the Committee of Sociology of the Polish Academy of Science. He recently published *The Meaning of Contemplation for Social Qualitative Research. Applications and Examples*. London, NY: Routledge, 2022.

Robert Perinbanayagam has taught at Hunter College of the City University of New York for several years and recently retired from it. He is the author of *Signifying Acts*, *Discursive Acts*, *Games and Sport in Everyday Life*, and *The Presence of Self*, which won the theory prize given by the theory section of the American Sociological Association and the Cooley Award from the Society for the Study of Symbolic Interaction. The latter society also conferred the G.H. Mead award for distinguished contribution to the field of interactional studies.

Joel O. Powell recently completed two terms on the Minnesota Board of Peace Officer Standards and Training. He is currently the Professional Peace Officer Education Coordinator at Minnesota State University Moorhead.

Cirus Rinaldi is an Associate Professor of Sociology of Law, Deviance, and Social Change in the Department of Cultures and Societies of the University of Palermo, Italy, where he also coordinates the "Bodies, Rights and Conflicts" Research Group. His research explores deviance theory, sociological theories of sexuality, male sex work, and LGBTQI+ issues. He is the author of the books *Sesso, Sè e Società. Per una sociologia delle sessualità* (2016), *Uomini che si fanno pagare: Genere, identità e sessualità nel sex work maschile tra devianza e nuove forme di normalizzazione* (2020), and "Sex and Sexuality," in *The Oxford Handbook of Symbolic Interactionism* (2024) in addition to many journal articles and contributions to edited collections.

Douglas P. Schrock is a Professor of Sociology at Florida State University. He has published research on many topics, including the transgender community and movement, violent men and intervention programs, and Donald Trump and his supporters. Much of his works addresses gender, sexuality, race, and class and focuses on culture and identity, emotion and embodiment, and personal and social change. What ties his works together is an enduring interest in how interactionism can help us better understand how inequality is reproduced and challenged.

David Schweingruber is an Associate Professor of Sociology at Iowa State University. He earned his PhD in Sociology from the University of Illinois at Urbana-Champaign. He has published research on internal conversations, the organization of door-to-door salespersons, engagement proposals, protest policing, family violence, introduction to sociology textbooks, and Internet addiction as a social problem. He teaches large sections of Introduction to Sociology. He is the 2022 winner of the Helena Lopata Mentoring Excellence Award given by the Society for the Study of Symbolic Interaction.

Eric O. Silva (PhD, University of California, Davis) is a Professor in the Department of Sociology and Anthropology at Georgia Southern University. He studies how actors construct reality in contentious situations. His substantive cases include Donald Trump, immigration, creationism, sports teams' use of Native American imagery, vaccines, and genetically modified organisms.

Andrea Voyer is a Docent and Associate Senior Lecturer in the Department of Sociology at Stockholm University. Andrea's research focuses on inequality associated with ethnicity, class, gender, and migration. She draws on two main theoretical foundations: Civil Sphere Theory, which emphasizes the symbolic social construction of the collective solidarity on the idea of shared values and morality; and Goffman's microsociological and symbolic interactionist theorizing on the significance of practical everyday behaviors. Her research has been funded by the Russell Sage Foundation, the US National Science Foundation, and the Swedish Research Council.

David W. Wahl, PhD, ABS, is an Assistant Professor of Sociology and Criminology at McMurry University and a board-certified sexologist. As a professor and a researcher, Dr Wahl's work focuses on issues of sex, gender, sexuality, sexual violence, human trafficking, and sex work.

FORWARD: AN ISSUE FOR A GENERAL SOCIOLOGY

Joel O. Powell

Minnesota State University, USA

ABSTRACT

This volume answers a call by the late David Maines for forums to showcase symbolic interactionism. Eight papers in this volume answer Maines' call by illustrating the value of interactionist approaches, defining and describing directions for research. Exploring a broad range of topics including accounts, identity, sex work, and yoga, the eight studies show the breadth and innovation that Maines saw as crucial to a general sociology.

Keywords: Symbolic interaction; David Maines; critical interactionism; accounts; Gerda Walther

Volume 57 of *Studies in Symbolic Interaction,* was Shing-Ling S. Chen's labor of respect for the life and career of David Maines. This volume, Volume 59, also salutes Maines. A formidable advocate for the interactionist project, Maines often called for forums and compendiums that would showcase symbolic interactionism as the best hope for a general sociology. He found this aspiration witnessing the many clumsy attempts of sociologists to reinvent concepts refined for decades by interactionist researchers. Because of a failure to genuinely engage with interactionism, Maines argued, the interactionist perspective is caricatured as a dissident, qualitative school limited to observations in microworlds (Maines, 2001; See also Schrock, this volume). Without irony, he observed that sociology is becoming more mature in the unreflective adoption of interactionist precepts.

Eight papers in this issue answer calls from Maines to illustrate the value of interactionist approaches by defining and describing directions for research. While none of these efforts will provide a definitive framework, each is a fine specimen of investigation, commentary, and speculation. Their common threads are bright. Society is enacted, so action and joined activity are always processes for study. People interpret one another as individuals and in their togetherness.

Essential Issues in Symbolic Interaction
Studies in Symbolic Interaction, Volume 59, 1–5

Published under exclusive licence by Emerald Publishing Limited
ISSN: 0163-2396/doi:10.1108/S0163-239620240000059001

Language is central to these processes. It is impossible to separate society from the individual, the individual from society, or micro- and macro-cosmic social worlds. While the research sites in these works range from sex work to yoga, and the topics from mind, to motive, to identity, to collective behavior, all examine the facts of people doing things together.

This action orientation is often counter-intuitive. People tend to see themselves and others as collections of traits or features that are mostly unchanging. In a courageous ethnography of male sex workers, Cirus Rinaldi rejects such a common sense, essentialist orientation. Sexuality is not a state of being, but an active, improvisational process. Rinaldi emphasizes the agency in becoming sexual in social contexts rather than the condition of being sexual. This permits scrutiny of crucial symbolic features of sexual orientation and activity. Much can be lost and gained in navigating the complex worlds of work, sex, and masculinity. The map and compass are vocabularies of motive, with which the sex worker guides others away from stigmatizing conclusions. The sex worker flounders in common sense understandings that men having sex with men means being gay or somehow less than masculine. In the examination of motive talk, Rinaldi pulls together the phenomena of individual agency and traumatic cultural pressures on self-definition.

The nebulous cultural definitions that people must manage reside alongside sharp, institutional labels that are no less essentialist, but carry additional scientific credence. Mehmet Bicacki explains how the psychological label of "gifted underachiever" fails to account for variations in context and the different ways in which people manage self-definition. Children may or may not see themselves as underachievers, but the definitions and experiences of underachieving are decidedly social. For example, students may deliberately underachieve to avoid stigma or garner acceptance. They can resist or accept definitions with a variety of accounts. Moreover, once the label of giftedness emerges and is widely available, many actors (along with the gifted ones) develop vocabularies of motive to explain the behavior of self and others. Institutional responses become selective and exclusive. Gifted educational programs could certainly be made available to everyone, but the privileges as well as the stigmas are reserved for children who have been matched with their definition. This happens, as Bicacki observes, in a field where definition and measurement are entirely problematic. So, the pointed, clinical estimation of the child takes on the appearance of objective assessment.

The paper in this volume taking the most direct approach to accounts is Eric Silva's discussion of United States (US) political culture. Accounts and stigma are conspicuous in political discourse, particularly in the "culture wars." In the hyper-mediated national conversation, people are confronted with more demands to account for their political views. Accounts for political worldviews are readily available – often as threadbare distortions of the views of the other – and arguments for why one political standpoint should dominate will simplify and satirize other views. But actors choose vocabularies and modify them in countless ways. By considering the construction of political reality as an act of agency, Silva resists the tendency to present US political strife as a simple struggle between right and left. Instead, Silva calls for deeper explorations of phenomena such as agreement across factions, intrafactional conflict, and the "dialogic ways opponents influence each other."

***

Perhaps the ease with which modern sociologists have dismissed interactionism as microcosmic stems from interactionist attempts to understand the self. Self seems a plain, assumed, even trivial piece of the human experience compared to theorizing geo-politics, world-economies, or social history. But the interactionist starting point for understanding self is that it is a developing social structure. More importantly, self does not exist except that it is minded, situated among others, and acting in and on society. David Schweingruber and David Wahl recognize this seamless joining of self and society and present a minded-self that moves in concert with the social world. They ask whether investigating internal conversations will help sociologists to understand society. Of course, it will. In the dialog with self, society is formulated and applied to immediate problems, plans for the future, reconstructions of the past, and vagrant daydreams. Scweingruber and Wahl are not content with these assumptions, however reasonable. They call for a systematic study of internal conversations and offer innovative methods for accessing continuing internal narratives.

Krzysztof Konecki notes that a minded self is also an embodied self. In an intriguing and detailed study of doing yoga, Konecki finds that bodily action in the company of others reveals minded selves to one another. Konecki's insight is inspired by Merleau Ponty in a compelling (and comforting) observation that the minds of others are not really hidden. This view of intersubjectivity through shared corporeal experiences is a reminder of the importance of phenomenological thought to the interactionist project, and harks back to a reappraisal of Husserl and Schutz by 20th century interactionists. It is a reminder, too, of the fundamental pluralism of interactionist thought. There is no definably human body, mind, or self that is not tethered to the company of others.

Robert Perinbanayagam considers another seemingly individualistic phenomenon, identity, and unites self and society with a grammar of naming. After reviewing extensive interactionist work on identity and providing several pertinent illustrations, Perinbanayagam concludes that identities are not only a set of socially provided names but also a complex dialectic of lumping and splitting (See also Zeerubavel, 1996) or a "unity of opposition." The Black American is not white, but also is not German. Here the simple example reveals that the grammar of identity is situational. However, the acknowledgment of identity is not a passive process. Instead, identity is a dynamic "from which one draws the rhetoric of motives that leads to the selected acts of the agent." Perinbanayagam shows the relevance of this with a stark reference to the murder of George Floyd. As onlookers pleaded with Derek Chauvin to release a suffocating George Floyd, Chauvin remained committed to an identity and course of action that resulted in Floyd's death. As Perinbanayagam observes, Chauvin's identity moved his acts, while at the same time his acts "nourished" his identity.

These works on accounts, selves, and identities may herald the promise of a critical interactionism. Douglas Schrock is content that many different interactionist approaches can flow into a critical project so long as they explore power and inequality. All the phenomena explored in this book are germane because power and domination involve bodies, minds, and identities. And Schrock sees the potential for understanding power in the interactionist commitment to "power as constituted by what people do together, how such actions shape what happens elsewhere, and the consequences for unequal relations." In contrast to Foucault's translucent view of power as determining relations, or the Exchange theorists' simplistic understanding of dependency, this transactional standpoint emphasizes power as a social accomplishment. Ultimately Shrock's hope is for an interactionism that breaks through the barriers of misunderstanding identified by Maines by consciously demonstrating its relevance to understanding systemic oppressions.

***

One feature of Mead's philosophy that endures in all interactionist thought and research is a pluralistic approach to mind, self, and society. Centuries of dualistic and monistic thinking were not adequate to a science that asked questions about mutual understanding, collective activity, and intersubjectivity. Understanding the connections of one to another is vital to any apprehension of the human condition.

In their article on collective intentionality, Zeynep Melis Kirgil, Andrea Voyer, and Gary Alan Fine revisit problems of mutuality and cooperation by rejecting a dualistic conception of self and other. They concentrate on the sense of collective membership that is felt by people acting in concert. While much of early social behaviorism focused on the mechanics of joined activity, such as how people divine what kinds of objects they are in a situation, Kirgl, Voyer, and Fine attend to the experiences of sharing intentions, objectives, and sensibilities sufficient for large social arrangements such as community. They credit the work of Gerda Walther as first and right on the matter of community life. Walther showed the way to understanding that people are joined by empathy and a meta-understanding that they are apprehending their situations in similar ways. This early formulation anticipates the work of Couch (1995) and his associates (Miller et al., 1975) who identified reciprocity and mutuality at the core of cooperative action – as people actively form social objectives based upon a shared focus of attention.

Kirgl, Voyer, and Fine do a real service to sociology with their continuing inquiries into the work of Gerda Walther and also in their call for research and analysis in the meso-domain. In communities, the people who are experiencing life together exist at the weld of grand social forces, intimate understandings, and unique social experiences. These things are inseparable, and Kirgl, Voyer, and Fine rightly insist that they be studied together.

***

David Maines observed that the accumulation of knowledge in sociology was inhibited by a lack of awareness of the theories and frames of knowledge in which sociologists were working. His particular concern was for the absence of engagement with interactionist research and commentary across a broad range of topics. He did his best to create opportunities for dialogue. This volume of *Studies* continues that effort.

REFERENCES

Couch, C. J. (1995). Presidential address: Let us rekindle the passion by constructing a Robust science of the social. *The Sociological Quarterly*, *36*(1), 1–14.

Maines, D. R. (2001). *The faultline of consciousness: A view of interactionism in sociology*. Aldine de Gruyter.

Miller, D. E., Hintz, R., & Couch, C. J. (1975). The elements and structure of openings. *The Sociological Quarterly*, *16*(4), 479–499.

Zeerubavel, E. (1996). Lumping and splitting: Notes on social classification. *Sociological Forum*, *11*(3), 421–433.

MALE SEX WORKING AS SEXUAL SCRIPTING: A SYMBOLIC INTERACTIONIST ACCOUNT

Cirus Rinaldi

University of Palermo, Italy

ABSTRACT

This chapter aims to outline the ways in which symbolic interactionism shifts the focus of inquiry into sex from being sexual *toward* becoming sexual, *which takes into account* doing *sexualities, rather than tracing their origins in a static conception of nature. This means that our being sexual varies according to the rituals and performances in which we are involved as part of our daily lives. Such is the case any time we perform a role to communicate our identity to one or more audiences from communicative, expressive, aesthetic, and verbal points of view. This process is particularly manifest in male sex working where social actors are involved in the use of excuses, justifications and, generally, motive talk that are useful to neutralize their own sexual conducts and negotiate the gender appearance and sexual practices. Using the late developments of sexualities' symbolic interactionist studies emphasized by sexual scripts theory, the chapter focuses on the theoretical necessity to understand that there are far more* reasons *to be sexual than* ways *to be sexual.*

Keywords: Male sex working; masculinities; sexual scripts; becoming sexual; sexual career

INTRODUCTION

The actual existence of a biological substratum, of impulses and physiological traits undoubtedly allows the construction of bodily and sexual experiences; however, these take full meaning only if they defined in *sexual terms* within social interactions and contexts. An *impulse* – any kind impulse – "works" as long as it

Essential Issues in Symbolic Interaction
Studies in Symbolic Interaction, Volume 59, 7–28

Published under exclusive licence by Emerald Publishing Limited
ISSN: 0163-2396/doi:10.1108/S0163-239620240000059002

can be *specifically named*, as long as it becomes the object of interpretative processes of experiences common to a specific group and, therefore, endowed with symbolic meanings.

In his seminal work, *The Philosophy of the Act*, George Herbert Mead following Dewey, rejected the behaviorist one-dimensional stimulus–response scheme favored by most behaviorists, in which stimulus and response were considered isolable events independent from the process that bonds the organism to its environment. Following Mead's ideas about the four stages of the act (impulse, perception, manipulation and consummation), the (sexual) act may be considered not as a linear and deterministic process, but mainly as a line of actions through which we shape and comprehend our own world (Mead, 1938).

If the biological dimension is a "brute fact," natural and immutable, why is it that every culture in every different historical time has attributed different meanings to sex – codifying and regulating sexualities in very different ways? Since our sexual organs themselves do not seem to have changed conspicuously in the last few centuries, why do sexual practices assume a high degree of variability? Our sexual existence only becomes meaningful as far as it is experienced in the form of symbolic communication (Gecas & Libby, 1976). Our sphincters and genital organs do not possess any trans-historical significance nor can sexual practices be regarded as trans-cultural manifestations, or sexual desires, which cannot be explained on the basis of constant motivations in every period of time and across every culture (Gagnon, 1999).We do indeed attribute meanings to impulses, stimuli and sensations that, although they are regularly considered as *objective and universal* characteristics, they have *different meanings* depending on the group considered, the cultural context, or different historical periods. We learn to attribute meanings to the stimuli we are *subjected* to, and we *learn* to feel effects in relation to physiological urges, drives, or desires. Obviously, perceptual organs *do* exist materially, but the same arousal is activated within cultural and symbolic contexts. We are able to interpret a "symptom" (*erection*) and give it a certain meaning in order to "feel something" or to be able to "do something" (*orgasm*) only when we have learned to respond to specific stimuli and learned a series of techniques, of modalities, related to *what to feel and how to enjoy*, not only in relation to our "desires" and "fantasies," but also because *we know how to stimulate ourselves properly, we know how to identify the effects and how to feel fulfilled and for what are the reasons and relative purposes* (which often they have nothing to do with specifically sexual matters).

Our sexual conducts are formed and directed according to our inner culturally defined experience: individuals must understand what is happening (they must be able to "name" their sensations, their own actions, those of others, and give a prompt response) (Rinaldi, 2016). They refer to "scripts," to metaphorical and dramaturgical dimensions that support human sociosexual actions (Gagnon & Simon, 1973).

Whereas "essentialist" or "naturalist" perspectives view sex/sexuality as something "given," as a set of immutable, "natural," fixed characteristics (Weeks, 1985), symbolic interaction(ism) engages with the idea that human sexuality is fundamentally unstable and variable. By definition, "sex" is the effect of society and of culture, one of many variables which are the effect of different arrangements and structures (like, for instance, gender, age, class, ethnicity, ability, etc.) – it is one element interconnected with many other factors defining society. Interactionist analysis allows us to grasp the full range of human sexualities as the result of the production, organization, negotiation, and transformation processes that occur in the social realm (Plummer, 2002, p. 1).

Since symbolic interactionism is mostly concerned with analyzing language and its capacity to typify, to classify, and to share experiences and events, it pays particular attention to the social reality of social-sexual worlds, conceived as the result of social interaction and negotiation, as well as of the *production of meanings*. This means that our being sexual varies according to the rituals and performances in which we are involved as part of our daily lives. Such is the case any time we perform a role to communicate our sexual identity and desire to one or more audiences from communicative, expressive, aesthetic, and verbal points of view. It follows that, like other spheres of social life, sexuality is based on a performative imperative and specific sexual scripts that make our socio-sexual actions accountable (Garfinkel, 1967).

Male sex workers who identify themselves as "straight" are potentially stigmatized individuals and are involved in "identity work" (Snow & Anderson, 1987) aiming to neutralize sexual stigma that derives from having sex with other men and to regain their "masculine" status. As we will discuss later, the analysis of sex workers' accounts will show that there are more *reasons* to be sexual than *ways* to be sexual (Simon & Gagnon, 1986).

SYMBOLIC INTERACTIONISM AND THE (HIDDEN) STUDY OF SEXUALITIES

The predicament of symbolic interactionism is that we develop a specific language, a series of names, and meanings defined as "sexual" that we employ to talk about and label a particular set of sensations, situations, subjects, and traits (Gecas & Libby, 1976). Symbolic interactionism developed within the work of the pragmatists at the Chicago School in the 1920s. The idea of *process* and of the possibility of multiple forms that a single process can take is central to symbolic interactionism. It follows that, as a theory, symbolic interactionism is concerned with the interactions, forms of adjustment, and the mutual influences between social actors and *environment(s)*, where both human and social life are seen as *emerging processes* (Mead, 1934). Key thinkers of this tradition, including George H. Mead and Robert E. Park, never dealt specifically with issues of sexuality; others, like William I. Thomas, produced works that touched on this subject tangentially, drawing from secondary sources mostly borrowed from anthropology that presented rather stereotyped notions of gender differences (Thomas, 1907). It is only in recent times that the role of the Chicago School has been reassessed, shedding light on its contribution to urban studies more generally, and specifically to understanding the city as "sexual laboratory" (Heap, 2003, p. 459), as well as to the study of sexual subcultures (Heap, 2009; Mumford, 1997; Rubin, 2002). In addition to unpublished research and reports, in their canonical texts the

Chicago School group has tended to focus more or less explicitly on sexual themes, though they did so within a moralist and pathologizing framework that ultimately failed to broaden the scope of a theory of sexualities in a meaningful way.[1] Having said this, the group never really treated the subject of sex without bespeaking their prudish discomfort, arguably springing from their position inside the academy, and from the predominant views on sexuality within the studies of the time, which focused exclusively on exploring (and condemning) social deviance. There are few exceptions. Florian Znaniecki in a paper he presented at the first International Congress for Sexual Research (Berlin, 10–16 October 1926) argued that "a sexual act is a social act when it bears upon a human being as its object and tends to provoke a conscious reaction of this being" (Znaniecki, 1927, p. 222), hence taking into account a series of strictly regulated activities. E. W. Burgess argued that human sexuality, unlike that of animals which remained the product of instincts, was the result of attitudes and values emerging from particular groups and social environments (Burgess, 1949); while Herbert Blumer in a review of *Sexual behavior in the human male* of Alfred C. Kinsey and colleagues (Kinsey et al., 1948) criticized the authors' exclusive focus on quantitative data, since they were interested into the mere distribution of sexual outlets and the biological occurrences of orgasm (Blumer, 1948). By doing so, Blumer believed that these authors were failing to consider that orgasm should be placed within a "framework of social definition and social practice" in order to grasp its social nature, while also allowing to recognize its different meanings according to specific situation. At the beginning of the Fifties, Manford H. Kuhn from the quantitative interactionist school of Iowa suggested that sexual actions, not unlike any other type of actions, are more carefully understood as social objects that determine the range of responses by social actors. Actors apply a predefined vocabulary of meanings based on the particular group to which they belong, as well as on the language and sexual motives borrowed from their own social roles. This also explains why meanings cannot be fully comprehended through the mere application of physiological factors to account for sexuality (Kuhn, 1954, p. 123).

SEXUAL SCRIPTING THEORY

Gagnon and Simon's work (1973) improved American Pragmatism by uniting a number of approaches. Their work led to a major change in sociological inquiry, through shifting the analytical framework of research on human sexuality away from biological, psychological, and medical approaches. Specifically, the two authors replaced the idea(s) of impulses and physiological activities which were typical of a bio-medical approach with that of *symbolic actions*. In other words, sexuality was no longer seen as "independent variable" but rather, as a "dependent" one, influenced by social categories, such as age, gender, class, ethnicity, sexual orientation, etc. For Gagnon and Simon, there are three distinct types of sexual scripts: first, *cultural scripts*, which refer to orientations, maps of instructions, and repertoires of meanings available in social life guiding individuals toward a suitable choice of specific roles to perform within a given relationship. Second, *interpersonal scripts* refer to the ways in which individual apply a certain cultural scenario based on a specific cultural of interactional context or situation. Finally, the so-called *intrapsychic scripts* conjure the desiring dimensions of subjects' intimate lives. Sexual conduct therefore results from the combination of the three kinds of scripts. However, for the most part, a certain relationship can be considered satisfactory only to the extent that it employs specific cultural codes as defined by cultural scripts. Although it is possible to proceed with an analytical definition of sexual scripts, each script is interrelated with the others. The theory of sexual scripts thus allows exploring subjects' own organization and building of individual sexual meanings and behaviors. Rather than merely responding to physiological and sexual sensations, subjects are motivated by their own symbolic system, which plays a fundamental role in the social organization of their sexual experience. The theory of sexual scripts has been subject to criticism on several grounds. Some have argued against its lack of consideration for more structural issues (Green, 2008); others have claimed that it does not adequately consider, for instance, the difficulties in predicting intrapsychic scripts due to the changing nature of people's desires (Green, 2014, p. 52); still others have added that this indeterminacy also extends to the possibility that unexpected sexual meanings may occur (Walby, 2012, Chapter 2, pp. 28–31). Despite this criticisms, sexual scripts nonetheless have offered a deeper understanding of the fact that there are more reasons to be sexual than ways of being sexual (Simon & Gagnon, 1986). Furthermore, the theory of sexual script has made it possible to move beyond what can be viewed as more simplistic aspects typical of a Freudian approach to sexuality that either naturalizes the sexual or sees it as the founding aspect of social behavior, while failing to consider that "social roles are not vehicles for the expression of sexual impulse but that sexuality becomes a vehicle for expressing the needs of social roles" (Gagnon & Simon, 1973, p. 33). Following from what has been discussed so far, the theory of sexual scripting shares a series of common traits with symbolic interactionism, including the following: (a) sexual meanings originate in our social interactions and that we learn about them and how to use them through others, not through our individual experiences; (b) sexual meanings are neither static nor are they assigned to things, people and objects once and for all, but rather, they change much like our perceptions of them; (c) the attribution of sexual meanings is not an automatic action, but rather, it is always the result of a self-reflexive and interpretative process, which also involves creativity; (d) we are always positioned within interactions soliciting our search for the "correct sexual meaning" of events, which is also the most appropriate in terms of context; (e) individuals become fully human through interacting with others; furthermore, becoming sexual is part of the development of the social self, of communicative processes, and of the forms of social organization; (f) all kinds of behavior, including sexual conduct, is the result of instincts, urges, and objects that we find in our environment, as well as of the definitions we use to describe them; (g) we refer to a set of rules and ways of feeling; not only do they allow us to frame our actions as members of a particular group within the context of the available cultural models but also they provide us with a repertoire of feelings that may be seen as desirable in a particular context; (h) it follows that our shaping of sexual behaviors is not based exclusively on physiological and biological impulses; rather, it emerges from the different contexts in which we are involved, as well as from the very processes of building, negotiating, and establishing the meaning of a certain situation with others.

TALKING SEX, BECOMING SEXUAL, AND HAVING SEX: SCRIPTING DESIRE

The two authors, in particular Gagnon, start from a general idea that, in its simplicity, challenged most of the essentialist analyses that had dominated the bio-psycho-social sphere until then: human beings are born sexual (that is, they have a chromosomal, gonadal, genetic and, therefore, biological make-up, although these dimensions often take on a normative character), and only within symbolic-cultural systems and through the symbolic mediation processes involved, they become sexual. In fact, we are born within a social context that provides us with cultural and sexual repertoires, *scripts* that we learn to use and a series of meanings that we use to *state* ourselves sexual, to *define* others sexual, and to understand when we *do* or *something* sexual happens to us, in order to *feel* in a sexual way. *So we do not become sexual all at once or once and for all.* Rather, we find ourselves within a *process of becoming* that we believe is illusorily dependent on the sex we *have* or *are*, but instead it is, in reality strongly conditioned by our gender, our ethno-racial group, our social class, our moral and religious beliefs, our education, etc.

Among the various influences of *sexual scripts*, as we can see from the reflections just enunciated, a significant place is given to the symbolic interactionism, to the extent that sexuality does not possess any intrinsic meaning but emerges within interactional and interpretational processes (Blumer, 1969), where language is also considered a "symbolic action." In fact, the processes underlying the naming, defining and communicating of sexuality contribute not only *to shaping it but also to creating it*: for instance, when we speak about sexuality to minors or instruct them with a specific "vocabulary of sexual motives," contributing to construct, directly or indirectly, their experience of the sexual (Gagnon & Simon, 1973). *Becoming sexual* means, above all, learning beliefs, representations, preferences, evaluation systems and practices, taking on specific roles and *vocabularies* within a process of sexual socialization that will last throughout our lives.

"Sexual talk"– "Talking Sex" – Sexual Motives and Vocabularies

As well as sexuality, which is constructed on the basis of meanings that are not purely sexual, language also does not rely exclusively on sexuality to produce and communicate sexual meanings: people, in fact, through the use of words in their interactions do not simply create the construction of their sexual identity but *do many other things* (Cameron & Kulick, 2006). When *we say and do* sexuality, we may want to reproduce gender and power asymmetries ("you're a female, you can't stay late at night!"), or enact forms of domination, violence ("I know you like it, shut up, and let me enjoy it!"), or producing love and intimacy ("doing it with you it's different, I've never felt the same way before"), or imposing bodily and racial stratifications ("black hookers like it, they never say no to you"), or displaying our social status and class affiliation ("you go after that one, she's a slut, she's not for you!"), etc. Through language, social actors understand what they do or should do while having sex; the words also allow us to think about what *is sexually possible, normal, or desirable* (Cameron & Kulick, 2006, p. 12).

As Mills points out, we use *vocabularies of motives* that are words, phrases and rhetoric that make our behaviors appear appropriate in different situations.

The individuals expressing or imputing motives are not merely describing their actions, or providing motives, but they are retrieving new reasons that will mediate their action: *their rationalization functions as a new social action* (Burke, 1965; Mills, 1940).

When using a certain type of "discourse of motives," we can intercept the sympathetic resonance of groups, categories of people, or the communities. We can be "understood" because we find ourselves using the same lexicons and cultural repertoires or because we use specific *motives* shared by the listeners. Our socioeconomic status or other characteristics (such as sexual orientation, gender, religion or ethno-racial characteristics) might allow us to appear in the eyes of others as a legitimate member ("After all, he's a good guy!"). In this way, according to Mills' (1940) indications, when subjects explain or justify what they have done, they are simultaneously accepting a set of reasons that can interpret that specific situation or circumstance, using vocabularies of motives that correspond to a specific historical time and social structure. Vocabularies of motives provide *accounts*, such as description and explanations that we can use to remedy broken interactions, inappropriate, questionable or improper actions.

They are *set* linguistic tools, used whenever our actions are subject to evaluation or to avoid potential conflict when we find ourselves bridging the potentially created gap between actions performed and social expectations (Lyman & Scott, 1970). Similarly, we are socialized within cultural contexts that provided us with "vocabulary of sexual motifs" – which we are expected to learn, indirectly or directly, implicitly or explicitly, and, of course, also to reject. This vocabulary is not necessarily associated with a specific sexual activity, but it has also contributed to educate us to a series of analogies, associations, and meanings even before we come into material contact with sexuality.

For instance, we can think of all the vernacular and vulgar expressions we have heard or hear at school, in the street, or written on walls, that have a useable value regardless of their use in concrete sexual situations (which anticipate most of the dominant social values). A teenage girl's apparent emancipated sexuality, her appearance or the way she dresses might lead someone to call her a "whore"; how the classmate who is shy, effeminate or does not play football is called a "faggot"; even expressions like "suck it" (referring to *fellatio,* to oral-genital intercourse) and "I fucked you" (describing penetration but used to describe one's cunning skills and the possibility of cheating on someone) may be used, even in goliardic terms, in challenges between males.

All these examples refer to forms of de-*contextualization of meanings* and their direct (purely sexual) application, which nevertheless produce feedback effects on the sexual image that the subjects possess of others and of themselves or that they want to display to others. These expressions do not immediately represent a sexual practice but serve as informal sexual socialization practices within which sexuality is the means of *saying and meaning* something not purely sexual (such as gender roles, subordination, different endowments of power, etc.).

Sexuality is expressed through language, and language contributes to producing sexualities. Language, moreover, allows acts, relationships, or situations to take on a clear sexual definition or, on the contrary, succeeds in *desexualzsing* them (think of jokes, in particular those ones that, while orienting us toward the values present in the social context or in the group to which we belong, diminish the tabooization of sexuality). This is because sexual conduct can originate from nonsexual motives, and conversely, sexual motives can lead to conducts that are not explicitly sexual.

"Becoming Sexual" – Sexual Careers

We learn to be sexual and become, among other possibilities, symbolic *producers and consumers of sexuality*. The prominence given to the processual dimension, linked to the symbolic interactionist lesson – very evident in above all Gagnon's (2004) contributions – makes it possible to abandon any static observation of human sexualities, any explanation considered in any aetiological or deterministic logic. Instead, in the processual complexity of each stage or step, representing interactional situations and contexts, it is possible to grasp symbolic practices and social exchanges, structural conditions, and subjective interpretative dimensions. It is no coincidence that Gagnon (2004), for instance, paid particular attention to the concept of career and the work of Everett C. Hughes, "the only real member of the Chicago School" (Kimmel, 2007, p. 10), present, at the time, at his sociological training in the famous Department.

Hughes (1971, 2010) had uncoupled the study of careers from exclusively professional activities and processes. He proposed it for the comparative study of very different activities, as well, in order to "*penetrate more deeply* into the personal and social drama of work, to understand the *arrangements* and the socio-psychological tools by which men make their work acceptable, or even glorious for themselves and others" (Hughes, 2010, pp. 272–273), whether it would be working in a "famous institution" or "dealing with rubbish."

Hughes' analysis made it possible to consider the concept of career in a processual method. His work takes into account both objective issues (status and functions that are eventually defined in structural terms) and subjective ones, with respect to perspectives that cannot be prefixed and that are "always in the making," through which the subject "sees his life and interprets the meaning of his different actions, attributes and everything that happens to him" (Hughes, 2010, p. 144). However, Erving Goffman and Howard Becker will explicate a proper theoretical reflection that indicates specific applications through the concept of "deviant careers." In particular, Goffman (1961) deals with *the moral career* of the psychiatric patient and the stigmatized person (Goffman, 1963), and

Becker specifies a model of deviant careers that considers "behaviour" as a *process that unfolds within phases and sequences* (Becker, 1966).

Even sexuality can be analyzed in terms of sequential paths. However, that analysis would not be deterministic nor predetermined or inevitable, not even exclusively subjective or purely perceptive – within which individuals "move" according to their own perspectives, experiences, relationships, and self-perceptions. Each career is conditioned by environmental, contextual and collective elements and by the meanings that the subjects produce or that "are assigned" to them rather than by uncontrollable impulses. Therefore, each career consists of a series of contingent factors, of both a structural type (the "objective" component) and of an individual type (the "subjective" component). These elements may favor or hinder, slow down or accelerate, intensify or diminish progression, both on a structural basis (meaning the dimension of control or regulation, for instance) and on a subjective basis, such as the individual's desires and projects.

As Goffman (1961) suggests, the concept of career is advantageous because it simultaneously offers "two sides": it allows us to consider both the personal dimension of self-image and sense of identity as well as the public dimension of status, role, and institutional and structural arrangements *external* to the individual. Career implies "moral aspects" insofar as it involves regular changes in a subject's self-image as well as in the judgment of self and others involved, directly and indirectly, within the career. In a way, anytime an individual is engaging in a sexual career she/he is both performing a specific moral character and acquiring an ongoing identity which is deeply situated to the emerging sexual meaning and to the duration of the performance itself.

The involvement of subjects within sexual careers, although characterized by very different activities, has similar structural elements with respect to "work" or "occupational" segments and "conventional" involvement experiences: "entry" or "recruitment," "replacements," "dismissals," "deaths," "retirement," "promotion," "demotions" or "career exit," to name a few.

The analysis is even more useful in the study of "sexual careers" because it can *demystify the study of sexuality* and analyze participation to this specific type of career like any other aspect of social life. It occurs when researchers focus on the previous experiences of the actors, when they consider the characteristics of the interactional contexts in which the subjects pursue their activities and the definitions of the situations in which the participants find themselves into.

"Having Sex" – Performance and Sexual Dramaturgy

When we conceive something or someone as "sexual" we do not merely apply meanings as if we were actors *trained* and *educated* for a role or mere *performers*. When we act within symbolic interactions, we become our own *scriptwriters* as we apply and shape meanings and relevant materials drawn from available cultural scenarios to conduct our actions by adapting them to the performance of a specific conduct (Simon & Gagnon, 1986).

For instance, if we consider the processes of sexual socialization, we realize that we are certainly socialized as an *audience* or as *apprentices* of the collectively available cultural repertoires. However, when we are asked to enact specific *scripts*, we encounter the demands of concrete situations, those of others', and of the existing ones, we have with them: in this case, we are not simply actors saying lines, but rather we become *improvisers* (Gagnon, 1990), *dramaturgs* of ourselves. Thus, sexuality too – like other aspects of social life – is based on a dramaturgical imperative: we must necessarily appear to others (Edgley, 2015, p. 56).

The *sexual scripts* owe this component both to Burke's *dramatism* approach and, more implicitly, to Erving Goffman's dramaturgical approach. Burke (1945), in particular, identifies five key elements: the act, the scene, the agent, the agency and the purpose. *The act*, in particular, implies the set of gestures, attitudes and performance that "give a name" to what happens. *The scene* is the background and context for the action, the situation in which it occurs, the coherent set of actions that in more mature reflections will be later called the "definition of the situation." *The agent* corresponds to the type of person (in terms of appearance, behavior, etc.) *who performs the act. The agency* refers, on the other hand, to the means or manners of action of the agents, and finally, *the purpose* intercepts the agents' motives, strategies and aims that they wish to achieve from the interaction.

Therefore, "being sexual" depends, primarily, on the rituals and performances in which we are constantly involved in everyday life situations whenever we play a role that, from a communicative, expressive, aesthetic, and verbal point of view, communicates our identity to one or several audiences. The moment of the transition from the *backstage to the limelight* in which the audience finds itself (or even in the opposite movement, as a presence in the audience to withdrawal to the backstage) offers the possibility to understand how the social actor "puts on" or "takes off" a particular role (Goffman, 1959).

When we are in co-presence with an audience, our intent is to display our behavior as *appropriate* and be *recognized* in the role we assume, to be *legitimized, competent or desirable*. In order to validate our definition of the situation, we need to self-manage our identity, by engaging in a general identity work so that we can manage the impressions of others and make our *self-presentation* (Goffman, 1959) succeed. Sociosexual interactions produce games of reciprocity and sociability (Simmel, 1949), within which social actors produce processes where the producers are also consumers and performers assume the role of audience.

The definition of the situation also provides a "program for co-operative activity" that follows and possesses "a precise moral character". Thus, when individuals project a definition of the specific situation, they are announcing that they are "a person of a certain type" and demand a consequential moral recognition; by doing so, they oblige their audience to evaluate and treat them in the manner appropriate to the situation (Goffman, 1959). Actors in their self-presentation rely on the dramaturgical qualities of realization (Goffman, 1959, p. 52), which is the accentuation and enhancement of their activity through signs in order to meaningfully convince the audience, during the interaction, to possess the announced or expected characteristics. In this sense, the social actor is engaged in *preventive or corrective* activities in order not to "lose face" and make "true" and "authentic" what he or she performs and represents. The activities of self-presentation show how "being a particular type of person does not only imply possessing the required attributes, but also maintaining the standards of conduct and appearance that the social group entails" (Goffman, 1959, p. 87), whereby our roles are not something we possess but they are scripts that must be *staged, illustrated, and realized.*

With regard to sexual conduct and interactions, which are specific activities that make it impossible for their actors "to be immediately involved in another interaction" (Goffman, 1959, p. 142), dramaturgical analysis allows us to consider behaviors that take place in the *spotlight* of the interactive scene (in front of an audience), in those contexts where we are most interested in maintaining a certain self-representation, and the *backstage* where we relieve the tensions caused by the performance. The bedroom is the backstage for our friends and guests, but it becomes the spotlight for sexual interactions with our partner. The bathroom is the backstage that allows us to prepare for the socio-sexual scene, where bodies are cleaned, prepared, and adorned. With regard to sexuality, space and environment in which the interaction takes place assume a central role precisely because backstage and spotlight and their boundaries help define the meaning of sociosexual action.

All our socio-sexual interactions must be *staged* in some way and have to be "tuned" in order to create the alignment of actions and the creation of a common definition. Having sex means *doing things together with others*; we can learn techniques and perform certain acts only if we enact them in the conversation we have with ourselves and in the interaction with others. Even when we have sexual fantasies, we are doing something with others, with the culture we have internalized.

MALE SEX WORK AS SEXUAL SCRIPTING: A SYMBOLIC INTERACTIONIST ACCOUNT

Much of my latest research attempts to explain how male sex workers begin and continue their careers and how they negotiate their masculinities within street sex work arenas. In this last section, I will apply what I consider the main contributions drawn from symbolic interactionism to male sex work, focusing mainly on how young males involved in sex work neutralize stigmatizing labels (Goffman, 1963; Weitzer, 2018) and build and exchange sexual capital by creating hierarchies of bodies, practices, and desire. The data are drawn from an ethnography conducted between 2011 and 2018 in two metropolitan cities in Southern Italy. About 80 hours of ethnographic observation were collected within some public sex environments such as public parks, train stations, porn cinemas and other cruising areas. Specifically, the following reflections and findings are drawn from an exploratory study conducted between 2011 and 2018. Specifically, it is based on approximately 80 hours of ethnographic observation within a series of public sex environments (PSEs) (public parks, stations, and other cruising areas) and three porn cinemas in two metropolitan cities in Southern Italy. A total of 25 in-depth interviews were collected among foreign sex workers and immigrants (8 Tunisians, 5 Moroccans, 4 Romanians, and 1 Albanian) and Italians (7) on the topics of entry and permanence in sex work careers, on the sexual activities and their emotional management. The average age of the interviewees was 23.5 years; all the majority – except for two subjects who described themselves as bisexual and one who perceived himself as homosexual – self-defined themselves as heterosexual; these were mainly subjects from working class and disadvantaged backgrounds and with low level of education, and migrants were clearly in a state of social marginality (see Rinaldi, 2020; Rinaldi & Bacio, 2022).

The commercialization of the male body and the sale of (homo)sexual sex have specific features compared to other types of sex work (such as escorting) (see Minichiello et al., 2013; Gagnon & Simon, 1974; Plummer, 1982). Because sex between men occurs within cognitive, interpretive, and cultural frames that define it as something "unnatural," sex between sex workers and clients can be explained by a series of motivations (Scott et al., 2014) and specific sexual scripts. These scripts do not necessarily depend on the "nature" of the sex workers involved. Instead, they tend to identify clients as predatory, insatiable, and depraved. In short, the scripts prevent male sex workers from identifying with the cultural enemy (namely, "the faggot" client), allowing them perform dramatizations of masculinity and sexuality that help them maintain their hegemonic masculine identity.

Straight self-defined male sex workers generally use the following sexual scripts: (1) A man must maintain his manly reputation and normative sexual status; if he is "active" and has a virile appearance, he can have sex with other men (adults or foreigners) without losing his virility; (2) Those who perform a "passive" role in anal intercourse or an "active" role in oral sex are considered a separate species and pigeonholed in a specific essentialist and racial category. They are seen as "faggots," "sick people," and "sinners" to be exploited, and their role is likened to that of an "available" female or a "social" female.

These are the reasons why for heterosexual male sex workers who sell sex to other men, being a public sex worker, receiving pay for sexual services, or receiving little monetary compensation (and, therefore, being depreciated) often means being attacked in their male respectability and being treated as "females." Italian male sex workers often interpret professionalization as a form of dependence on the client, on another male. This dependence reveals their deficiency as a male, which makes them appear less masculine, a man with a deficit.

For these reasons, the sexual-economic exchange must appear as a concession that the sex worker himself grants to the client, a willing choice. Sex workers do not want to view the sexual exchange as something the client would grant to the sex worker. The following attitude is typical from the side of the sex worker: "I can come with you, but you have to pay me, if you didn't have money you'd make me sick, and still, with all the money you have, you make me sick anyway" (Anonymous, cinema, bathrooms).

The following interview extract may help clarify what I am discussing here:

> I do never solicit them [i.e., my clients]. That's embarrassing for me. It's them who must come to me, not the other way round. If they waste time ... coming back and forth, that pisses me off big time. So I stop them and say: "Bro, what do you want?" [He brushes the tip of his forefinger with that of his thumb, indicating money.] "You must pay to come with me." See, I don't ask them, it's them who must come to me. They must knee down. [He says this in Sicilian dialect, alluding to oral sex.] I can't look like the needy type, like I'm a girl. Otherwise, I'd look like a fucking whore. Hammouda, 22, Tunisian

If you feel "depreciated" or "devalued," then you must preserve your respectability and "save your face" (Goffman, 1967). According to an expression used in the field, male sex workers usually achieve this goal by "making a scene," lest they are seen and identified as a "scafazzato" – that is, a "bum," a person "devoid of self-respect," "with no dignity" because they "charge little" and perform "indecent" sexual activities (such as passive anal intercourse, active fellatio, or masturbation). Therefore, they must always preserve their reputation as a man: It is an advantage from a privileged situation, an "incorporated capital" (Bourdieu, 1997). Both the sex workers and the clients constantly monitor and add value to masculinity, which is under a permanent threat. Sex workers fashion themselves so to appear as individuals exerting a direct control of their context and interactions, playing the "active part" and functioning as the decision-making center of the exchange. This active and spasmodic control of the sexual interaction makes us understand how sex work poses a constant threat to the sex worker's sexual and gendered self.

Becoming Sex Worker: Justifying and Negotiating Masculinities

Entering the sex work scene often coincides with embarking on a "career" as a sex worker. As the worker takes up this role, he has to negotiate it constantly, because he risks losing his virile reputation (Connell & Messerschmidt, 2005). At the outset of their career, nonprofessional sex workers (that is, street prostitutes) – who are mostly people of lower social status, working-class individuals, and racialized migrants – often construct legitimizing accounts of their conduct. These narratives are an attempt to neutralize the effects or repair the breach of social expectations (including the gender order) caused by the sex workers' participation in behaviors that they and others label as "deviant." Sex workers feel the need to justify to themselves and to others why they do what they do and why they intend to do what they intend to do. Individuals engage in a discourse on motives when they consider what is happening as questionable, inconsistent, problematic, inappropriate, unsolicited, and/or awkward. Accordingly, we can say that sex workers, as potentially stigmatized individuals, engage in "identity work" (Snow & Anderson, 1987) to create and sustain social acceptance among the other males involved in the "trade" by rationalizing any allegedly unacceptable masculine behavior. By doing so, sex workers can regain their status as legitimate, *masculine men.*

The most common justifications that sex workers give to legitimize their behaviors revolve around neutralizing the stigma that derives from having sex with other men. Their accounts show that sex workers subscribe to dominant social values and sexual norms, including the moral and social sanctions against homosexual conduct. Consequently, in attempting to neutralize their actions, they try to show their commitment to those dominant social values and to convince the "conventional others" that male sex workers should not be classified as deviants or "queers." This process suggests that sex workers, while enacting the scripts of a specific sexual subculture, work within a broader regulatory system of values. Therefore, the world of sex work and the "conventional" world (that is, the setting in which men despise the other men with whom they have sex) intersect at many points. Sex workers come to learn when they can violate sexual norms and use that knowledge in a twofold way: after selling sex, to mitigate shame and sense of guilt, and before selling sex, to anticipate the transgressive action in order to facilitate it.

Sex workers from my sample used four main "motives" to explain and justify why they became sex workers and continue pursuing this career: (1) "To make money"; (2) "I'd rather do this than get into even worse trouble with the police"; (3) "It's an easy job/easy money" and (4) "It's the only thing I can do"

The first motive, "to make money," is associated with an impersonal activity whose moral sanctions are neutralized by a monetary exchange. The respondents justify their involvement by neutralizing any emotional or physical urge for offering their services:

> I started when I realized I could make some money ... I'd never done it before, I started doing it when I saw the money. Antonio, 19, Italian
>
> I don't like sex with men, but I need the money. I live with my mum, my father is dead. I am responsible for my family. Abdul, 21, Moroccan
>
> I don't like it ... you know ... it's the easiest way to make money. Roberto, 22, Italian

The second motive, "I'd rather do this than get into even worse trouble with the police," is the most popular among illegal immigrants and young "offenders" involved in other illegal activities. They are usually forced to limit their visibility in public and semi-public areas so to reduce as much as possible their contact with the local authorities:

> So, as a boy, I went down a wrong path ... you know, petty crime. Then, I realized that it was not the right path. So in order to make some money, I began, as they say, my career as a hustler. Roberto, 22, Italian

The third motive, "It's an easy job/easy money," is the most popular among Italian sex workers, who consider selling their body a second job. This motive is common among individuals from disadvantaged backgrounds and lower social classes, who go in search of extra money over the weekends. Others choose prostitution according to a basic cost-benefit analysis:

> Doing it is not just another way to make money; you can make a lot of money doing it, in a very short time, and in a very simple way: You don't even know how easy it is. You don't even have to move. They just come to you, as if you were all covered in honey. You don't even have the time to cum, that others lineup. You don't even realize that. What do you do, then? You

> "babbii" with them [Sicilian dialect for "joking"] until you have them blow you. Money … I'd leave with a lot of money. Totò, 24, Italian

Sex workers use the fourth motive, "It's the only thing I can do," in order to solicit solidarity and sympathy from what George H. Mead called the "generalized other" (1934). This motive focuses on social inequalities and a lack of opportunities:

> I came here to change my life, to find a job, to make a lot of money. I wanted to change my family's life in Tunisia. Moving to Italy could have been an opportunity to do so … I went around, looking for a job but didn't find one. Rachid, 20, Tunisian

> I don't have a visa, this is the only thing I can do. I can't go elsewhere or look for a job. I can only stay here and wait for a client. Abdul, 20, Moroccan.

> We stay here, on the street…. A real job could change our lives … this [sex work] is useless…. What are my dreams? I have some dreams … to have a home, a girlfriend, a family … if I find a good job, once I've found it … I'll never look back and forget everything. Arian, 22, Albanian

The stories that are based on "lack of opportunities" also draw on of victimization-based rhetoric strategies, which aim to elicit "sympathy" to sacrificed masculinity. The third and fourth motives can be included within a specific class of justifications called "sad tales" (Scott & Lyman, 1968). "Sad tales" are based on a reconstructed past described as terrible, painful, or sad. The goals of such accounts are to make heterosexuality appear essential, natural, and normal and to reinforce traditional ideas about normative masculinity (Simon, 1996). Thus, the practice of homosexuality becomes either a temporary, necessary activity replacing the heterosexual relationship, or its training phase. Homosexuality is tolerated to the extent that it does not preclude heterosexual relationships and marriage and to the extent it does not turn into a loving relationship that replaces marriage or leads to embracing a new identity.

DOING IT

The study of male sex work entails a detailed analysis of the presentation of the masculine self and the negotiations that the actors undertake to define "what is happening" and to avoid sexual stigma. In sex work settings, we can identify several important types of negotiation, including definitions of the situations in which the sexual activity takes place, means of access to the sexual experience, and instructions about social roles and statuses (race, gender, and class) and group roles.

Individuals who identify as heterosexual and who want to "be part of the trade" have to bypass the assumption that only "queers" take part in the sex work business. Therefore, they need to authorize themselves to participate in the sexual acts and experiences required by this work. In most cases, the explanation is chiefly economic, although other factors may play a part, including curiosity, latent homosexual fantasies, or "pleasure for its own sake." Sex workers become "scriptwriters" or "adapters." At the same time, they draw categories and materials from existing cultural norms in order to turn their actions into scripts for specific behaviors (Gagnon & Simon, 1986). The sex worker, then, participates in a dramaturgical production of the sexual act that demands an exhibition of unfeigned sexual signs (erection and orgasm), which require them to learn specific techniques (learning to feel pleasure, perceiving the positive effects):

> After some time it [my penis] started to work, I was going crazy.... But, in the end, I pulled it off. Abdul, 25 Moroccan

Sex workers behave in ways that question the representation of human sexuality as a mere reaction to stimulation. In fact, they prove how we attach meaning to what we feel on the inside (as well as what we perceive from outside) and how we are involved in a symbolic translation process that translates feelings into names, labels, and other linguistic categories. Male sex workers are almost always able to exercise some degree of voluntary control over their inner symbolic processes and to speed up, slow down, or completely inhibit their sexual responses and reactions. They have to learn how to achieve a symptomatic condition (an erection), interpret it, and assign to it a precise meaning so that they can "feel something," manage to "do something" (get an orgasm), or "work" without being identified as "faggots." To achieve these goals, they can adopt various learning techniques, including the dissembling or simulation of the sexual act:

> Q: "Can you explain to me how you do it?"
>
> I: "You trick them, have them on ... without them realizing!"
>
> Q: "So what do you do exactly?"
>
> I: "Well in short ... you need to ... do lots of different things ... or the fake cum shot."
>
> Q: "And how do you do that?"
>
> I: "So, for the fake cum shot, you can just fake it and cum on their ass, you spit on their ass and then rub your hand over it, you rub your dick, so that he can't tell, but you get some people that do get it and don't tell you, and others that normally ...it's not like they don't get it, but they're so much into dick that they just don't realize it." Luigi, 19, Italian

The previous excerpts prove that when we manage our bodily sensations and physiological urges we are also, at the same time, performing individual and collective actions like giving names, labels, and meanings to ourselves and to others. In other words, we are creating sensorial and corporeal codes that allow us not only to assign meanings to our actions, desires, and sensations, but also to interpret other people's perceptive behavior (Schwalbe & Mason-Schrock, 1996, p. 115; Snow & Anderson, 1987). When we bring in our senses to the so-called social-sexual interactions (touch, sight, hearing, smell, and taste) we are enacting a series of practices and reflexive processes rather than just responding to external inputs or urges. In this case, we are making these inputs, urges, and desires *meaningful*, which would otherwise remain vague and ambiguous, just like we are *signifying* our "shared common socio-physiological natural capacities" (Mead, 1962, as cited in Dingwall et al., 2015, p. 75). We could paraphrase Becker and say that *our sensorial and physical experiences of sexual inputs emerge from our conceptualization of sexuality and its uses, within the development of our experiences of what is socially defined as sexual* (Becker, 1966, p. 42). There are no universal inputs and urges that produce general, universal, homogenous responses, because we all depend from the dynamic, complex interrelations of culture, interaction, and subjectivity. This is not to deny the materiality of our perceptive organs, but rather to argue that sexual arousal originates within cultural and symbolic contexts and that through interpreting meanings we enrich our physiology. In other words, we experience sexual arousal only as the product of a mediation involving social structures, cultures, interactions, and social contexts. Our sexual conducts are shaped and organized according to culturally mediated inner experiences (Lindesmith et al., 1975): individuals must become aware of what is happening to them, that is to say, they must learn to develop a vocabulary in order to name their (and other people's) sensations, actions, as well as to provide answers if required. Our physiological reactions constitute the raw material subject to processes of interpretation involving the shared common experiences of a particular group; as such, they *can be perceived* only according to certain modalities and they "function" *only when* endowed with symbolic meanings. We are not reacting suddenly to a given input; rather, we are providing meanings to what is happening *inside* (as well as *outside*) ourselves, whereby we translate these sensations into names, labels, and linguistic categories. Nothing can be seen as inherently or ontologically sexual that belongs to social and human life (Parker, 2010, p. 58). This also applies to solitary sex and related masturbatory fantasies, in that they both originate in an erotic imaginary, a language, names and labels that are internalized, together with social influences and previous experiences, as well as future projects. All these aspects perform a regulatory function on social behavior and by extension, sexual behavior. Subjects are always in the position to be able to control somehow their own internal symbolic processes; this means that, to varying degrees, their sexual responses and reactions can always be accelerated, slowed down, or inhibited completely (Lindesmith et al., 1975, p. 506). In one way or another, even when we think we are surrendering to desire in its most solitary and intimate form, we are transforming our culture into the internal language of symbolic mediation, which is also to say that we are creating, more or less deliberately, an (absent) audience for our own activity (Goffman, 1959, pp. 170–175). We are dealing with cultural repertoires that are acted upon in two different ways: on one hand, we learn and internalize them as part of the values, norms, and sexual codes available within a particular historical context; on the other, we mobilize our internal resources to influence and be influenced by them. The analysis carried out so far is evidence of the fact that fantasies and intrapsychic processes are firmly embedded in personal contexts and cultural scenarios that are symbolically mediated by actors (in this case, by referring to gendered structures).

When sex workers "do it," they are not just doing mere sex; they are doing a specific form of masculinity, and, in a way, they are doing "normality," so to say they are doing "heterosexuality" doing "homosexual acts," they are reproducing conventionality accessing to "deviant" resources.

The Sexual Hierarchy Within the Field

Sex workers' self-positioning as "heterosexual" enables them to assert their traditional masculinity, showing contempt for the client or – as in the example – trying to swindle him. The convergence of traditional male gender roles, ethnic-sexual moral rhetorics ("We are the real [Italian] men"), and hetero-normativity ("I do it, but only as a top. I'm a man. I'm not like them, they're faggots" or "I'm a man") allows sex workers to distance themselves from the abject other, as we see in the following excerpts:

> There are lots of queers, they fall in love with you and help you. Some of my friends manage to get loads of money from them, they have a car, a house a job . . . everything . . . they got lucky, you know? They're like women, they treat you like women do, they take care of you, they fall in love with you. Roberto, 20, Romanian
>
> I'm a top, I'm a real man . . . they're faggots. Aziz, 24, Tunisian
>
> I'm a total top, they're sick, they like to be abused [be receptive in the sexual act]. Antonio, 19, Italian
>
> I've made mistakes in my life, I always get into trouble . . . I've been also in jail but I could never be a faggot. Richard, 22, Albanian
>
> No, I've never bottomed. Never. Once, one wanted to pay me 500 Euros [*sic*] just to give him head but . . . as soon as . . . I just . . . I'd just put a condom on his dick and I was already going to kneel down when . . . I can't help. . .. My body doesn't accept to bottom.
>
> [Q: Not even if they offered you a shitload of money?]
>
> No, I can't . . . I can't even pretend. I just can't do it. Maybe putting . . . or licking him, . . . like . . . my dick against his, well that's something I usually do. [D: And what about masturbating him?].
>
> Yes, I did that, sometimes. Every day, when my clients come, I happen to do it. While I fuck them from behind, I grab his dick and jerk him off, until he cums. [Q: Are there boys that bottom? Like S., the guy you spoke to me about before. Is it easy to speak about it with the other boys?] Uhm . . . as far as I am concerned, it's not that easy. Roberto, 22, Italian

The sex work field is highly specialized field. Its actors are unequally equipped with sexual capital (which depends on physical traits, self-presentation, and other characteristics that acquire monetary and symbolic value within the sex field) and therefore occupy different spaces in the hierarchy of sexual work, the "levels and layers of desirability" (Green, 2014). Effeminate gay men are considered "lower class" sexual actors as opposed to racialized men or those who possess characteristics that are culturally associated with manliness. Based on the data collected, we can make the following generalizations about "erotic capital": (1) Male sex workers are sharply differentiated according to the sexual practices offered (bottom vs. top). By overtly despising effeminate individuals, male sex workers take a virile and contemptuous attitude, which clients especially value within the sexual exchange; (2) The most attractive (profitable) sex workers have the ability to perform anal insertive intercourse; a virile body; specific racialized characteristics (skin color, the fact of being exotic or "Mediterranean"); traits associated with a lower-class status (a certain accent, defiant attitude, gait, and coarseness of manners); and specific bodily features (large penis size; height; a fit, lean, and young body); (3) Local (Italian) sex workers consider themselves more trustworthy than foreign sex workers, whom they stereotype as unclean or as thieves, and (4) Other factors associated with the sexual hierarchy include the qualities and "styles" of the sex offer. The sex workers highest in the hierarchy work to maintain privacy for their clients and for themselves; take a subtle approach to hooking up (not flashy or exaggerated) and offer sex in a comfortable or quasi-private location (never outdoors, never in the train station public toilets because women and children may catch you in the act)

> Cos today the client comes and says I am the best at this. Tomorrow he meets a Tunisian boy that for 5 Euros does the same things I do. Still, with the Italian boys, including me, things are different: If you give me 20 Euros you will find a clean and honest person . . . I mean, you don't risk to catch some disease, while if you go with the Tunisian boy you get the same pleasure but can get some disease, because he's not a clean person aesthetically and physically. Antonio, 19, Italian
>
> They come here and steal away our clients.
>
> Aldo, 22, ItalianThey're all dirty.
>
> Anonymous Italian male sex worker Never trust them: They might be even sick. Sergio, 25, Italian
>
> However, foreign sex workers sometimes successfully differentiate themselves on the basis of their offers and physical traits: Italians are all bottoms. Momo, Moroccan, 20
>
> I don't use condoms. Don't need them. I'm not a faggot. . .. They [the local sex workers] can get sick, not me. Lilian, Tunisian, 21
>
> Italians have small dicks. Rico, Tunisian, 21

CONCLUSIONS

Males endowed with a specific "physical" and "attractive" capital characterized by certain mannerisms, education, lifestyles, and cultural habits are naturalized, classed, sexualized, and/or racialized according to the same features that lead to the marginalization of less desirable male sexual partners or sex workers. Within homosexual communities and societies at large, a "class" of treacherous, disgusting, and threatening individuals is constructed, whose dangerous and virile features cause attraction and repulsion. Sex work can threaten their respectability as males and their masculinity, leading sex workers to cultivate a hypermasculinity that compensates for their sacrificed masculinity. Male sex workers convey this hypermasculinity through aggressive manners and virile physicality. The study of male sex work in Southern Italy allows us to understand what it means to perform a subordinate masculinity in between the old and the new, between the need for "a real man" to provide for a woman (and for himself) and the inability to acting like a "traditional man" as a result of limited opportunities and career choices. Because, as Luigi (22, Italian) says, "As soon as I make enough money, I need to buy new clothes, get some weed, and look for fimmini ['girls' in Sicilian dialect] . . . I wanna bring a girl to the disco, and if you don't have money enough, what would you give her?". At the same time, following the main insights from symbolic interactionism, we can consider how all forms of sexualities are "unnatural," since just like any other human behavior, they don't not include a set of predetermined, fixed forms and contents; as any other human behavior, sexuality is a complex condition originating from the purely human capacity/ability to think, to act, and to remember, as well as from people's needs to live with other human beings to do things together. In this sense, sexual scripts prove that we are not *merely* sexed but, rather, that we *become sexual*. That sex is never "just sex."

NOTE

1. These are mostly PhD and MA theses, ethnographic notes, or even just life stories, which are collected and then transcribed. The wide majority is held at the Regenstein Library, University of Chicago and at the Ernest W. Burgess Fund, Special Collections Research Center of the University. See Heap (2003), p. 458 note 5 and Heap (2009).

REFERENCES

Becker, H. S. (1966). *Outsiders. Studies in the sociology of deviance*. The Free Press.

Blumer, H. (1948). A sociologist looks at the "Kinsey Report". Sexual behavior in the Human male by Alfred C. Kinsey, Wardell B. Pomeroy, Clyde E. Martin. *Ecology*, *29*(4), 522–524.

Blumer, H. (1969). *Symbolic interactionism: Perspective and method*. Prentice-Hall.

Bourdieu, P. (1997). The form of capital. In A. H. Halsey, H. Lauder, P. Brown, & A. Stuart Wells (Eds.), *Education: Culture, economy, society* (pp. 46–58). Oxford University Press.

Burgess, E. W. (1949). The sociological theory of psychosexual behaviour. In P. Hoch & J. Zubin (Eds.), *Psychosexual developments in health and disease* (pp. 227–243). Grunn and Stratton.

Burke, K. (1945). *A grammar of motives*. Prentice-Hall.

Burke, K. (1965). *Permanence and change: An anatomy of purpose*. Bobbs-Merrill.

Cameron, D., & Kulick, D. (2006). General introduction. In D. Cameron & D. Kulick (Eds.), *The lenguage and sexuality reader* (pp. 11–12). Routledge.

Connell, R., & Messerschmidt, J. W. (2005). Hegemonic masculinity: Rethinking the concept. *Gender & Society*, *19*(6), 829–859.

Dingwall, R., Nerlich, B., & Hillyard, S. (2015). Determinismo Biologico e Interazionismo Simbolico: correnti eraditarie e percorsi culturali. In R. Rauty (Ed.), *L'interazionismo simbolico: caratteristiche e prospettive* (pp. 55–82). Kurumuny.

Edgley, C. (2015). Sex as theatre: Action, character and the erotic. In T. S. Weinberg & S. Newmahr (Eds.), *Selves, symbols and sexualities. An interactionist anthology* (pp. 55–72). Sage.

Gagnon, J. H. (1990). The explicit and implicit use of the scripting perspective in sex research. *Annual Review of Sex Research*, *1*(1), 1–43.

Gagnon, J. H. (1999). Sexual conduct: As today's memory serves. *Sexualities*, *2*(1), 115–126.

Gagnon, J. H. (2004). Revisiting the text: An interview with John Gagnon. In J. H. Gagnon (Ed.), *An interpretation of desire. Essays in the study of sexuality* (pp. 275–288). University of Chicago Press.

Gagnon, J. H., & Simon, W. (1973). *Sexual conduct. The social sources of human sexuality*. Aldine Publishing Company.

Gagnon, J. H., & Simon, W. (1974). *Sexual conduct: The social sources of human sexuality*. Aldine.

Gagnon, J. H., & Simon, W. (1986). Sexual scripts: Permanence and change. *Archives of Sexual Behavior*, *15*(2), 97–120.

Garfinkel, H. (1967). *Studies in ethnomethodology*. Prentice-Hall.

Gecas, V., & Libby, R. (1976). Sexual behavior as symbolic interaction. *The Journal of Sex Research*, *12*(1), 33–49.

Goffman, E. (1959). *The presentation of self in everyday life*. Anchor Books.

Goffman, E. (1961). *Asylums*. Anchor Books.

Goffman, E. (1963). *Stigma: Notes on the management of spoiled identity*. Prentice-Hall.
Goffman, E. (1967). *Interaction ritual: Essays in face-to-face behavior*. Aldine.
Green, A. I. (2008). Erotic habitus. Toward a sociology of desire. *Theory and Society*, *37*(6), 595–626.
Green, A. I. (2014). The sexual fields framework. In A. Green (Ed.), *Sexual fields: Toward a sociology of collective sexual life* (pp. 25–56). University of Chicago Press.
Heap, C. (2003). The city as a sexual laboratory: The queer heritage of the Chicago school. *Qualitative Sociology*, *26*(4), 457–487.
Heap, C. (2009). *Slumming. Sexual and racial encounters in American nightlife, 1885–1940*. University of Chicago Press.
Hughes, E. C. (1971). *The sociological eye: Selected essays*. Transaction.
Hughes, E. C. (2010). *Lo sguardo sociologico* (Edited by M. Santoro). Il Mulino. Original work published 1958/1984.
Kimmel, M. S. (2007). Introduction. John Gagnon and the sexual self. In M. S. Kimmel (Ed.), *The sexual self. The construction of sexual script* (pp. 7–15). Vabderbilt University Press.
Kinsey, A. C., Pomeroy, W. B., & Martin, C. E. (1948). *Sexual behavior in the human male*. W.B. Sanders Co.
Kuhn, M. (1954). Kinsey's view on human behaviour. *Social Problems*, 119–125.
Lindesmith, A. R., Strauss, A. L., & Denzin, N. K. (1975). *Social psychology*. The Dryden Press.
Lyman, S. M., & Scott, M. B. (1970). Accounts. In S. M. Lyman & M. B. Scott (Eds.), *A sociology of the absurd* (pp. 111–143). Appleton-Century-Crofts.
Mead, G. H. (1934). *Mind, self, and society: From the standpoint of a social behaviorist*. University of Chicago Press.
Mead, G. H. (1938). *The Philosophy of the Act* (Edited by C. W. Morris). University of Chicago Press.
Mead, G. H. (1962). *Mind, self, & society* (Edited by C. W. Morris). University of Chicago Press.
Mills, C. W. (1940). Situated actions and vocabularies of motive. *American Sociological Review*, *5*(6), 904–913. https://doi.org/10.2307/2084524
Minichiello, V., Scott, J., & Callander, D. (2013). New pleasures and old dangers: Reinventing male sex work. *The Journal of Sex Research*, *50*(3–4), 263–275.
Mumford, K. (1997). *Interzones: Balck/White sex districts in Chicago and New York in the early twentieth century*. Columbia University Press.
Parker, R. (2010). Reinventing sexual scripts: Sexuality and social change in the twenty-first century. *Sexuality Research and Social Policy*, *7*, 58–66.
Plummer, K. (1982). Symbolic interactionism and sexual conduct: An emergent perspective. In M. Brake (Ed.), *Human sexual relations. Toward a redefinition of sexual politics* (pp. 223–241). Pantheon Books.
Plummer, K. (2002). General introduction, sexualities. Critical concepts. In K. Plummer (Ed.), *Sociology, Vol. 1: Making a sociology of sexualities* (pp. 1–24). Routledge.
Rinaldi, C. (2016). *Sesso, Sè, e Società. Per una Sociologia delle Sessualità*. Mondadori.
Rinaldi, C. (2020). *Uomini che si fanno pagare. Genere, identità e sessualità nel sex work maschile tra devianza e nuove forme di normalizzazione*. DeriveApprodi.
Rinaldi, C., & Bacio, M. (2022). Becoming male sex worker, doing masculinities. Socio-sexual interactions and gender production in men selling sex to men in Italy and Sweden. *Italian Journal Of Sociology Of Education*, *14*, 7–30. https://doi.org/10.14658/PUPJ-IJSE-2022-2-2
Rubin, G. S. (2002). Studying sexual subcultures. Excavating the ethnography of gay communities in urban North America. In E. Lewin & W. Leap (Eds.), *Out in theory. The emergence of lesbian and gay anthropology* (pp. 17–68). University of Illinois Press.
Schwalbe, M. L., & Mason-Schrock, D. (1996). Identity work as group process. *Advances in Group Processes*, *13*, 113–147.
Scott, J., Callander, D., & Minichiello, V. (2014). Clients of male sex workers. In V. Minichiello & J. Scott (Eds.), *Male sex work and society* (pp. 82–105). Harrington Park Press.
Scott, M. B., & Lyman, S. M. (1968). Accounts. *American Sociological Review*, *33*(1), 46–62.
Simmel, G. (1949). The sociology of sociability. *American Journal of Sociology*, *553*, 254–261.
Simon, W. (1996). *Postmodern sexualities*. Routledge.
Simon, W., & Gagnon, J. H. (1986). Sexual scripts: Permanence and change. *Archives of Sexual Behavior*, *15*, 97–120.

Snow, D. A., & Anderson, L. (1987). Identity work among the homeless: The verbal construction and avowal of personal identities. *American Journal of Sociology*, *92*, 1336–1371.

Thomas, W. I. (1907). *Sex and society. Studies in the social psychology of sex*. University of Chicago Press.

Walby, K. (2012). *Touching encounters. Sex, work & male-for-male internet escorting*. University of Chicago Press.

Weeks, J. (1985). *Sexuality and its discontents*. Routledge.

Weitzer, R. (2018). Resistance to sex work stigma. *Sexualities*, *21*(5–6), 717–729.

Znaniecki, F. (1927). The sexual relation as a social relation and some of its changes. In A. Marcus & W. Weber (Eds.), *Verhandlungen des I Internationalen Kongresses für Sexualforschung, Berlin, vom 10 bis 16 Oktober 1926* (pp. 222–230). Marcus & Weber.

BRIDGING THE MISSING LINK ON GIFTEDNESS AND UNDERACHIEVER LABELS RESEARCH: EMBRACING SYMBOLIC INTERACTIONISM

Mehmet Bicakci

Friedrich-Alexander Universität, Germany

ABSTRACT

In this chapter, I will outline the labels of giftedness and underachievement and present the theoretical debates surrounding these labels. A historicist examination of these labels follows, highlighting how the gifted underachievement (GUA) label emerges through the negation of "giftedness." Subsequently, I explore the concept of GUA and its negative connotations, stemming from the positive valuation inherent in the term "giftedness" and its implications for what is considered "normal." This chapter also reviews perspectives on shifting the focus away from the individual within the current paradigm of labeling giftedness and explores insights from systemic thinking and symbolic interactionism (SI). The conclusion underscores the necessity of a symbolic interactionist perspective to address the gaps in research on the labeling of giftedness and underachievement. Finally, I propose a generic definition that can be used in GUA research in the light of SI.

Keywords: Gifted underachievement; self-fulfilling prophecy; teacher-student interaction; Pygmalion effect; self-concept

INTRODUCTION

Though identified as gifted, Deniz (a pseudonym) navigated his high school years as an underachiever. His belief in his innate abilities made him complacent, assuming success required little effort. This attitude persisted until the critical

Essential Issues in Symbolic Interaction
Studies in Symbolic Interaction, Volume 59, 29–67

Published under exclusive licence by Emerald Publishing Limited
ISSN: 0163-2396/doi:10.1108/S0163-239620240000059003

national university admission exam in Turkey, where, against all odds, Deniz excelled, securing a place in a prestigious medical school – a remarkable feat given the competition of roughly 2 million candidates for about 15,000 spots. Deniz claimed that his success was not just academic but a "rejection" of his past underachievement, fueled by a desire to "prove" his potential. Deniz's story underscores the significant impact of one's environment on academic identity. His transformation was a conscious departure from his "previous self," contrasting sharply with his best friend, who "accepted" the underachiever label.

My encounter with Deniz led to a discussion that profoundly influenced my PhD research direction. This discussion in late 2021 resonated with my experiences, motivating me to explore the subject more deeply. Reflecting on my school years, I recognized my struggle with the educational system, marked by a lack of engagement and conflict with teachers. Like in Deniz's case, I secured a place in a reputable local high school despite minimal preparation. This unexpected success challenged my teachers' low expectations and branded me as a "gifted underachiever," a label that also defined my high school experience. After turbulent high school and university years, I started a master's degree in gifted education to understand more about this topic. My comprehensive literature review on GUA during my master's degree revealed numerous areas needing investigation (Bicakci & Baloğlu, 2021). However, although my review answered some of my questions, it raised more questions that needed to be answered. When I decided to commit myself to this field, the main topic of my PhD thesis was clear: How does the label "GUA" function?

An Overview of Giftedness

The modern educational use of the "gifted" term is often credited to Guy. M. Whipple (Henry, 1920). This term was proposed about 15 years ago when the *g*-factor was introduced (Spearman, 1904), while the concept of IQ was still in its earlier version (see., Stern, 1912). Such educational labeling, especially in the realm of special education, has been a major focus in the literature since the end of the 20th century. When we look closer, the term "gifted" embodies a broad spectrum of definitions and perspectives. This diversity, while offering researchers a multitude of frameworks to guide their investigations, simultaneously poses a challenge in formulating a clear and operational definition of the concept. The concept of giftedness should be characterized uniquely across different contexts, but in a way that aligns logically and consistently with the prevailing realities in each setting (Borland, 1989, as cited in Borland, 1990).

The designation of "giftedness" and its various iterations are imbued with a convoluted history and multifaceted connotations. These canonizations have changed over time with theoretical insights. In the most general terms, the changes have taken place around individual and environment-oriented perspectives. Along with the post-positivist paradigm, most contemporary theories (Balestrini & Stoeger, 2018; Boncquet et al., 2022; Chowkase, 2022; Dai, 2020; Glück & Tischler, 2021; Renzulli, 2011b, n.d.; Renzulli & Delcourt, 2018; Sternberg, 2007a, 2007b, 2017, 2018, 2022b; Sternberg & Karami, 2021;

Stoeger et al., 2018; Vialle & Ziegler, 2015; Ziegler et al., 2018; Ziegler & Phillipson, 2012; Ziegler & Stoeger, 2017) like the systemic view of giftedness, which has gained traction since the 2000s (Ziegler & Stoeger, 2017), offer an alternative perspective that transitions the focus from the individual to the context in which giftedness emerges (Ziegler, 2005; Ziegler & Stoeger, 2017; Ziegler, Stoeger, & Vialle, 2012). This understanding constitutes the theoretical framework of this study. In other words, in this study, the concept of giftedness was defined within the framework of systemic thinking. Nevertheless, the systemic theory of giftedness does not doctrines an absolute definition of giftedness. Yet briefly, this approach generally defines giftedness as "potential for extraordinary achievement" (Ziegler & Stoeger, 2017, p. 191). To put it simply,

> ...by decoupling giftedness from the either-or reductionist psychometric model that simplifies giftedness as a static condition, emerging thoughts on giftedness see it: (a) as a socially constructed entity that constantly evolves with our society (i.e., different forms of giftedness emerge in different times and/or societies), (b) as an inclusive nonnormative guiding framework that seeks out each individual's unique giftedness and talents, and (c) as a recursive person-in-situation realization that depends on the complexity of a system and the dynamism between an individual and his or her environment. (Lo & Porath, 2017, p. 351)

An Overview of Gifted Underachievement

As a researcher focused on the critical issue of GUA, which affects an estimated 15%–50% of gifted students (Abu-Hamour & Al-Hmouz, 2013; Bennett-Rappell & Northcote, 2016; Iniesta et al., 2017; Kim, 2008; Mayes et al., 2020; Mazrekaj et al., 2022; Veas et al., 2016). I recognize its far-reaching consequences for individual students' well-being and broader global issues, such as education and economics (Ceci et al., 2009; Emerick, 1992). This is particularly alarming, as gifted students constitute the top 10% of the general population (National Association for Gifted Children., n.d.) and GUA affects them regardless of socioeconomic status, race, culture, or residential area (Blaas, 2014; Neihart, 2006; Nooman et al., 2015; Schober et al., 2004; Siegle & McCoach, 2020). Despite its importance, research on GUA remains relatively scarce compared to the overall field of gifted education (Albaili, 2003; Bennett-Rappell & Northcote, 2016; Dai et al., 2011). However, the field is evolving, with an increasing acknowledgment of the need to better understand and address GUA (Wiley, 2020) and numerous up-to-date reviews highlighting its severity and significance (Bicakci & Baloğlu, 2021; Ridgley et al., 2020; Siegle & McCoach, 2020).

Given the lack of agreement on a common definition of GUA, which has fueled ongoing debates in various fields such as sociology, psychology, law, and policy, identifying GUA has proven to be a complex task (Jackson & Jung, 2022). Additionally, significant variations in identification methods have led to inconsistent research findings, affecting the comparability, validity, and applicability of results for many years (Dowdall & Colangelo, 1982; Jackson & Jung, 2022; Mofield & Parker Peters, 2019; White et al., 2018). Lastly, defining GUA requires the integration of definitions of both "giftedness" and "achievement," making it inherently complex (Jackson & Jung, 2022).

In the broadest sense, GUA refers to fluctuations in performance, either objective or subjective, over time. Various criteria are used to define GUA, such as school performance (Butler-Por, 1987), observed performance (Dowdall & Colangelo, 1982), and having lower grades (Whitmore, 1980). The time factor, whether temporary or situational, is also considered in some definitions (Clark, 1992). GUA has been operationalized using various criteria for various factors. For example, Ziegler, Ziegler, and Stoeger (2012) operationalize GUA as possessing an IQ score within the top 4% and an achievement rate of 50% or less. In contrast, Colangelo et al. (1993) utilize a combination of American College Test (ACT) scores in the 95th percentile or higher and a grade point average (GPA) of 2.25 or lower to define GUA. However, the ongoing diversity and debate surrounding objectivist definitions of GUA remain unresolved. In short, although the definitions introduced above are objectivist, GUA, by its very nature, cannot be defined in the same way as such concepts in the mechanistic natural sciences. Especially researchers who want to examine experiences in qualitative research resort to a concept that can be defined as "relative underachievement" (Desmet et al., 2020; Desmet & Pereira, 2022).

Labeling the Gifted

In the statistical type of definition, the *rareness* of a given concept or behavior is a distinctive classification notion for being regarded as "deviant." Deviations under this definition do not contain value judgments (such as having double-colored eyes). Due to its statistical prevalence (e.g. 1%, 5%, or 10% of the population), the giftedness field could be categorized under this approach. Having to say that, giftedness is the study field of individuals statistically regarded as *outliers*, as they are represented mainly by being at the right end of the normal (see., Gauss, 1809) distribution. Another simple but frequently used definition type of deviance is identifying a concept or behavior by its *pathological* characteristics. Becker (1963) used the *dysfunctional organ* analogy for the latter approach and defined it as "distance from a healthy state." In gifted education, for example, *disharmony hypothesis* (i.e. mad genius stereotype) research continues to produce findings on how negative stereotyping might have an influence (e.g. Baudson, 2016; Simonton, 2014). Last but not least is the *relativistic* type of deviance definition. In this type, deviance is defined as one's adjustment or maladjustment from the given group rules. Therefore, labeling the deviance then becomes a socio-cultural process.

Students can be labeled "gifted" through formal and informal processes. The formal process typically involves a diagnostic assessment administered by an educational institution or qualified professional (Heller, 2004; Lohman, 2009; Robinson, 1986; Sternberg, 2010; Ziegler & Stöger, 2004). This assessment may include tests or evaluations to measure the student's abilities, knowledge, or potential. On the other hand, the informal process of labeling a student as "gifted" may involve recognition by family, teachers, or peers based on the student's abilities or potential (Gagne, 2015; Renzulli, 2000, 2011a; Tannenbaum, 1983; Ziegler & Stoeger, 2012; Ziegler & Stöger, 2004). This informal recognition may not involve any formal assessment or evaluation, but it can still have significant consequences for the student's education and development. Once a student is formally or informally labeled as "gifted," they may receive specialized education or support to meet their unique needs and abilities. In conclusion, labeling students as "gifted" can occur through both formal and informal processes, and the consequences of this labeling can vary widely depending on the context and the specific nature of the label.

By the 2000s, views on giftedness are vastly different, yet the term has continued to be used without much alteration in its meaning (Sternberg & Desmet, 2022). The label is still in use since its early days. The main reason for this semantical stability over time could be the positive value judgments within the label (Robinson, 1986). *Semantic stability* implies "tolerance to deviations or perturbations in time" and "implicit consensus" on the given concept (Wagner et al., 2014, p. 108). Thus, value judgments are often related to the nearest stereotypes (i.e. implicit consensus) about the given label and the individual's behaviors (Bernburg, 2019). Consequently, the fundamental premise in the current research paradigm is labeling and, eventually, identification procedures for gifted students needed to undergo paradigm shifts, as has been repeatedly stressed for the last two decades. A clear, nondiscriminatory label (or no label at all) that *de-emphasize* the "individual" and a dynamic, development-focused, cyclical, self-monitoring/checking identification paradigm is being sought (Sternberg & Desmet, 2022). The gifted label, which had been cursorily studied in the early 20th century, has since sprouted its scientific roots. Nonetheless, whereas our scientific progress on this label since then has been logarithmic, it still presents a challenging picture. These problems are from general to specific (Lo, 2014; Rist, 2017);

- It takes a long time to transfer the sociology and philosophy of educational labeling to practice and application.
- Labeling theories might not always work well in educational settings, especially in special education.
- We have little knowledge about the label of giftedness and its variants.

An Overview of Core Challenges

Since the beginning of the 21st century, it has been said that labeling is one of the most important problems in the field of giftedness. Indeed, even in the first two decades of the 21st century, the "*labeling problem* is continually mentioned" (Heller, 2004, p. 307, italics in original). Several renowned researchers argue that it should be dispensed with altogether, while others still defend it (Ziegler & Bicakci, 2023). Ultimately, although labels suppress the uniqueness of the individual, we are nevertheless driven to use it (Gallagher, 1972). Hence, instead of revisiting the field's longstanding issues, it is essential to reassess the core challenges and scrutinize them from a novel viewpoint in the context of giftedness. The discussion of these core challenges in labeling is happening on following fronts: (a) objective vs relative labeling, (b) formal vs informal labeling (c) terminological confusions, and (d) stereotyping.

Objective vs Relative Labeling

Historically, most of the methodologies that have been applied in psychology, because of their origin in the natural sciences, do not work well because, for example, in the natural sciences, there is no such concept as "normativity"; therefore, what we need to do is to develop new conceptualizations (Valsiner, 2019). In other words, the 19th-century mechanistic (e.g. Lewin, 1931) understanding of social sciences, which developed under the influence of classical physics (von Bertalanffy, 1968), is no longer adequate today (see., Nobel Prize in Physics 2022 by, The Royal Swedish Academy of Sciences, 2022). To put it simply, most of the methodologies in psychology struggle to explain contextual variations. Ideas grounded in the objectivist ontological stance inherited from classical physics (or at least assumed to be so, Crotty, 1998) may not work well.

As defined above, briefly, "giftedness is context-bound and inseparable from the particularities of time and place, as well as from the multiple constructed realities that obtain within a specific social unit, such as a school system" (Borland, 1990, p. 163). Considering that the behavioral norm of "giftedness" is mainly formed by a comparison of the behaviors of *average* individuals (Bernburg, 2010; Desmet et al., 2020; Desmet & Pereira, 2022; Guskin et al., 1986; Jackson & Jung, 2022; Kavish et al., 2016; Matsueda, 1992; Robinson, 1986), the relativistic type of deviance could be considered for the giftedness field. Gifted individuals thereby become vulnerable to being judged by others for being *deviant* from the *norm* (Baudson, 2016; Baudson & Preckel, 2016; Kosir et al., 2016; Lenvik, 2022). As a result, due to the norm shift, deviant behavior is more likely to resonate negatively as a result of the relativistic comparison.

Both gifted individuals and "gifted underachievers" might be perceived as deviants as a result of comparisons by others. That is to say, the reason appears to be that the norm of comparison in the "gifted underachievement" case shifted to "being gifted." (Reis & McCoach, 2000). Thus, individual-centered theories that function with factors based on trait-based explanations (e.g. motivation, self-regulation, and entity beliefs) cannot cover most elements of the system, such as teacher–student relationships. For example, Desmet et al. (2020) highlighted that the literature has not adequately addressed teacher-student relationships in the context of underachievement. They draw upon Eccles (1983) who proposed that "significant others," such as parents, peers, and educators, play a crucial role in shaping students' self-perceptions.

Formal vs Informal Labeling

The gifted label is often used in educational settings for its practical purposes. However, we cannot always refer to formal labels. On the other hand, informal labels may not serve practical purposes either. For example, parents and officials may perceive teachers' assessments as subjective, leading to a reliance on standardized tests for their ability to provide clear, prescriptive evaluations (Mehan, 1978). This leads to the use of labels as a regulatory tool in the educational system, assigning certain characteristics to students as if they are predetermined, much like astrological signs. Can we address the distrust that arises from the conflict between teacher subjectivity and standardized tests, which may not accurately measure many children due to cultural or gender biases, or vice versa? That is to say, the functions and meanings of labels can vary significantly from one individual to another, highlighting the complexity and subjectivity of labeling processes.

Terminological Confusions

Labels in educational settings can often cause confusion because of their subjective nature and the differing value judgments placed on them (Siegle, 2018). Besides the fact that negative educational labels are often characterized as deviant (Aneshensel & Phelan, 1999), they can often be confused with each other. For example, learning disability (LD) can be perceived as laziness, and attention deficit and hyperactivity disorder (ADHD) can be labeled as underachievement and so on. Therefore, terminological problems not only fail to reflect individual differences but can also lead to semantic shifts. However, often reactions to labels with positive connotations, such as "giftedness", can be blended with emotional reactions and associated with more negative connotations in order to protect the label-giver's own perceived sense of worth (David, 2023).

Stereotyping

The complexity and diversity of contextual implications in educational labeling have led to a wide range of stereotypes. It has been suggested that educational labels can serve important positive functions, such as fostering a common language among professionals, raising awareness about the label, and enhancing educational and social opportunities for the labeled individual (Winzer, 1996). However, these same labels can also produce negative effects, such as heightened expectations, stigmatization, and emotional dilemmas for the student, ultimately causing undesirable psychosocial consequences (Coleman, 1985; Coleman & Cross, 1988).

In summary, labeling can have various implications, including positive aspects (like creating a shared language and raising awareness), negative outcomes (potentially leading to increased expectations, stigmatization, and undesired psychosocial responses for the student), and neutral consequences (unresponsiveness or occasional presence of positive or negative thoughts, since some students may remain unaffected by the label). However, to the best of our knowledge, we cannot make assumptions about how the labeling works for the label "gifted underachiever." To conclude, there is no theory in the literature that predicts a process for the development of the label "GUA" and its impact on the individual's behavior.

Recommendations for Solutions

In the past two decades, various solutions have been proposed to address the issue of "conception of giftedness," with arguments primarily focused on the problem of labeling. However, despite the nearly half a century-long history of the labeling field, the findings of research conducted as early as 1953 (see. Epstein, 1953) remain relevant today (Berlin, 2009). The overarching goal of these ideas has been to reduce the label's excessive focus on the individual and to reap the benefits of identification without being exposed to the label's potential harm. However, the complexity of the problem can make these proposed solutions vulnerable.

The main debates about the labeling of giftedness have been shaped by concerns that the functionality of the label "gifted" may be erratic. For example, Borland (2005) addressed "… we can, and should, have gifted education without gifted children." and called for a shift to a program-oriented approach (p. 3). Through this approach, the emphasis was shifted from the individual to the education program. Dixson et al. (2020) painted an illustration of an approach focused on getting the maximum benefit from educational opportunities. They suggested that it would be more advantageous to embrace the "maximizing learning" approach in gifted education. From another perspective, Ziegler and Stoeger (2017) argued that identifying the "learning pathway" might eliminate the unwanted effects of labeling. This approach concentrates on the structure of the actiotopes in an individual's talent development, suggesting a more dialectical understanding of the "education" and "gifted" concepts. This is consistent with the constructivist approach.

To sum, the "gifted underachiever" label, entangled with the gifted label, is often perceived as a deviant label due to abovementioned challenges. Here, a paradigm shift is required to consider underachievement as a concept that develops through interaction rather than just an individual situation. Therefore, it becomes more necessary to unravel the "nature" of the label as a phenomenon not only from the particular or universal but from an interactionist perspective in relation to its contextual characteristics (Lo, 2014). In other words, a systemic and symbolic interactionist paradigm shift to explore their lived experiences and develop effective interventions (Ziegler, 2005; Ziegler & Stoeger, 2017; Ziegler, Stoeger, & Vialle, 2012).

Toward an Interactionist Approach to Giftedness Labels

In terms of social dynamics, the gifted label can lead to peer exclusion or a susceptibility to social feedback (Albaili, 2003; Ford & Thomas, 1997; Govan, 2012). These factors may cause some gifted students to intentionally underachieve to avoid standing out or to fit in with their peers. This represents a paradox where the gifted individual rejects their privilege to fulfill a need for social acceptance. Underachievement can also be influenced by motivational and self-regulation issues (Albaili, 2003; Cakir, 2014; Hebert & Olenchak, 2000; Kim & VanTassel-Baska, 2010; Maddox, 2014; McCoach & Siegle, 2003; Morisano & Shore, 2010; Obergriesser & Stoeger, 2015; Rayneri et al., 2006; Renzulli, 2011a; Richer, 2012; Schober et al., 2004; Snyder & Linnenbrink-Garcia, 2013; Snyder et al., 2014). Negative attitudes toward giftedness from the student themselves, teachers, or family can further demotivate these students, resulting in underachievement (Delisle, 2002; Ferrer-Wreder et al., 2014; Mofield et al., 2016; Peterson, 2001; Rimm & Lowe, 1988).

GUA indeed represents an antinomy – a contradiction between two seemingly reasonable beliefs or conclusions. While giftedness suggests significant capabilities above the norm, underachievement indicates performance below potential. When these terms combine to create "gifted underachievers," we encounter a paradox: those who are expected to display exceptional abilities (giftedness) but do not perform up to those expectations (underachievement). This contrast is a stark reminder of the complexities that encompass the idea of giftedness, which calls for continuous dialog, research, and a flexible understanding of the term. In conclusion, the coexistence of positive and negative perspectives on giftedness and its associated labels presents an antinomy that underscores the complexity of giftedness as a concept. As such, GUA is not just a personal failing or a lack of effort, but rather a complex phenomenon resulting from a confluence of societal and individual factors.

Theoretical Landscapes

The conflicting results and dispersed views on labeling research with gifted individuals may be that the theoretical guidelines on which labeling research is based are described for the behaviors of different samples (Robinson, 1986). For example, since gifted individuals deviate positively from the norm, it has been argued that the classical for modified labeling theories and stigmatization approaches did not work well (Adams & Evans, 1996; Robinson, 1986; Zimmerman, 1985). And also, social psychological theories about gifted individuals are scarce (Zimmerman, 1985). Thus, labeling researchers either have to try out various theories in order to put them on their theoretical research grounds, or they have to organize their ideas to fit them to the appropriate theory (i.e. procrustean bed, Borland, 1990). As a result of this, Lo (2014) addressed there has been broadly three main theoretical foundations for the research on gifted labeling (a) classical sociological theories (e.g. labeling theories or social-bonding theory), (b) social psychological theories (e.g. Pygmalion effect, Matthew effect, or halo effect), and self-psychology (e.g. self-concept or self-worth). Because of this plurivocality, theoretical approaches to the labeling of gifted and underachievers are in a logjam. The need can be clearly defined as follows:

> To extend the research on the educational experiences of those students who are differentially labeled by teachers, what is needed is a theoretical framework which can clearly isolate the influences and effects of certain kinds of teacher reactions on certain types of students, producing, certain typical outcomes. (Rist, 2017, p. 174)

As painted above, the field of GUA embodies a complex and multifaceted landscape, encompassing a myriad of issues and challenges. Among these are philosophical and conceptual inquiries, measurement and definition hurdles, and ongoing debates regarding the long-term ramifications of labeling and behaviors contributing to labels (Ferrer-Wreder et al., 2014; Govan, 2012; Matthews &

McBee, 2007; Reis & McCoach, 2000; Rubenstein et al., 2012; Siegle & McCoach, 2020; Steenbergen-Hu et al., 2020). However, past research within this domain has encountered numerous obstacles, such as questions surrounding causality, label semantics, label formation processes, and the operationalization of societal reactions to labels (Lo, 2014; Rist, 2017). To solve this stalemate, Schultz (2002) reasoned that "broadening the philosophical research focus can provide and enhance understanding and promote additional dialog between gifted underachievers and individuals attempting to meet these diverse learners' needs" (p. 205).

Reconsidering the Philosophical Underpinnings. Philosophical research requires a critical examination of existing theories and practices. In the context of Kantian critical philosophy, the term "critique is not precisely a criticism, but a critical analysis" (Durant, 1933, p. 289). Therefore, to gain a deeper understanding of GUA, it is essential to study how the label operates within various systems. To better understand the contextual and systemic nature of the GUA label, examining the concept of "interactionism" from sociology, as proposed by Mead (Blumer, 1966; Mead, 1934/1972) and Cooley (1902), could prove beneficial (Lo, 2014). This approach aligns with the constructivist epistemological stance (c.f., Borland, 1990). Yet research on giftedness labels has often been conducted on the theoretical basis of self-fulfilling prophecy (SFP).

The concept of the SFP, also known as Thomas's theorem or definition of the situation, was first introduced in sociology literature by William Isaac Thomas (Merton, 1995). This theorem, which states that "if individuals define situations as real, they are real in their consequences" (Thomas & Thomas, 1928, p. 572), suggests that people's expectations and perceptions of a situation can shape its outcome. This idea has been influential in sociological research and has been applied to a wide range of social phenomena.

Conceptual Nuances. It is important to distinguish between the definition of the situation, which focuses on the expectations and situations (Thomas & Thomas, 1928), and symbolic interactionism (SI), which looks at how people's behaviors and attitudes are influenced by their social interactions (Mead, 1934/1972). These two frames of view do, however, diverge and converge at several key points. First, Thomas's first idea is about the situation, not the interaction. Thus, in the SFP approach, the expectations of "others" are thought to have an effect on the behavior of the individual. By definition, "the self-fulfilling prophecy is, in the beginning, a false definition of the situation, evoking a new behavior which makes the originally false conception come true." (Merton, 1948, p. 506). However, in SI, the "others" and the "individual" produce and test the reality as being mirrors of each other (Carter & Fuller, 2016). In this view, people's behaviors and attitudes are shaped by their social environment (Blumer, 1969). In addition to these differences, there are also similarities. For example, both involve long-term exposures. Moreover, just as not all deviant behavior leads to labels and not all labels lead to deviant behavior, not all expectations will be fulfilled. In other words, simply because teachers have expectations about students' performance does not mean that students will always fulfill those expectations (Good &

Lavigne, 2018). If we compare, SI is a more comprehensive theory, which also predicts the effects of expectations on the student's self-concept.

Pygmalion, Golem, and Galatea Effects. In their groundbreaking study, Rosenthal and Jacobson (1968) conducted an experiment in 1965 in a public elementary school to investigate the "effects of one person's expectations on another's behavior." The researchers randomly selected students and told the teachers that some of the students were "growth spurters," without using any test results. As a result of the study, the Pygmalion effect was established as an effect in which a teacher's initial expectations about a student can result in the student fulfilling those expectations over time. This nondirect-interactional effect proposes that high expectations can lead to positive change in individuals by influencing the behavior of teachers, such as by providing students with challenging tasks, educational resources, and opportunities for new intellectual experiences. Subsequent research has expanded on the Pygmalion effect, leading to the development of the Golem and Galatea effects. The Golem effect refers to the idea that people's low expectations of someone's ability or performance can influence the person's actual ability or performance (Babad et al., 1982; Oz & Eden, 1994). On the other hand, the Galatea effect refers to the influence of expectations on performance more broadly, regardless of whether the expectations are positive or negative (Babad et al., 1982; Oz & Eden, 1994).

THEORETICAL FOUNDATIONS

Constructivism encompasses multiple theoretical perspectives such as social constructionism/constructivism or SI. *Social constructionism/constructivism* is, "a theoretical perspective that assumes that people create social reality(ies) through individual and collective actions" (Charmaz, 2006, p. 189). This perspective focuses on how people in a particular time and place create their own perceptions of reality. Instead of assuming that reality exists independently of us, social constructionists "view that social properties are constructed through interactions between people, rather than having a separate existence" (Robson & McCartan, 2016, p. 24). SI is another perspective that also aligns with the ideas of social constructionism, as it suggests that the meanings and realities we experience are the product of our collective interactions and processes, rather than being inherent in the world (Charmaz, 2006).

The Origins and Principles of Symbolic Interactionism

In Scotland, David Hume proposed that "the minds of men are mirrors to one another, not only because they reflect each other's emotions, but also because those rays of passions, sentiments, and opinions may be often reverberated, and may decay away by insensible degrees" (Hume, 1739/1960, p. 365). This concept is considered the first seed of the notion that people's minds shape their behaviors by mirroring each other. Similarly, in Britain, Adam Smith employed the mirror metaphor, stating that people could not comprehend the implications of their thoughts "with no mirror [of others] which can present them to his [their] view" (Smith, 1761, p. 199). Moreover, rooted in Hegel's "Phenomenology of Spirit," human existence depends on mutual recognition for self-awareness and social meaning (Hegel, 1979; Solomon, 1988). Hegel emphasizes the importance of a balanced, reciprocal relationship, where both parties acknowledge each other's autonomy, promoting self-consciousness development (Solomon, 1988).

By the beginning of the 20th century, the mirror metaphor had been adapted and reintroduced into the field of sociological research (Jahoda, 2007). Charles Horton Cooley (1902) coined the term "looking-glass self," focusing on the self-concept within the interactionist view. Cooley perceived society as a living organism, with individuals playing unique roles, akin to small pigments in a complete painting. He argued that an individual's behavior develops as involuntary reactions until they observe their actions in the mirror (Cooley, 1902). Although the core idea can be found in the thoughts of Hume, Smith, Hegel, and Cooley, George Herbert Mead's *Mind, Self, and Society* is often cited (Kuhn, 1964) as the foundation of the symbolic interactionist school (Blumer, 1966, 1969; Kavish et al., 2016; Matsueda, 1992; Mead, 1934/1972). Nevertheless, central to the arguments of these thinkers is the concept of mutual recognition.

The mirror metaphor was incorporated into many theoretical perspectives such as SI. Briefly, SI explores "the nature of human society" (Blumer, 1966, p. 535). In this perspective, the core argument is that reality or truth is constructed through in vivo, meaningful, and dynamic interactions (Blumer, 1969; Carter & Fuller, 2016; Charmaz, 2021; Glaser & Strauss, 1964, 1967). That is to say, individuals continuously evaluate themselves and their circumstances, adjusting their behaviors accordingly (Becker, 1963; Blumer, 1966; Mead, 1934/1972). All in all, this perspective maintains that repeated interactions between individuals build and sustain society (Carter & Fuller, 2016).

In order to better understand the current state of SI, in the context of this chapter, it is necessary to explain the following concepts: (a) formal and informal labels, (b) primary and secondary deviances, and (c) role-taking. When an individual is officially labeled as deviant within an educational or legal mechanism, it is a formal label; if those do it without authority, it is an informal label (Kavish et al., 2016). Lemert's (1951) contribution was to the separation of primary and secondary deviations. Lemert argues that an individual exhibits primary deviance as long as they are unaware of their label and do not intentionally perform the behaviors expected by the label. However, whenever the individual uses their deviance as a social tool and develops a conception of self, it is secondary deviance (Bernburg, 2010). Lastly, Stryker (1957) placed the role-taking approach within the framework of interactionism and tried to explain the patterns of behavior of individuals in social interaction.

Labeling

The concept of "label" is a central topic in social bias research, and researchers have offered a variety of definitions for this term. However, there is a general consensus that labels are concepts that socially represent human differences in a way that makes them salient (Link & Phelan, 2001). In society, labels that do not contain any discriminatory language or negative stereotypes are referred to as "social labels," while those that do, such as "criminal," are referred to as "deviant labels" (Bernburg, 2019).

Formal and Informal Labels. Deviant behavior might be ubiquitous, but labeling does not always happen. In other words, there is not reciprocal relationship between deviant behavior and labeling, and other factors, such as individual characteristics and social context, may also influence these processes (Lemert, 1967). The labeling process can be divided into stages or components, focusing on the role of official institutions or authorities, to understand better its various factors and impact on individuals. The official types of a label refer to whether the assessment is carried out formally by institutions with authorities to label an individual as deviant (such as the *rites of matrimony*, or *passage*), or informally within a community (such as labeling someone as "nerd").

Authority and Consequences. Formal labels can have significant consequences and privileges for the individual and may alter their deviant status (Bernburg, 2019; Erikson, 1966). However, individuals may also be informally labeled as deviant by their social milieu based on contextual factors (Matsueda, 1992). In contrast to formal labels, which are typically applied by institutions with the authority to define deviant behavior, informal labels are often applied by individuals or groups without this authority (Kavish et al., 2016). However, both formal and informal labels can have the same power in terms of their impact, regardless of their official status. In some cases, an individual's official label may not have a significant impact on their life if it is kept secret from the school or community, whereas informal labels can have significant consequences (Bernburg, 2019). This means that deviant behavior can be defined differently in different contexts, and the impact of labeling can vary widely.

Deviance. The concept of deviance is central to the study of sociology and is defined as behavior or beliefs that violate the norms, values, and expectations of a particular society or group (Becker, 1963). According to Becker (1963), "...*social groups create deviance by making the rules whose infraction constitutes deviance* and by applying those rules to particular people and labeling them as outsiders" (p. 10, italics in original). Therefore, it is important to understand the context and recognize the various types of deviance definitions, including statistical, pathological, and relativistic. Statistical deviance is defined by rarity, while the distance from a healthy state defines pathological deviance. Relativistic deviance is defined by an individual's adjustment or maladjustment to group rules, and labeling deviance becomes a socio-cultural process. In conclusion, deviance is a multifaceted concept that is shaped by the norms, values, and expectations of a particular society or group and can take many forms.

The Origins and Principles of Systemic Theory of Giftedness

In the last 30 years, systemic thinking, which focuses on wholism instead of reductionism, has become widely used (Ziegler & Stoeger, 2017). This way of thinking has become more popular in the field of gifted education due to the chaotic complexity of an individual's talent development. Recently, the need to cover developmental pathways that reductionist views cannot explain has been the main goal of researchers. Trying to bring operational definitions closer to the theoretical definitions, or "unifying" them, has become the "philosopher's stone" of researchers in the fields of intelligence and giftedness in order to find the best way of measuring their ambiguous theoretical framework. But these efforts have been condemned as being "procrustean" by the nature of this research area (Dai, 2016). Since the development of an individual's talent is started to consider more complex, the individual-oriented theories, which are prepared from a reductionist view by taking into account the "measurability criteria," are regarded as insufficient. This is the basis for the formation of systemic thinking.

From a contextual point of view, Ziegler and Phillipson (2012) described the actiotope model of giftedness based on a systemic approach. "An actiotope includes an individual and the material, social and informational environment with which that individual actively interacts." (Ziegler et al., 2013, p. 3). The actiotope model of giftedness has emerged the necessity of devising a theory that encompasses the individual and the environment (Ziegler et al., 2017). This model suggested that "analysis of the nexus of individual and context" would be helpful to understanding how excellence develops (Ziegler et al., 2013; Ziegler & Stoeger, 2017). This research will be based on the "circular causation principle" of a systemic approach to giftedness. As Ziegler and Stoeger (2017) addressed that underachievement occurs due to the dysfunction of the entire structure of the system.

Bridging the Theoretical Foundations

SI and systemic theory of giftedness are theoretical perspectives or frameworks that can be used to understand and explain different aspects of giftedness from different angles. SI focuses on the importance of social interactions and meaning-making in shaping individual experiences, while systemic theory of giftedness emphasizes the complex interactions between different systems in shaping giftedness. To justify briefly,

> (. . .) given the fact that labeling is very personal experience, it would be meaningful to conduct a symbolic interactionist study focusing on how students with label(s) internalize the meaning of the label(s). (Lo, 2014, p. 81)

A Summary of Ontological, Epistemological, and Theoretical Assumptions

This study assumes that there is no single truth or reality and that reality is fluid and somewhat indeterminate (Crotty, 1998) It posits that social reality is constructed through social interactions, with individuals' experiences and meanings actively shaped by the social context in which they occur (Blumer, 1969; Carter & Fuller, 2016; Charmaz, 2021; Glaser & Strauss, 1964, 1967). The study also argues that the label "gifted underachiever" is not a fixed or objective reality, but rather a dynamic, socially constructed phenomenon influenced by the interactions and experiences of gifted students (Berlin, 2009; Desmet et al., 2020; Desmet & Pereira, 2022; Jackson & Jung, 2022; Jenkins-Friedman & Murphy, 1988; Lo, 2014; Shifrer, 2013;

Zimmerman, 1985). It also assumes that those labeled as "gifted underachievers" have agency and actively participate in the construction of their own identities (Blumer, 1966, 1969; Kavish et al., 2016; Matsueda, 1992; Mead, 1934/1972) and experiences within the system (Hegel, 1979; Solomon, 1988). Consequently, the study assumes that individuals' interactions and experiences shape the meaning and functions of the label within a particular system (Ziegler et al., 2013; Ziegler & Stoeger, 2017). Briefly, this study assumes that social interactions shape the fluid, socially constructed concept of "gifted underachiever" and individuals' experiences within that context.

By examining the theoretical insights so far, I have completed one side of the bridge I promised in the title. From here, I will review the literature and explain why this particular gap in research has been created by the absence of SI from the equation.

HISTORICAL PERSPECTIVES ON GIFTEDNESS LABELS

The Use of Labeling Theories in Gifted Education

Labeling researchers in sociology have different, but not contradictory, understandings of labeling and deviance, with different constructs and definitions (c.f., Becker, 1963; Lemert, 1951; Matsueda, 1992; Schur, 1965; Tannenbaum, 1938). For many years, the nomenclature of labeling was borrowed from sociology and adapted to education by academics who seek to explore this subject as a new branch in educational sciences. Extensions, modifications, and direct adaptations of these labeling theories have been used in mental health and educational labeling research. In addition to this plurivocality, gifted education researchers also traditionally borrowed and adapted different theoretical concepts when examining the "gifted" label (see., Coleman, 1985; Cross et al., 1991; Tercan & Yıldız-Bıçakçı, 2022; Zimmerman, 1985). However, in past research, there is scarcely any reference to the which labeling theory they have used, or the findings on deviance were falsely attempted, for example deviant behaviors explained with "expectation bias" approaches such as Pygmalion, or vice versa. As a result, it has become impossible to compare and discuss the findings of past research since it was unclear which particular type of deviance is being referred to. As a result, theoretical richness has become an obscuring factor.

In order to understand the use of labeling theories in the field of gifted education, it is necessary to have good knowledge about the original theories, as their way of defining deviance and assumptions sometimes diverges. For example, classical labeling theories describe a scene when behavior is dramatized as an *evil act* (Tannenbaum, 1938). These classical theories assume that label-bearing individuals self-sabotage themselves because of negative stereotypes and difficulties they are experiencing just because they are stigmatized by others (Becker, 1963). Additionally, in labeling theories, deviance usually refers to behaviors that are negatively perceived by society as rule-breaking (Bernburg, 2019; Zimmerman, 1985). Moreover, although it is also one of the classical theories, "self-concept" was added to the labeling theories later. It was Lemert (1967) who argued that individuals' self-concepts are affected by the label. Since giftedness is seen as positive deviance and Pygmalion refers to the behavior of others rather than the individual, it is problematic to read these findings on the same theoretical basis. Therefore, it has become more difficult to draw an overall picture of the results from past research. All in all, when interpreting the findings of previous research, it is essential to take into account the theoretical underpinnings and the behaviors that are considered deviant.

How Past Research on the Labeling the Gifted Should Read?

In reviewing the findings of past research in labeling the gifted field, a researcher should consider (a) the type of deviant behavior that the research refers to, (b) the concordance between the theory and the research hypothesis, and (c) the research context (focus and result of the research, sample characteristics, and overall perception about the label). The reasons for considering these features in reviewing research are threefold: First, labeling (formally or informally) an individual as "gifted" is dependent on a norm (relativistic approach of deviance). Second, the weight of judgment in a label determines how it affects the person (stigmatization). Third, since the label's function may vary, it may be fair to consider the "gifted" labels assigned in each unique individual system (context of labeling). For example, calling someone "gifted" might be referred as saying that "they cannot do better," and calling as "underachiever" refer "they can do better." Since the meaning and effects of the label are multifaceted, its evaluation should be contextualized.

Ancient Canonizations

The meanings ascribed to concepts are intrinsically linked to their context (Wittgenstein, 1953). For instance, while "gifted" and "genius" are different terms (with genius typically associated with adulthood and a higher degree of giftedness), their meanings are shaped by contextually and culturally influenced values (Simonton, 2022). Although the term "giftedness" doesn't appear in ancient literature, it can be inferred that the historical portrayal of this concept can be understood by examining the positive, negative, or neutral value judgments inherent in its semantics. As a result, ancient literature can be scrutinized from two angles: mythological and theological.

From a mythological standpoint, the positive connotations associated with "hero" figures may provide an initial point for tracing the origins of the "gifted" label. Heroes of various myths, such as Gilgamesh, Enūma Eliš, the Dagda, or the Odyssey, are perceived as having exceptional abilities. From a theological perspective, which is also positive, the concept of "giftedness" can be located within theological traditions, particularly early Christian discourses (Gellel & Camilleri, 2022; Saarinen, 2022). As noted by Malabou (2005), "The emergence of modern subjectivity is, for Hegel, fundamentally and profoundly connected to the advent of Christianity" (p. 79). Moreover, when the causal attributions in both mythological and theological canonizations are examined, similar motifs appear.

Here, the term's etymological journey underlines associations with being "endowed with exceptionality" by God or being "born lucky" in a genetic sense (Glaveanu & Kaufman, 2022). In summary, both mythological and theological interpretations associate superior and positive characteristics with the idea of genius.

Conversely, the image of the "mad genius" has a history as long as that of the labels of gifted and genius. This term often serves a cynical function in psychological attribution. This negative stereotype can be traced back to Christian theological tradition, as evidenced by St. Augustine's claim that humans are born sinful and thus need correction (Howley et al., 1999). Moreover, history abounds with examples of "geniuses" who faced psychological and social difficulties due to a fragile temperament, such as Vincent Van Gogh, Sylvia Plath, Wolfgang Amadeus Mozart, and Ludwig van Beethoven (Jamison, 1993). Up until the 18th century, the term was used in mystical, romantic, and religious contexts (e.g., "demon" or "mania" in Greek); its "rational" use became more common following the Enlightenment (Becker, 1978). From that point forward, the term adopted more neutral semantics although it retained the potential to oscillate between positive and negative connotations.

The "Enlightened" Labels

There are different views on how the gifted label, which comes from a long mystical and theological history, became what it became during the 18th and 19th centuries. The change in the use of the term gifted in modern era can be explained by the increased importance attached to the mind (De Condorcet, 1795; Rauscher, 2022). Descartes could be considered the founder of the individual-oriented etiology of giftedness even though his thought still has theological overtones (Hacking, 2013; Shadish et al., 2002). Descartes' *lumen naturale* view could be interpreted as "faculty of the mind" (Daniel, 1978, p. 92). This view stresses that one can find the truth with one's mind, with the light "ignited" into one. Later, the English and Scottish Empiricists, led by David Hume, John Locke, and George Berkeley, were Immanuel Kant's ideas' preparatory figures.

Kant, the most important protagonist of the Enlightenment, became the symbol of the individual's use of reason. In his position paper (*Beantwortung der Frage: Was ist Aufklärung?*), he addressed that a proper Enlighten attitude is "daring to use one's own mind," spreading the slogan "*Sapere Aude!*" (Kant, 1784/2004, p. 5, italics in original). This slogan triggered exploration, experimentation, and reasoning in intellectual circles. In the books published during the Enlightenment Era alongside Kant, it was frequently emphasized that truth could be found through reason. The thinking pattern was established around the idea that a well-educated and "adult" mind is a runner in finding the truth.

A century later, by the same token, Auguste Comte argued that intellectual evolution occurs in three stages: "the primitive theological state, the transient metaphysical, and the final positive state" (Comte, 1858, p. 522). He has described this evolution with a double analogy: the earth's position in the solar system, thus in the universe, and human's position in everything around them and childhood, youth, and adulthood stages of mental and scientific development. Often, however, this idea is communicated in the history of science. It must be said that philosophers in search of truth have worked on and thought about the history of science and, ipso facto, the history of intelligence.

Comte suggests that his theory can be applied to the history of science and the process of individual development. Hither, there is an important emphasis on optimizing the individual's mental development, on bringing the mind to its *best* state. However, these discourses still contain the discourse of the "gift" when it comes to the etiological examination of giftedness (Becker, 1978). In this era, giftedness has come to be seen as "self-evident." Hence, the emphasis has shifted from Socratic demonic views (Simonton, 2014, 2022) in pre-Kantian discourses to Aristotelian melancholics views (Schlesinger, 2009; Silverman, 2013). This discourse, in turn, laid the foundations for our image of the gifted or the mad genius today (i.e. Jamison, 1993; Lombroso, 1895). Furthermore, these views were almost common among professionals working in the field of psychiatry (Becker, 1978; Schlesinger, 2009). I mean that was the general consensus of contemporary science at the time. This overemphasis on the individual has inevitably led to the formation of an accusatory discourse. This indirectly led to the development of the post-structuralist idea of "*controlling deviant individuals.*"

For the "labeling as a control mechanism" perspective, for example, Borland (2005) and (Gallagher, 1999) argue that giftedness is an invention, not a discovery, drawing on Foucault (1995)'s ideas on discipline and punishment through norming. "Since the 18th century, it [norming] has joined other powers-the Law, the Word (Parol) and the Text, Tradition" (Foucault, 1995, p. 184). The main reasoning in this discourse was, in a world where populations are managed by knowledge (as a power), the emergence of such a label was inevitable. Due to the increased emphasis on the mind during Enlightenment Era, the gifted label was produced for both classification and, therefore, control of the public, they argued. We can find support for this view in the fact that one of the most important dimensions of giftedness is norming. While the control argument holds some merit, the essence of the giftedness label could be understood as a phenomenon resulting from the interplay between the individual and the society, rather than being attributed solely to one aspect (Arnorld, 2011; Hegel, 1896; von Bertalanffy, 1968; Ziegler & Phillipson, 2012; Ziegler & Stoeger, 2017). Moreover, the Enlightenment fostered arguments that focused on the interaction between the two poles – society and the individual – rather than on either one alone(e.g. Hegel, 1896; Hume, 1739/1960; Smith, 1761).

Gemeinschaft

From the Gemeinschaft perspective, it can be inferred that the community developed the gifted label to address its burgeoning needs. As Borland (2005) and (Gallagher, 1999) suggest, the giftedness label has connotations of control. This approach predominantly focuses on the "need" aspect of the gifted label, aiming to provide resources and support. Sternberg (2022a) posits that "the whole basis for the gifted-education movement, historically, has been that there exists a subset of the population that can be identified as gifted, which then can be provided with special instruction that matches their special educational needs" (p. 135). Although catering to the needs of gifted individuals is the primary objective of education, there exists an inherent contradiction in the label's meaning. As I will elaborate below, people may not consistently associate positive emotions with the label of intellectual disability (Jenaro Río et al., 2018), whereas they might attach positive emotions to the gifted label (Bicakci & Ziegler, In preperation; Dixson, 2022). While I recognize the needs of gifted individuals, my aim is to demonstrate the presence of a Hegelian dialectic negation within the giftedness label itself.

Gesselschaft

From the "Gesselschaft" standpoint, it becomes evident that individuals within society navigate their personal lives autonomously, albeit in relation to society itself. Consequently, the label of giftedness is intrinsically tied to individuality. This idea echoes the "principle of subjective freedom" found in Plato's The Republic (Lumsden, 2020). I argue that, from this perspective, modern giftedness can be likened to "individual salvation," serving as a counterweight to what Foucault described as "the submission of subjectivity" (Huijer, 2017). However, in the contemporary context of giftedness, relying solely on one of these two viewpoints will not result in a holistic understanding or solution. In Hegelian terms, there is a dialectical process between the particular and the universal.

Bürgerliche Gesellschaft

Rather than adhering to the notion of pure individuality, there is a more interactive concept in labeling. According to Hegel, "civil society (*bürgerliche Gesellschaft*) is best conceived as an aggregate of individuals pursuing their specific needs" (italics in original, Lumsden, 2020, p. 3). Adopting this perspective ensures that the gifted label evolves and adapts to address the intricate and multifaceted nature of gifted label more effectively. By doing so, it considers the diverse experiences that shape both the universal and particular aspects of giftedness while respecting the unique needs and aspirations of each person. This approach promotes a more inclusive and comprehensive understanding of the concept, which ultimately benefits the individuals it seeks to describe and support. Consequently, in alignment with structural linguistics influenced by Hegel's *Geist* notion, the definition of a concept encompasses "not only what is explicitly stated but also what remains unsaid" (Sapir, 1921). Applying this to giftedness, the label can be seen as encompassing both the privilege associated with exceptional ability and the specific needs that come with it, even if these aspects are not always explicitly recognized. That is to say, *giftedness* is a concept that is immanent in the perception of both a privilege and a need.

Privilege vs Need

From the perspective of privilege, the label of giftedness often implies a high expectation, which can sometimes be a burden rather than a privilege. This is especially true in the context of societal and educational pressures (Peterson, 2001; Pyryt, 2004; White et al.). In certain socioeconomic contexts, such as low-income families (Gibbons et al., 2012; Neihart, 2006) or rural areas (Azano et al., 2017; Nooman et al., 2015), the privilege of giftedness may not be fully realized due to limited resources or opportunities. Cultural, racial, or ethnic differences can further complicate this scenario (Diaz, 1998; Earp, 2012; Ford, 1998, 2012, 2014; Ford & Thomas, 1997; Moore et al., 2005). From the need discourse, underachievement can be viewed as a void or absence of fulfilled needs in the gifted individual's education. The lack of challenge, or the perception of school as boring or not challenging enough, can lead to underachievement (Davis et al., 2014; Kanevsky & Keighley, 2003; O'Boyle, 2008; Snyder & Linnenbrink-Garcia, 2013; Tsai & Fu, 2016). Asynchronous development or less developed fine motor skills might also result in underachievement, as they might not align with the standardized expectations for their age or grade level (Zeidner & Shani-Zinovich, 2011; Ziegler & Stoeger, 2010).

METHODOLOGICAL APPROACHES IN GIFTEDNESS LABELS RESEARCH

Traditional Approaches and Their Limitations

Presently, research within the GUA subfield has primarily focused on three key areas: (a) understanding, (b) identifying underlying causes, and (c) reversing underachievement (Steenbergen-Hu et al., 2020). Furthermore, the overall themes of GUA research mainly focus on two main areas: (a) the nature of the phenomenon and (b) the interactive structure of contributing factors (Siegle & McCoach, 2020; Snyder et al., 2021). These foci appear from the assumption that underachieving gifted students deviate from the norm, with their underachievement stemming from various, often complex, combinations of individual and environmental factors (Desmet et al., 2020; Desmet & Pereira, 2022; Reis & McCoach, 2000; Siegle & McCoach, 2020; Snyder et al., 2021; White et al., 2018). Put simply, as Schultz (2002) poignantly remarked, "historically, underachieving gifted students in the classroom have been viewed as defective merchandise in need of repair" (p. 204).

Although some knowledge exists about the workings of the GUA label, a more comprehensive understanding is needed. Although researchers acknowledge that students may receive the "gifted underachiever" label based on specific behaviors, a consensus on these "signaling behaviors" remains elusive (Siegle & McCoach, 2020). Adding to that, one intriguing idea posits that underachiever "behavior" may serve as a "defense mechanism" (Wiley, 2020, p. 1534). Moreover, current research suggests that individuals labeled as "gifted underachievers" often have low self-concepts (Figg et al., 2012; Obergriesser & Stoeger, 2015; Van Boxtel & Mönks, 1992), and perceive the label negatively or as "defective" (Hoffmann, 2020). Labeling may also expose students to stigmatization, negatively affecting family dynamics and sibling relationships (Winzer, 1996). Besides, gifted underachievers could experience a higher risk of peer rejection compared to other gifted students (Desmet et al., 2020;

Desmet & Pereira, 2022; Lutz & Lutz, 1980). Accordingly, the label not only pertains to the individual student but is also shaped by the social context in which it is applied (Kolb & Jussim, 1994). As a result, numerous students may face challenges and fail to receive adequate support and resources within the educational system.

All in all, individuals still continued to be categorized *formally* or *informally* as "gifted" or "underachievers" based on internal and external factors or both (Dai, 2020; Feldhusen & Heller, 1986; Reis & McCoach, 2000). Steenbergen-Hu et al. (2020) recent meta-analysis emphasizes the need for further research to explore the potential interactions between students' mindsets and their educational contexts within the GUA field. Moreover, interventions aimed at reversing underachievement frequently emphasize the individual while neglecting broader systemic factors (Cavilla, 2017). As previously mentioned, existing perspectives are trait-based and do not offer broader insights. Furthermore, the current literature lacks a theory that can predict the behaviors of this unique population based on the theoretical foundations of labeling. In conclusion, the gifted underachiever label is collectively constructed based on the value load, norms, terminological background, and behavioral characteristics of the gifted individual, with the underlying assumption that these individuals are not performing or unable to perform at their full potential.

Assuming the Structural Valances of Labels

The concept of giftedness has been subjected to a variety of stereotypes, with research demonstrating a range of positive, negative, and neutral perspectives associated with the "gifted" label (Robinson, 1986). Despite the potential stigma, reviews have been suggesting that it isn't always perceived negatively. Society may view giftedness as a desirable trait (Dixson, 2022), and studies show that the "gifted" label and giftedness are often viewed as positive attributes (Berlin, 2009; Dixson, 2022; Heller, 2004; Kosir et al., 2016; Lee et al., 2012). However, negative labels or "name-calling" have also been reported, with stigmatization research indicating significant consequences for individuals labeled as such. Academic achievers, for instance, may be stigmatized as "unpopular" (Rentzsch et al., 2011). To put it briefly, it has been demonstrated unequivocally that giftedness is statistically and socially a deviant concept but its direction is kaleidoscopic (Jackson & Jung, 2022).

Globally, students with high academic merit have been labeled with stigmatizing words like "nerd", "Streber" in Germany, "Hnun" in Israel (Rentzsch et al., 2013), and similar terms in other countries (e.g., "İnek" in Turkey, "Зубър" (Zaitseva et al., 2018) in Bulgaria, "خرخون،" (Khar Khoon) in Iran, "Ñoño" in Mexico, "书呆子" (Shudaizi) in China, "Mọt sách" in Vietnam, and "Plugghëst" in Switzerland). These labels often carry negative connotations, often using animal names, and emphasize negative deviance (e.g. horse, worm, cow,and donkey). This highlights the paradoxical nature of giftedness and the complex societal perceptions surrounding it.

The literature on this topic swings between positive and negative views, with some neutral stances where one perspective doesn't dominate. These perspectives aren't necessarily sequential or evolving but can exist concurrently. My claim here is not to posit that the gifted label is entirely positive but to emphasize its resistance to being solely negative. It can be a source of social status (Dixson, 2022) and a "benevolent/desirable" label (Lo, 2014). However, it can also lead to self-sabotage to avoid stigmatization and stereotypes, like being labeled "nerds," "brainiacs," or "geeks" (Cross et al., 2019; Tannenbaum, 1983). Historically, it's been associated with negative connotations, such as insanity during Medieval times, and later, racism and eugenics (Gentry, 2022). Despite this, the gifted label has persisted, unlike other labels in special education. A reason for this persistence may lie in the distinctive functioning of the gifted label.

All in all, gifted individuals are often regarded as positively deviant (Robinson, 1986; Zimmerman, 1985) leading many to view the gifted label in a positive light (Adams & Evans, 1996; Heller, 2004; Lo, 2014). Consequently, the term itself does not inherently become a pejorative label. This perspective resonates with Foucault (1984)'s later arguments on self. Post-structuralist concept of "creating one's self as a work of art implies that one refuses given subjectivities, imposed by knowledge and power systems" (Huijer, 2017, p. 325). This view challenges the notion that labeling serves only to control society, suggesting instead that it can be used as a tool for positive self-creation.

Previous Studies

Zimmerman (1985) was one of the first academics to question the borrowing labeling theories to explain the positive deviance of gifted students. In Zimmerman's theoretical review, four different labeling approaches (see., Becker, 1963; Lemert, 1951; Scheff, 1966; Schur, 1971) were analyzed for their applicability to artistically talented students. The researcher has selected Schur's (1971) theory, among other theories, and exerted to adapting it to gifted education. The most convincing reason for the researcher to adopt this view was that Schur's theory sees deviance as "deviating from the norm" rather than "breaking the rule." However, for exactly the same reasons that the researcher criticized at the beginning of the article, he put a caveat on the use of the adopted version. The researcher stated that this theory, too, "does not wholly reflect an unbiased approach" and can be lackluster in describing both positive and negative deviations from the norms (p. 35).

Lo (2014) conducted a realistic (classical) grounded theory research on the "twice exceptional" label, which is a method that "focuses on capturing facts and mechanisms in the external social reality and striving to achieve a higher level of generalizability" (p. 284). This research aimed to provide a conceptual framework of how dual labeling affects individuals (giftedness and ADHD). The focus of Lo's research was on the three aspects of the effects of labeling – psychological, social-emotional development, and academic performance. Moreover, another substantial aim was to seek coping strategies used toward labeling used by twice-exceptional students. Of the 12 students, two were adults, and the rest was student participants who were between grades 7–12. This conceptual model underscores how personal autonomy, environmental influences, and developmental factors intertwine in educational labeling, an action rooted in a societal setting that dictates specific views and policies about labels. It suggests that such labeling, through transient emotional responses, initiates a process of self-understanding formation that directly influences successful academic and social behavior, thereby bridging the collective understanding of reality and individual lived experiences.

Significant Others

Some important research findings on the function of the label in relation to what sociological theory calls "significant others." Jenkins-Friedman and Murphy (1988) conducted research on actual/idealized and actual/public self-concept discrepancies among gifted students. The sample consisted of 128 gifted students in classes from four to eight in a Midwestern school. Self-concept is measured with a 21-item scale asking for status assessments between "me" and "ideal me." The adjustment evaluated by teachers was measured by a scale of 11 bipolar items on whole behaviors such as goal setting or perfectionism. Well-adjusted students were found to show higher coherence between their Goffmanian aspects of self-concept. What is found in this research is that the stigmatization of "significant others" is related to students' self-concept discrepancy. In another study on "significant others," in her seminal research, Berlin (2009) conducted her research on gifted students' perceptions of how others perceive their giftedness. 66 students, aged 12–14 years old and grades from sixth to eighth, participated in the study. The researcher found that gifted students find the label positive since it is a key to opening the doors of special experiences, teachers, opportunities, and enriched curricula. However, the most frequent negative thoughts about labeling centered around the expectations of parents, teachers, other people, and even the students feeling pressured by their internal drive to "be good." What was found in this research, traits characterized by individuals' perception of themselves through the eyes of others are similar to traits that others see as "maladaptive."

Teacher–Student Interactions

Teachers' expectations, judgments, and perceptions are influenced by a variety of factors, such as standardized test scores, previous academic performance, personal characteristics, and socioeconomic status (Rist, 2017). SI (Blumer, 1966, 1969; Kavish et al., 2016; Matsueda, 1992; Mead, 1934/1972) posits that this information, reflecting students' attributes, is echoed back to the teachers in a cycle of interaction. Yet, establishing causality in these teacher–student interactions, however, remains challenging (Ready & Wright, 2011; Rist, 2017). On the one hand, "for teachers, judgments on their students' characteristics shape how they plan and implement instructional activities in order to offer individual learning support" (see also., Biddle & Anderson, 1986; Huber & Seidel, 2018, p. 1). On the other hand, for students, teachers' judgments "can crucially influence individual students' academic careers and self-concepts" (Südkamp et al., 2012, p. 743). Despite uncertainty regarding the direction of causality, previous research provides valuable insights into the landscape of these interactions: reciprocal effects. For example, Skinner and Belmont (1993) found reciprocal effects, with students who initially showed higher behavioral engagement receiving more teacher support subsequently.

Early research investigated how teachers' behaviors are influenced by their perceptions of student ability, a topic of interest dating back nearly 50 years (Brophy & Good, 1970; Carr & Kurtz-Costes, 1994; Flanders, 1974; Harris & Rosenthal, 1985). These studies indicated a tendency among teachers to offer more praise to students they perceive as having higher ability, thereby encouraging them to fully realize their potential (Brophy & Good, 1970; Carr & Kurtz-Costes, 1994). In an interesting twist, by the means of SI's premises, the assessment process is not a one-way street. Göncz et al. (2014) research highlighted that a student's personality traits can significantly shape their perception of a teacher's personality, contributing to approximately 20% of the shared variance. This reciprocal influence underscores the complex dynamics of the teacher-student relationship. Furthermore, Pielmeier et al. (2018) examined the impact of teacher judgment accuracy on verbal interactions in German mathematics classrooms, drawing on early research and theoretical insights (Hattie & Timperley, 2007; Kaiser et al., 2013; Ready & Wright, 2011; Südkamp et al., 2012). They found that the accuracy of a teacher's judgment of student pre-achievement negatively correlated with the frequency of their elaborate questioning. This suggests an adaptation for students with lower preachievement levels, whereas no significant correlation was found with the overall verbal interactions and the teacher's judgment accuracy of students' characteristics. To put it blankly, as Ready and Wright (2011, p. 354) eloquently argued, "teachers' perceptions influence their interactions with and expectations of their students; they drive important decisions, especially those related to student placements into academic programs; and they have meaningful consequences for children's immediate and long-term opportunities."

I have critically examined numerous studies exploring the impact of teachers' perceptions of students on their teaching behaviors. I've drawn attention to the complex, dynamic nature of teacher–student interactions, highlighting that students' behaviors can significantly shape teachers' perceptions and vice versa. I found a considerable number of research papers on the topic, some directly related, some providing indirect empirical data, and some making arguments through conceptual discussions. "However, the educational sciences have not developed theoretical explanations for the varying quality of teachers' assessments that have been investigated empirically" (Krolak-Schwerdt et al., 2013, p. 217). Although some studies have developed competent models that can shed light on teachers' processes of judgment, they have not included the reciprocity in their models (e.g. Herppich et al., 2018).

From seminal early research to recent investigations, I found that teachers' perceptions and expectations, particularly those formed during initial interactions, can unintentionally reinforce their existing biases, with significant implications for the learning environment and student outcomes (for a book-length discussion see., Krolak-Schwerdt et al., 2014). However, the accuracy of these perceptions is not uniform, especially when it comes to assessing nonacademic attributes such as motivation and personality traits. Moreover, "biases in judgments due to expectations are more likely to occur when there is an incentive to confirm an expectation or a striving to rapidly reach a particular conclusion" (Krolak-Schwerdt et al., 2013, p. 216).

DISCUSSION

Labeling the gifted encompasses both social and individual aspects, characterized by a complex interplay between the individual and society (Adams & Evans, 1996; Heller, 2004; Lo, 2014). Various terms from different theoretical sources are used within the field of giftedness. However, they ultimately converge on a single concept: the "gifted" and, subsequently, the "gifted underachiever" label. But these labels are not negations of each other. Therefore, despite numerous theories addressing underachievement, there is a significant gap in examining the underachievement label itself. Adding to that, the use of different theoretical underpinnings has great potential to cause diverging results.

The prevailing theoretical paradigm in giftedness emphasizes the need to shift focus from the individual, as overemphasis can impose a significant burden on gifted individuals (Sternberg & Karami, 2021) extending to the subfield of GUA. Just as there is harm in attributing "giftedness" solely to the individual, there is undoubtedly harm in attributing "underachiever" exclusively to the individual as well. This unbalanced focus implies that gifted individuals' failures stem from their own inadequacies. It is evident that there is an urgent need to shift the focus from the individual to systems, as current perspectives often implicitly blame the individual for their lack of success and "dysfunction." Consequently, research on gifted underachievers has concentrated on individual characteristics, yielding a literature that delineates common traits such as low self-efficacy, motivation, goal valuation, negative attitudes toward school and teachers, and inadequate self-regulation skills (Rimm, 2008; Siegle & McCoach, 2020; White et al., 2018).

The "paradigm shift" that has been frequently discussed in the last decade should extend beyond reductionist understanding of giftedness (Ziegler & Stoeger, 2017). The systemic theory of giftedness offers a promising perspective that examines the interplay among individual, social, and environmental factors, but there is still a lack of understanding concerning the labeling of gifted underachievers (Lo & Porath, 2017; Ziegler, 2005; Ziegler & Stoeger, 2017; Ziegler, Stoeger, & Vialle, 2012). Whilst this systemic paradigm holds promise for a more comprehensive and nuanced understanding of giftedness (Dai, 2020; Dixson et al., 2020; Maker, 2021; Sternberg, 2017; Ziegler & Stoeger, 2017), additional research is required to explore its ramifications for various subfields of giftedness, including GUA. To break this impasse, scholars such as Schultz (2002) advocate for a philosophical approach to address these persistent issues in GUA field. In essence, there is an urgent call for a perspective transcending the prevailing paradigm by scrutinizing the term's ambiguity and examining the workings of GUA as a phenomenon (Steenbergen-Hu et al., 2020). Overall, it is hard not to agree with the prediction made by James H. Borland nearly 34 years ago when we take a look at the current theories: "In the end, the field of the gifted may be inherently postpositivist, whether we like it or not" (Borland, 1990, p. 167). At the project's beginning, I encountered literature in the throes of this paradigmatic transition. So, I had to delve into history, philosophy, methodology, and sociology.

Upon examining the existing body of research, I have discerned two key themes pertaining to the notion of giftedness: *privilege* and *need*. Recognizing the interwoven nature of these perspectives, I employ a dialectical approach to unravel the complexities and subtleties of this multifaceted concept, as well as its implications. This dialectical exploration enabled me to develop a more holistic understanding of giftedness that acknowledges the intricate interplay between individual capabilities and societal expectations. Moreover, my analysis has led me to conclude that, irrespective of which theme (privilege or need) is emphasized in the context of giftedness, the phenomenon of GUA stands in contradiction to the concept itself. This negation can be interpreted as a form of deviance, as suggested by various scholars (Becker, 1963; Cooley, 1902; Kavish et al., 2016; Lemert, 1951; Matsueda, 1992; Schur, 1965; Tannenbaum, 1938).

Although limited knowledge exists concerning the "GUA" label as a phenomenon, it is vital to understand its functions in order to identify appropriate interventions, helping gifted underachievers reach their full potential (Reis & McCoach, 2000; Ritchotte et al., 2014). This knowledge gap complicates the process of accurately identifying these students' needs (McCoach & Siegle, 2014). Moreover, there is limited knowledge about its informal identification, nature, functions, and effects (Reis & McCoach, 2000). Typically, GUA labels rely on observable behavior and encompass both formal and informal labeling processes based on specific characteristics or abilities (Bernburg, 2010; Guskin et al., 1986; Kavish et al., 2016; Matsueda, 1992; Robinson, 1986). While formal labeling adheres to predetermined criteria, informal labeling is more subjective and varies among individuals (Bernburg, 2010; Lemert, 1967). As a result, employing various forms of data and research methodologies is essential for gaining a more comprehensive understanding of this multifaceted phenomenon (Steenbergen-Hu et al., 2020). All in all, in this composite label, problem arises, "due to the difficulty in defining underachievement, it appears that the concept of underachievement may be regarded as a subjective, rather than an objective, classification" (Reis & McCoach, 2000, p. 163). Therefore, it becomes more necessary to unravel the "nature" of the label as a phenomenon not only from the particular or universal, but from an interactionist perspective in relation to its contextual characteristics (Lo, 2014).

CONCLUSION

Conceptual definitions offer insights into the criteria and comparison units employed in assigning the GUA label, informing the identification of gifted individuals who underachieve. Put simply, as for the identification process, it involves converting conceptual definitions into measurable units via standardized tests, evaluations, or other assessment forms, with numerous operational definitions available, such as the absolute split, simple difference, regression, and nomination methods (Jackson, 2017). Beyond objective identification or labeling, *informal labels* ultimately involve value judgments made by educators or researchers (Desmet et al., 2020; Desmet & Pereira, 2022; Reis & McCoach, 2000).

Gifted individuals are diverse, and their experiences of underachievement may manifest in different ways. Therefore, it is essential to recognize that underachievement in gifted populations can be relative. In some cases, students may achieve at moderate or high levels but still fall short of their potential or perceive themselves or be perceived as underachieving (Desmet et al., 2020; Desmet & Pereira, 2022; Snyder & Adelson, 2017). To avoid epistemological mistakes, researchers should rely on self-identification from participants or nomination by others rather than using objective criteria when analyzing a social label like GUA (Desmet et al., 2020; Desmet & Pereira, 2022; Jackson & Jung, 2022).

Toward a Generic Definition of Gifted Underachievement

Desmet and Pereira (2022) defined and described "relative underachievers" as "students, often gifted, who achieve at objectively high standards, but below what we expect, are called relative underachievers compared to absolute underachievers (p. 2). Along the same lines, the term of "perceived underachievement refers to a person's perception of the degree to which there is a discrepancy between their perceived ability and their perceived accomplishment" (Snyder & Adelson, 2017, p. 1), meaning that students can be identified through self-identification or nomination. Self-identification is the feeling of not achieving one's potential, while nomination is based on observations by others, such as teachers (Desmet et al., 2020; Jackson & Jung, 2022). Therefore, in this study, I defined the term GUA as the perceived (by the individual and/or others) deviation from expected levels of achievement in individuals formally and/or informally identified as gifted, resulting from the interplay between individual characteristics and environmental factors.

The generic definition, which I think can break the deadlock in giftedness and GUA research by bringing in SI, can be operationalized as follows:

- *Self-identified gifted underachievers:* Students who perceive a discrepancy between their abilities and their accomplishments. They believe they are capable of achieving more than they currently are, but feel they are falling short of their potential (Desmet et al., 2020; Desmet & Pereira, 2022; Snyder & Adelson, 2017).
- *Other-identified gifted underachievers:* Students who achieve at relatively high standards but are perceived by "significant others" (i.e. teachers) as not reaching their full potential. These individuals may not necessarily view themselves as underachievers, but others in their environment may hold this perception (Berlin, 2009; Desmet et al., 2020; Desmet & Pereira, 2022; Jackson & Jung, 2022; Jenkins-Friedman & Murphy, 1988; Lo, 2014; Shifrer, 2013; Zimmerman, 1985).

- *Bidentified gifted underachievers:* Students who not only recognize within themselves the potential for high achievement but are also identified by others (i.e. both self-identified and other-identified gifted underachievers) as not reaching their full potential (Desmet et al., 2020; Desmet & Pereira, 2022; Jackson & Jung, 2022; Snyder & Adelson, 2017).

REFERENCES

Abu-Hamour, B., & Al-Hmouz, H. (2013). A study of gifted high, moderate, and low achievers in their personal characteristics and attitudes toward school and teachers. *International Journal of Special Education*, *28*(3), 5–15.

Adams, M. S., & Evans, T. D. (1996). Teacher disapproval, delinquent peers, and self-reported delinquency: A longitudinal test of labeling theory. *The Urban Review*, *28*(3), 199–211. https://doi.org/10.1007/BF02355337

Albaili, M. A. (2003). Motivational goal orientations of intellectually gifted achieving and underachieving students in the United Arab Emirates. *Social Behavior and Personality*, *31*(2), 107–120. https://doi.org/10.2224/sbp.2003.31.2.107

Aneshensel, C. S., & Phelan, J. C. (1999). The sociology of mental health: Surveying the field. In C. S. Aneshensel & J. C. Phelan (Eds.), *Handbook of the sociology of mental health* (pp. 3–18). Kluwer Academic/Plenum.

Arnorld, D. (2011). Hegel and ecologically oriented system theory. *Journal of Philosophy: A Cross-Disciplinary Inquiry*, *7*(16), 53–64. https://doi.org/10.5840/jphilnepal201171616

Azano, A. P., Callahan, C. M., Brodersen, A. V., & Caughey, M. (2017). Responding to the challenges of gifted education in rural communities. *Global Education Review*, *4*(1), 62–77.

Babad, E. Y., Inbar, J., & Rosenthal, R. (1982). Pygmalion, Galatea, and the Golem: Investigations of biased and unbiased teachers. *Journal of Educational Psychology*, *74*, 459–474. https://doi.org/10.1037/0022-0663.74.4.459

Balestrini, D. P., & Stoeger, H. (2018). Substantiating a special cultural emphasis on learning and education in East Asia. *High Ability Studies*, *29*(1), 79–106. https://doi.org/10.1080/13598139.2017.1423281

Baudson, T. G. (2016). The mad genius stereotype: Still alive and well. *Frontiers in Psychology*, *7*(9), 368. https://doi.org/10.3389/fpsyg.2016.00368

Baudson, T. G., & Preckel, F. (2016). Teachers' conceptions of gifted and average-ability students on achievement-relevant dimensions. *Gifted Child Quarterly*, *60*(3), 212–225. https://doi.org/10.1177/0016986216647115

Becker, H. S. (1963). *Outsiders: Studies in the sociology of deviance*. Free Press.

Becker, G. (1978). *The mad genius controversy: A study in the sociology of deviance*. Sage.

Bennett-Rappell, H., & Northcote, M. (2016). Underachieving gifted students: Two case studies. *Issues in Educational Research*, *26*(3), 407–430.

Berlin, J. E. (2009). It's all a matter of perspective: Student perceptions on the impact of being labeled gifted and talented. *Roeper Review*, *31*(4), 217–223. https://doi.org/10.1080/02783190903177580

Bernburg, J. G. (2010). Labeling and secondary deviance. In J. H. Copes & V. Topalli (Eds.), *Criminological theory: Readings and retrospectives* (pp. 340–350). McGraw Hill.

Bernburg, J. G. (2019). Labeling theory. In M. D. Krohn, N. Hendrix, G. Penly Hall, & A. J. Lizotte (Eds.), *Handbook on crime and deviance* (pp. 179–196). Springer International Publishing. https://doi.org/10.1007/978-3-030-20779-3_10

Bicakci, M., & Baloğlu, M. (2021). Gifted underachievement: Characteristics, causes and intervention. *Ankara University Faculty of Educational Sciences Journal of Special Education*, *22*(3), 771–798. https://doi.org/10.21565/ozelegitimdergisi.607979

Bicakci, M., & Ziegler, A. (In preperation). *Investigating special education student teachers' emotional reactions to the gifted label and its relation with their label preferences*.

Biddle, B. J., & Anderson, D. S. (1986). Methods, knowledge, and research on teaching. In M. C. Wittrock (Ed.), *Handbook of research on teaching* (pp. 42–64). Macmillan.

Blaas, S. (2014). The relationship between social-emotional difficulties and underachievement of gifted students. *Australian Journal of Guidance and Counselling*, *24*(2), 243–255. https://doi.org/10.1017/jgc.2014.1

Blumer, H. (1966). Sociological implications of the thought of George Herbert Mead. *American Journal of Sociology*, *71*, 535–544. https://doi.org/10.1086/224171

Blumer, H. (1969). *Symbolic interactionism: Perspective and method*. University of California Press.

Boncquet, M., Lavrijsen, J., Vansteenkiste, M., Verschueren, K., & Soenens, B. (2022). "You are so Smart!": The role of giftedness, parental feedback, and parents' mindsets in predicting students' mindsets. *Gifted Child Quarterly*, *66*(3), 220–237. https://doi.org/10.1177/00169862221084238

Borland, J. H. (1989). *Planning and implementing programs for the gifted*. Teachers College Press.

Borland, J. H. (1990). Postpositivist inquiry: Implications of the "New philosophy of science" for the field of the education of the gifted. *Gifted Child Quarterly*, *34*(4), 161–167. https://doi.org/10.1177/001698629003400406

Borland, J. H. (2005). Gifted education without gifted children: The case for no conception of giftedness. In J. E. Davidson & R. J. Sternberg (Eds.), *Conceptions of giftedness* (2nd ed., pp. 1–19). Cambridge University Press. https://doi.org/10.1017CBO9780511610455.002

Brophy, J. E., & Good, T. L. (1970). Teachers' communication of differential expectations for children's classroom performance: Some behavioral data. *Journal of Educational Psychology*, *61*(5), 365–374. https://doi.org/10.1037/h0029908

Butler-Por, N. (1987). *Underachievers in school: Issues and intervention*. John Wiley & Sons.

Chowkase, A. A. (2022). Three C's conception of giftedness: A call for paradigm shift. *Gifted Education International*. https://doi.org/10.1177/02614294211064703

Cakir, L. (2014). The relationship between underachievement of gifted students and their attitudes toward school environment. In S. Besoluk (Ed.), *Erpa International Congress on Education* (Vol. 152, pp. 1034–1038). Elsevier Science Bv. https://doi.org/10.1016/j.sbspro.2014.09.269

Carr, M., & Kurtz-Costes, B. E. (1994). Is being smart everything? The influence of student achievement on teachers' perceptions. *British Journal of Educational Psychology*, *64*(Pt 2), 263–276. https://doi.org/10.1111/j.2044-8279.1994.tb01101.x

Carter, M. J., & Fuller, C. (2016). Symbols, meaning, and action: The past, present, and future of symbolic interactionism. *Current Sociology*, *64*(6), 931–961. https://doi.org/10.1177/0011392116638396

Cavilla, D. (2017). Observation and analysis of three gifted underachievers in an underserved, urban high school setting. *Gifted Education International*, *33*(1), 62–75. https://doi.org/10.1177/0261429414568181

Ceci, S. J., Williams, W. M., & Barnett, S. M. (2009). Women's underrepresentation in science: Sociocultural and biological considerations. *Psychological Bulletin*, *135*(2), 218–261. https://doi.org/10.1037/a0014412

Charmaz, K. (2006). *Constructing grounded theory: A practical guide through qualitative analysis*. Sage.

Charmaz, K. (2021). The genesis, grounds, and growth of constructivist grounded theory. In J. M. Morse, B. J. Bowers, K. Charmaz, A. E. Clarke, J. Corbin, C. J. Porr, & P. N. Stern (Eds.), *Developing grounded theory: The second generation revisited* (2 ed., pp. 153–187). Routledge. https://doi.org/10.4324/9781315169170

Clark, B. (1992). *Growing up gifted*. Maxwell Macmillan International.

Colangelo, N., Kerr, B., Christensen, P., & Maxey, J. (1993). A comparison of gifted underachiever and gifted high achievers. *Gifted Child Quarterly*, *37*(4), 155–160. https://doi.org/10.1177/001698629303700404

Coleman, L. J. (1985). *Schooling the gifted*. Addison-Wesley.

Coleman, L. J., & Cross, T. L. (1988). Is being gifted a social handicap? *Journal for the Education of the Gifted*, *11*, 41–56.

Comte, A. (1858). *The positive philosophy* (H. Martineau, Trans.). Calvin Blanchard.

Cooley, C. H. (1902). *Human nature and the social order*. Scribner's.

Cross, T. L., Coleman, L. J., & Terhaar-Yonkers, M. (1991). The social cognition of gifted adolescents in schools: Managing the stigma of giftedness. *Journal for the Education of the Gifted*, *15*(1), 44–55. https://doi.org/10.1177/016235329101500106

Cross, J. R., Vaughn, C. T., Mammadov, S., Cross, T. L., Kim, M., O'Reilly, C., Spielhagen, F. R., Pereira Da Costa, M., & Hymer, B. (2019). A cross-cultural study of the social experience of giftedness. *Roeper Review*, *41*(4), 224–242. https://doi.org/10.1080/02783193.2019.1661052
Crotty, M. (1998). *The foundations of social research: Meaning and perspective in the research process.* Sage.
Dai, D. Y. (2016). Envisioning a new century of gifted education: The case for a paradigm change. In D. Ambrose & R. J. Sternberg (Eds.), *Giftedness and talent in the 21st century: Adapting to the turbulence of globalization* (10th ed., pp. 45–63). Sense Publishers. https://doi.org/10.1007/978-94-6300-503-6_3
Dai, D. Y. (2020). Rethinking human potential from a talent development perspective. *Journal for the Education of the Gifted*, *43*(1), 19–37. https://doi.org/10.1177/0162353219897850
Dai, D. Y., Swanson, J. A., & Cheng, H. (2011). State of research on giftedness and gifted education: A survey of empirical studies published during 1998-2010 (April). *Gifted Child Quarterly*, *55*(2), 126–138. https://doi.org/10.1177/0016986210397831
Daniel, S. H. (1978). Descartes' treatment of 'lumen naturale'. *Studia Leibnitiana*, *10*(1), 92–100. http://www.jstor.org/stable/40693840
David, H. (2023). Should we continue to use the term "giftedness"?. *Australasian Journal of Gifted Education*, *32*(1), 28–32. https://doi.org/10.21505/ajge.2023.0004
Davis, G. A., Rimm, S. B., & Siegle, D. (2014). *Education of gifted and talented* (6th ed.). Pearson.
De Condorcet, M. (1795). Future progress of mankind. In *Outlines of an historical view of the progress of the human mind: Being a posthumous work of the late M. De Condorcet* (pp. 316–372). J Johnson. https://doi.org/10.1037/11670-010
Delisle, J. R. (2002). Underachiever or selective consumer? In J. Delisle & J. Galbraith (Eds.), *When gifted kids don't have all the answers: How to meet their social and emotional needs* (pp. 167–190). Free Spirit.
Desmet, O., & Pereira, N. (2022). Gifted boys' perceptions of their academic underachievement. *Gifted Education International*, *38*(2), 229–255. https://doi.org/10.1177/02614294211050294
Desmet, O. A., Pereira, N., & Peterson, J. S. (2020). Telling a tale: How underachievement develops in gifted girls. *Gifted Child Quarterly*, *64*(2), 85–99. https://doi.org/10.1177/0016986219888633
Diaz, E. I. (1998). Perceived factors influencing the academic underachievement of talented students of Puerto Rican descent. *Gifted Child Quarterly*, *42*(2), 105–122. https://doi.org/10.1177/001698629804200205
Dixson, D. D. (2022). Moving beyond the gifted label in gifted education: An equity perspective. *Gifted Education International*, *38*(3), 425–430. https://doi.org/10.1177/02614294211065217
Dixson, D. D., Peters, S. J., Makel, M. C., Jolly, J. L., Matthews, M. S., Miller, E. M., Rambo-Hernandez, K. E., Rinn, A. N., Robins, J. H., & Wilson, H. E. (2020). A call to reframe gifted education as maximizing learning. *Phi Delta Kappan*, *102*(4), 22–25. https://doi.org/10.1177/0031721720978057
Dowdall, C. B., & Colangelo, N. (1982). Underachieving gifted students: Review and implications. *Gifted Child Quarterly*, *26*(4), 179–184. https://doi.org/10.1177/001698628202600406
Durant, W. (1933). *The story of philosophy* (New revised ed.). Garden City Publishing Co. Inc.
Earp, B. (2012). *Early academic self concepts and the racial achievement gap* (Vol. 5, pp. 3–24). Oxford Mosaic Publications.
Eccles, J. (1983). Expectancies, values, and academic behaviors. In J. T. Spence (Ed.), *Achievement and achievement motives: Psychological and sociological approaches* (pp. 75–146). W. H. Freeman.
Emerick, L. J. (1992). Academic underachievement among the gifted: Students' perceptions of factors that reverse the pattern. *Gifted Child Quarterly*, *36*(3), 140–146. https://doi.org/10.1177/001698629203600304
Epstein, M. (1953). Teachers look at gifted children. *Peabody Journal of Education*, *31*(1), 26–34. http://www.jstor.org/stable/1489610
Erikson, K. T. (1966). *Wayward puritans: A study in the sociology of deviance*. Wiley.
Feldhusen, J. F., & Heller, K. A. (1986). Introduction. In K. A. Heller & J. F. Feldhusen (Eds.), *Identifiying and nurturing the gifted.* Hans Huber Publishers.

Ferrer-Wreder, L., Wänström, L., & Corovic, J. (2014). Midlife outcomes of educationally under-achieving Swedish adolescents with above average generalized intelligence. *Research in Human Development*, *11*(3), 217–236. https://doi.org/10.1080/15427609.2014.936172

Figg, S. D., Rogers, K. B., McCormick, J., & Low, R. (2012). Differentiating low performance of the gifted learner: Achieving, underachieving, and selective consuming students. *Journal of Advanced Academics*, *23*(1), 53–71. https://doi.org/10.1177/1932202X11430000

Flanders, N. A. (1974). *Interaction analysis: A technique for quantifying teacher influence*. ERIC. https://eric.ed.gov/?id=ED088855. Accessed on Jul 24.

Ford, D. Y. (1998). The underrepresentation of minority students in gifted education: Problems and promises in recruitment and retention. *The Journal of Special Education*, *32*(1), 4–14. https://doi.org/10.1177/002246699803200102

Ford, D. Y. (2012). Ensuring equity in gifted education: Suggestions for change (again). *Gifted Child Today*, *35*(1), 74. http://search.ebscohost.com/login.aspx?direct=true&db=edb&AN=75281271&lang=tr&site=eds-live&authtype=uid

Ford, D. Y. (2014). Underrepresentation of african american and hispanic students in gifted education: Impact of social inequality, elitism, and colorblindness. *Advances in Special Education*, *26*, 101–126. https://doi.org/10.1108/S0270-4013(2014)0000026005

Ford, D. Y., & Thomas, A. (1997). *Underachievement among gifted minority students: Problems and promises* [ERIC Digest E544 - ED409660]. ERIC Clearinghouse on Disabilities and Gifted Education. https://eric.ed.gov/?id=ED409660

Foucault, M. (1984). On the genealogy of ethics: An overview of work in progress. In P. Rabinow (Ed.), *The Foucault reader: An introduction to Foucault's thought* (pp. 340–372). Penguin Books.

Foucault, M. (1995/1975). *Discipline and punish: The birth of the prison [Surveiller et punir: Naissance de la prison]* (A. Sheridan, Trans.). Vintage Books.

Gagne, F. (2015). From genes to talent: The DMGT/CMTD perspective. *Revista de Educación*, *368*, 12–39. https://doi.org/10.4438/1988-592x-re-2015-368-289

Gallagher, J. J. (1972). The special education contract for mildly handicapped children. *Exceptional Children*, *38*(7), 527–535. https://doi.org/10.1177/001440297203800702

Gallagher, S. (1999). An exchange of gazes. In J. L. Kinchloe, S. R. Steinberg, & L. E. Villeverde (Eds.), *Rethinking intelligence* (pp. 69–84). Routledge.

Gauss, C. F. (1809). *Theoria Mmotus corporum coelestium in sectionibus conicis solem ambientium*. ABC Books.

Gellel, A.-M., & Camilleri, R. (2022). Cultivating intellectual abilities and talents: The 'forgotten' Catholic contribution. *Gifted Education International*, 1–14. https://doi.org/10.1177/02614294221129360

Gentry, M. (2022). Excellence, equity, and talent development: Time to retire the g-word. *Gifted Education International*, *38*(3), 373–378. https://doi.org/10.1177/02614294211054203

Gibbons, M. M., Pelchar, T. K., & Cochran, J. L. (2012). Gifted students from low-education backgrounds. *Roeper Review*, *34*(2), 114–122. https://doi.org/10.1080/02783193.2012.660685

Glaser, B. G., & Strauss, A. L. (1964). Awareness contexts and social interaction. *American Sociological Review*, *29*(5), 669–679. https://doi.org/10.2307/2091417

Glaser, B. G., & Strauss, A. L. (1967). *The discovery of grounded theory: Strategies for qualitative research*. Aldine Pub. Co.

Glaveanu, V., & Kaufman, J. C. (2022). Building off creativity to move from gifted to gifting. *Gifted Education International*, *38*(3), 386–390. https://doi.org/10.1177/02614294211050149

Glück, J., & Tischler, K. (2021). How to save the World: Replacing "Giftedness" with "Giftingness" based on individual strengths and interests. *Gifted Education International*. https://doi.org/10.1177/02614294211058921

Göncz, A., Göncz, L., & Pekić, J. (2014). The influence of students' personality traits on their perception of a good teacher within the five-factor model of personality. *Acta Polytechnica Hungarica*, *11*, 65–86. https://doi.org/10.12700/APH.11.03.2014.03.5

Good, T. L., & Lavigne, A. L. (2018). *Looking in classrooms* (11th ed.). Routledge.

Govan, C. M. (2012). *Exploring the underachievement of elementary gifted students: An analysis of classroom achievement and standardized test performance* (Publication Number 35444665) [Doctoral dissertation]. Texas A&M University-Commerce. ProQuest Dissertations and Theses database.

Guskin, S. L., Okolo, C. M., Zimmerman, E., & Peng, C.-Y. J. (1986). Being labeled gifted or talented: Meanings and effects perceived by students in special programs. *Gifted Child Quarterly*, *30*, 61–65.

Hacking, I. (2013). *The taming chance* (15th ed.). Cambridge University Press.

Harris, M. J., & Rosenthal, R. W. (1985). Mediation of interpersonal expectancy effects: 31 meta-analyses. *Psychological Bulletin*, *97*, 363–386.

Hattie, J., & Timperley, H. (2007). The power of feedback. *Review of Educational Research*, *77*(1), 81–112. https://doi.org/10.3102/003465430298487

Hebert, T. P., & Olenchak, F. R. (2000). Mentors for gifted underachieving males: Developing potential and realizing promise. *Gifted Child Quarterly*, *44*(3), 196–207. https://doi.org/10.1177/001698620004400307

Hegel, G. W. F. (1896). *Philosophy of right*. Dover Publications.

Hegel, G. W. F. (1979/1807). *Phenomenology of spirit* (A. V. Miller, Trans.). Oxford University Press..

Heller, K. A. (2004). Identification of gifted and talented students. *Psychology Science*, *46*(3), 302–323.

Henry, T. S. (1920). *Classroom problems in the education of gifted children. The nineteenth yearbook of the National Society for the Study of Education (Part II)*. University of Chicago Press.

Herppich, S., Praetorius, A.-K., Förster, N., Glogger-Frey, I., Karst, K., Leutner, D., Behrmann, L., Böhmer, M., Ufer, S., Klug, J., Hetmanek, A., Ohle, A., Böhmer, I., Karing, C., Kaiser, J., & Südkamp, A. (2018). Teachers' assessment competence: Integrating knowledge-, process-, and product-oriented approaches into a competence-oriented conceptual model. *Teaching and Teacher Education*, *76*, 181–193. https://doi.org/10.1016/j.tate.2017.12.001

Hoffmann, J. P. (2020). Academic underachievement and delinquent behavior. *Youth & Society*, *52*(5), 728–755. https://doi.org/10.1177/0044118x18767035

Howley, A., Spatig, L., & Howley, C. (1999). Developmentalism deconstructed. In J. L. Kinchloe, S. R. Steinberg, & L. E. Villeverde (Eds.), *Rethinking intelligence* (pp. 27–51). Routledge.

Huber, S. A., & Seidel, T. (2018). Comparing teacher and student perspectives on the interplay of cognitive and motivational-affective student characteristics. *PLoS One*, *13*(8), e0200609. https://doi.org/10.1371/journal.pone.0200609

Huijer, M. (2017). A critical use of Foucault's art of living. *Foundations of Science*, *22*(2), 323–327. https://doi.org/10.1007/s10699-015-9441-z

Hume, D. (1739/1960). *A treatise of human nature* (L. A. Selby-Bigge, Ed.) Clarendon Press.

Iniesta, A. V., Lopez-Lopez, J. A., Corbi, R. G., Perez, P. M., & Costa, J. L. C. (2017). Differences in cognitive, motivational and contextual variables between under-achieving, normally-achieving, and over-achieving students: A mixed-effects analysis. *Psicothema*, *29*(4), 533–538. https://doi.org/10.7334/psicothema2016.283

Jackson, R. L. (2017). *Validation of methods to identify and measure the underachievement of gifted students* [Unpublished doctoral dissertation]. The University of New South Wales.

Jackson, R. L., & Jung, J. Y. (2022). The identification of gifted underachievement: Validity evidence for the commonly used methods. *British Journal of Educational Psychology*, *92*(3), 1133–1159. https://doi.org/10.1111/bjep.12492

Jahoda, G. (2007). *A history of social psychology: From the Eighteenth-century enlightment to the second world war*. Oxford University Press.

Jamison, K. R. (1993). *Touched with fire: Manic-depressive illness and the artistic temperament*. The Free Press.

Jenaro Río, C., Flores Robaina, N., & López Lucas, J. (2018). Utilización de la técnica del diferencial semántico para evaluar estereotipos hacia personas con discapacidades: La relevancia de la calidez y competencia [Using the semantic differential technique to assess stereotypes toward individuals with disabilities: The relevance of warmth and competence]. *Universitas Psychologica*, *17*(4), 1–12. https://doi.org/10.11144/Javeriana.upsy17-4.usdt

Jenkins-Friedman, R., & Murphy, D. L. (1988). The Mary Poppins effect: Relationships between gifted students' self concept and adjustment. *Roeper Review: A Journal on Gifted Education*, *11*, 26–30. https://doi.org/10.1080/02783198809553155

Kaiser, J., Retelsdorf, J., Südkamp, A., & Möller, J. (2013). Achievement and engagement: How student characteristics influence teacher judgments. *Learning and Instruction*, *28*, 73–84. https://doi.org/10.1016/j.learninstruc.2013.06.001

Kanevsky, L., & Keighley, T. (2003). To produce or not to produce? Understanding boredom and the honor in underachievement. *Roeper Review*, *26*(1), 20–28. https://doi.org/10.1080/02783190309554235

Kant, I. (1784/2004). Beantwortung der Frage: Was ist Aufklarung? *Utopie Kreative*, *159*, 5–10. (Berlinische Monatsschrift, DezemberHeft 1784, S. 481-494).

Kavish, D. R., Mullins, C. W., & Soto, D. A. (2016). Interactionist labeling: Formal and informal labeling's effects on juvenile delinquency. *Crime & Delinquency*, *62*(10), 1313–1336. https://doi.org/10.1177/0011128714542504

Kim, K. H. (2008). Underachievement and creativity: Are gifted underachievers highly creative? *Creativity Research Journal*, *20*(2), 234–242. https://doi.org/10.1080/10400410802060232

Kim, K. H., & VanTassel-Baska, J. (2010). The relationship between creativity and behavior problems among underachieving elementary and high school students. *Creativity Research Journal*, *22*(2), 185. http://search.ebscohost.com/login.aspx?direct=true&db=edb&AN=50791459&lang=tr&site=eds-live&authtype=uid

Kolb, K. J., & Jussim, L. (1994). Teacher expectations and underachieving gifted children. *Roeper Review*, *17*(1), 26–30.

Kosir, K., Horvat, M., Aram, U., & Jurinec, N. (2016). Is being gifted always an advantage? Peer relations and self-concept of gifted students. *High Ability Studies*, *27*(2), 129–148. https://doi.org/10.1080/13598139.2015.1108186

Krolak-Schwerdt, S., Böhmer, M., & Gräsel, C. (2013). The impact of accountability on teachers' assessments of student performance: A social cognitive analysis. *Social Psychology of Education*, *16*(2), 215–239. https://doi.org/10.1007/s11218-013-9215-9

Krolak-Schwerdt, S., Glock, S., & Böhmer, M. (Eds.). (2014). *Teachers' professional development: Assessment, training, and learning*. Sense Publishers.

Kuhn, M. H. (1964). Major trends in symbolic interaction theory in the past twenty-five years. *The Sociological Quarterly*, *5*(1), 61–84. http://www.jstor.org/stable/4105182

Lee, S.-Y., Olszewski-Kubilius, P., & Thomson, D. T. (2012). Academically gifted students' perceived interpersonal competence and peer relationships. *Gifted Child Quarterly*, *56*(2), 90–104. https://doi.org/10.1177/0016986212442568

Lemert, E. (1951). *Social pathology*. McGraw-Hill.

Lemert, E. (1967). *Human deviance, social problems and social control*. Prentice-Hall.

Lenvik, A. K. (2022). *Gifted education in Norway: A mixed-method study with teachers and students in Norwegian comprehensive school*. Doctoral dissertation. University of Bergen, Skipnes Kommunikasjon.

Lewin, K. (1931/1930). The conflict between Aristotelian and Galileian modes of thought in contemporary psychology. *The Journal of General Psychology*, *5*(2), 141–177. https://doi.org/10.1080/00221309.1931.9918387

Link, B. G., & Phelan, J. C. (2001). Conceptualizing stigma. *Annual Review of Sociology*, *27*, 363–385. https://doi.org/10.1146/annurev.soc.27.1.363

Lo, C. O. (2014). Labeling and knowing: A reconciliation of implicit theory and explicit theory among students with exceptionalities. *The Journal of Educational Research*, *107*(4), 281–298. https://doi.org/10.1080/00220671.2013.807490

Lo, C. O., & Porath, M. (2017). Paradigm shifts in gifted education: An examination vis-à-cis its historical situatedness and pedagogical sensibilities. *Gifted Child Quarterly*, *61*(4), 343–360. https://doi.org/10.1177/0016986217722840

Lohman, D. F. (2009). Identifying academically talented students: Some general principles, two specific procedures. In L. V. Shavinina (Ed.), *International handbook on giftedness*. Springer Science+Business Media. https://doi.org/10.1007/978-1-4020-6162-2_49

Lombroso, C. (1895). *The man of genius*. Walter Scott.

Lumsden, S. (2020). Community in Hegel's social philosophy. *Hegel Bulletin*, *41*(2), 177–201. https://doi.org/10.1017/hgl.2017.12

Lutz, F. W., & Lutz, S. B. (1980). Gifted pupils in the elementary school setting: An ethnographic study. In Paper presented at the *Annual Meeting of the American Educational Research Association*. Boston.

Maddox, M. (2014). *Exploring teachers' experiences of working with gifted students who underachieve* (Publication Number 3611208) [Ed.D., Walden University]. ProQuest Dissertations & Theses Global.

Maker, C. J. (2021). Exceptional talent in the 21st century context: Conceptual framework, definition, assessment, and development. *Gifted Education International*, *37*(2), 158–198. https://doi.org/10.1177/0261429421995188

Malabou, C. (2005). *The future of Hegel: Plasticity, temporality and dialectic* (L. During, Trans.). Routledge. (Original work published 1996).

Matsueda, R. L. (1992). Reflected appraisals, parental labeling, and delinquency: Specifying a symbolic interactionist theory. *American Journal of Sociology*, *97*, 1577–1611.

Matthews, M. S., & McBee, M. T. (2007). School factors and the underachievement of gifted students in a talent search summer program. *Gifted Child Quarterly*, *51*(2), 167–181. https://doi.org/10.1177/0016986207299473

Mayes, S. D., Waschbusch, D. A., Calhoun, S. L., & Mattison, R. E. (2020). How common are academic overachievement and underachievement in children with autism or ADHD? *Journal of Developmental and Physical Disabilities*, *32*(5), 775–783. https://doi.org/10.1007/s10882-019-09719-8

Mazrekaj, D., Witte, K. D., & Triebs, T. P. (2022). Mind the gap: Measuring academic underachievement using stochastic frontier analysis. *Exceptional Children*, *88*(4), 442–459. https://doi.org/10.1177/00144029211073524

McCoach, D. B., & Siegle, D. (2003). The school attitude assessment survey-revised: A new instrument to identify academically able students who underachieve. *Educational and Psychological Measurement*, *63*(3), 414–429. https://doi.org/10.1177/0013164403063003005

McCoach, D. B., & Siegle, D. (2014). Underachievers. In J. A. Plucker & C. M. Callahan (Eds.), *Critical issues and practices in gifted education: What the research say* (2 ed., pp. 691–706). Prufrock Press.

Mead, G. H. (1934/1972). *Mind, self, and society: From the standpoint of a social behaviorist*. University of Chicago Press.

Mehan, H. (1978). Assessing children's school performance. In J. Beck, C. Jenks, N. Keddie, & M. F. D. Young (Eds.), *Toward a sociology of education* (pp. 161–180). Transactional Books.

Merton, R. K. (1948). The self-fulfilling prophecy. *Antioch Review*, *8*(2), 193–210. https://doi.org/10.2307/4609267

Merton, R. K. (1995). The Thomas Theorem and the Matthew effect. *Social Forces*, *74*(2), 379–422. https://doi.org/10.2307/2580486

Mofield, E., & Parker Peters, M. (2019). Understanding underachievement: Mindset, perfectionism, and achievement attitudes among gifted students. *Journal for the Education of the Gifted*, *42*(2), 107–134. https://doi.org/10.1177/0162353219836737

Mofield, E., Peters, M. P., & Chakraborti-Ghosh, S. (2016). Perfectionism, coping, and underachievement in gifted adolescents: Avoidance vs. Approach orientations. *Education Sciences*, *6*(3), 22. https://doi.org/10.3390/educsci6030021

Moore, J. L., Ford, D. Y., & Milner, H. R. (2005). Underachievement among gifted students of color: Implications for educators. *Theory Into Practice*, *44*(2), 167–177. https://doi.org/10.1207/s15430421tip4402_11

Morisano, D., & Shore, B. M. (2010). Can personal goal setting Tap the potential of the gifted underachiever? *Roeper Review*, *32*(4), 249–258. https://doi.org/10.1080/02783193.2010.508156

National Association for Gifted Children. (n.d.). *What is giftedness*. https://www.nagc.org/resources-publications/resources/what-giftedness. Accessed on 18 May, 2022.

Neihart, M. (2006). Achievement/affiliation conflicts in gifted adolescents. *Roeper Review*, *28*(4), 196–202. https://doi.org/10.1080/02783190609554364

Nooman, S., Hanif, R., & Saeed, A. (2015). Assessing academic underachievement and high achievement among Pakistani secondary school students. *Pakistan Journal of Psychological Research*, *30*(2), 377–391.

O'Boyle, M. W. (2008). Mathematically gifted children: Developmental brain characteristics and their prognosis for well-being. *Roeper Review*, *30*(3), 181–186. https://doi.org/10.1080/02783190802199594

Obergriesser, S., & Stoeger, H. (2015). The role of emotions, motivation, and learning behavior in underachievement and results of an intervention. *High Ability Studies*, *26*(1), 167–190. https://doi.org/10.1080/13598139.2015.1043003

Oz, S., & Eden, D. (1994). Restraining the Golem - Boosting performance by changing the interpretation of low scores. *Journal of Applied Psychology*, *79*(5), 744–754. https://doi.org/10.1037/0021-9010.79.5.744

Peterson, J. S. (2001). Gifted and at risk: Four longitudinal case studies of post-high-school development. *Roeper Review*, *24*(1), 31–39. https://doi.org/10.1080/02783190109554123

Pielmeier, M., Huber, S., & Seidel, T. (2018). Is teacher judgment accuracy of students' characteristics beneficial for verbal teacher-student interactions in classroom? *Teaching and Teacher Education*, *76*, 255–266. https://doi.org/10.1016/j.tate.2018.01.002

Pyryt, M. (2004, June). Helping gifted students cope with perfectionism. *Parenting for High Potential*, 10–14.

Rauscher, F. (2022). *Kant's social and political philosophy*. The Stanford Encyclopedia of Philosophy. https://plato.stanford.edu/archives/fall2022/entries/kant-social-political/

Rayneri, L. J., Gerber, B. L., & Wiley, L. P. (2006). The relationship between classroom environment and the learning style preferences of gifted middle school students and the impact on levels of performance. *Gifted Child Quarterly*, *50*(2), 104–118. https://doi.org/10.1177/001698620605000203

Ready, D. D., & Wright, D. L. (2011). Accuracy and inaccuracy in teachers' perceptions of young children's cognitive abilities: The role of child background and classroom context. *American Educational Research Journal*, *48*(2), 335–360. https://doi.org/10.3102/0002831210374874

Reis, S. M., & McCoach, D. B. (2000). The underachievement of gifted students: What do we know and where do we go? *Gifted Child Quarterly*, *44*(3), 152–170. https://doi.org/10.1177/001698620004400302

Rentzsch, K., Schröder–Abé, M., & Schütz, A. (2013). Being called a 'Streber': The roles of personality and competition in the labelling of academically oriented students. *European Journal of Personality*, *27*(5), 411–423. https://doi.org/10.1002/per.1884

Rentzsch, K., Schütz, A., & Schröder-Abé, M. (2011). Being labeled "nerd": Factors that influence the social acceptance of high-achieving students. *The Journal of Experimental Education*, *79*(2), 143–168. https://doi.org/10.1080/00220970903292900

Renzulli, J. S. (2011a). More changes needed to expand gifted identification and support. *Phi Delta Kappan*, *92*(8), 61. https://doi.org/10.1177/003172171109200813

Renzulli, J. S. (2000). The identification and development of giftedness as a paradigm for school reform. *Journal of Science Education and Technology*, *9*(2), 95–114. https://doi.org/10.1023/A:1009429218821

Renzulli, J. S. (2011b). Theories, actions, and change: An academic journey in search of finding and developing high potential in young people. *Gifted Child Quarterly*, *55*(4), 305–308. https://doi.org/10.1177/0016986211421875

Renzulli, J. S., & Delcourt, M. A. B. (2018). Gifted behaviors versus gifted individuals. In C. M. Callahan & H. L. Hertberg-Davis (Eds.), *Fundamentals of gifted education: Considering multiple perspectives* (pp. 36–48). Routledge.

Renzulli, J. S. (n.d.). *The other goal of gifted education: Promoting emotional development and social responsibility through the use of co-cognitive skills [Essay]*. https://gifted.uconn.edu/wp-content/uploads/sites/961/2022/04/The_Other_Goal_of_Gifted_Education.pdf

Richer, E. T. (2012). *Motivational interviewing and its effect on underachieving high potential adolescents* (Publication Number 3493776) [Ed.D., Teachers College, Columbia University]. ProQuest Dissertations & Theses Global.

Ridgley, L. M., Rubenstein, L. D., & Callan, G. L. (2020). Gifted underachievement within a self-regulated learning framework: Proposing a task-dependent model to guide early identification and intervention. *Psychology in the Schools*, *57*(9), 1365–1384. https://doi.org/10.1002/pits.22408

Rimm, S. (2008). *Why bright kids get poor grades and what you can do about it: A six-step program for parents and teachers* (3rd ed.). Great Potential Press.

Rimm, S., & Lowe, B. (1988). Family environments of underachieving gifted students. *Gifted Child Quarterly*, *32*(4), 353–359. https://doi.org/10.1177/001698628803200404
Rist, R. C. (2017). On understanding the processes of schooling. In A. R. Sadovnik, J. P. W. Cookson, S. F. Semel, & R. W. Coughlan (Eds.), *Exploring Education: An introduction to the foundations of education* (5th. ed., pp. 165–176). Routledge. https://doi.org/10.4324/9781315408545
Ritchotte, J. A., Matthews, M. S., & Flowers, C. P. (2014). The validity of the achievement-orientation model for gifted middle school students: An exploratory study. *Gifted Child Quarterly*, *58*(3), 183–198. https://doi.org/10.1177/0016986214534890
Robinson, A. (1986). The identification and labeling of gifted children. In K. A. Heller & J. F. Feldhusen (Eds.), *Identifying and nurting the gifted* (pp. 103–109). Huber Publ.
Robson, C., & McCartan, K. (2016). *Real world research: A resource for users of social research methods in applied setting* (4th ed.). Wiley.
Rosenthal, R., & Jacobson, L. (1968). Pygmalion in the classroom. *The Urban Review*, *3*(1), 16–20. https://doi.org/10.1007/BF02322211
Rubenstein, L. D., Siegle, D., Reis, S. M., McCoach, D. B., & Burton, M. G. (2012). A Complex quest: The development and research of underachievement interventions for gifted students. *Psychology in the Schools*, *49*(7), 678–694. https://doi.org/10.1002/pits.21620
Saarinen, R. (2022). Christian excellence in history. From heroic saints to educated experts (1500–1800). *Gifted Education International*. https://doi.org/10.1177/02614294221128106
Sapir, E. (1921). *Language: An introduction to the study of speech*. Brace and World.
Scheff, T. J. (1966). *Being mentally ill*. Aldine.
Schlesinger, J. (2009). Creative mythconceptions: A closer look at the evidence for the "mad genius" hypothesis. *Psychology of Aesthetics, Creativity, and the Arts*, *3*, 62–72. https://doi.org/10.1037/a0013975
Schober, B., Reimann, R., & Wagner, P. (2004). Is research on gender-specific underachievement in gifted girls an obsolete topic? New findings on an often discussed issue. *High Ability Studies*, *15*(1), 43–62. https://doi.org/10.1080/1359813042000225339
Schultz, R. A. (2002). Understanding giftedness and underachievement: At the edge of possibility. *Gifted Child Quarterly*, *46*(3), 193–208. https://doi.org/10.1177/001698620204600304
Schur, E. M. (1965). *Crime without victims*. Prentice-Hall.
Schur, E. M. (1971). *Labeling deviant behavior: Its sociological implications*. Harper & Row.
Shadish, W. R., Cook, T. D., & Campbell, D. T. (2002). *Experimental and quasi-experimental designs for generalized causal inference*. Houghton, Mifflin and Company.
Shifrer, D. (2013). Stigma of a label: Educational expectations for high school students labeled with learning disabilities. *Journal of Health and Social Behavior*, *54*(4), 462–480. https://doi.org/10.1177/0022146513503346
Siegle, D. (2018). Understanding underachievement. In S. I. Pfeiffer (Ed.), *Handbook of giftedness in children: Psychoeducational theory, research, and best practices* (pp. 285–297). Springer International Publishing. https://doi.org/10.1007/978-3-319-77004-8_16
Siegle, D., & McCoach, B. (2020). Underachievers. In J. A. Plucker & C. M. Callahan (Eds.), *Critical issues and practices in gifted education: A survey of current research on giftedness and talent development* (3rd ed., pp. 521–534). Routledge.
Silverman, L. K. (2013). *Giftedness 101*. Springer.
Simonton, D. K. (2014). The mad-genius paradox: Can creative people be more mentally healthy but highly creative people more mentally ill? *Perspectives on Psychological Science*, *9*(5), 470–480. http://www.jstor.org/stable/44290034
Simonton, D. K. (2022). Giftedness from the perspective of research on genius: Some precautionary implications. *Gifted Education International*, *38*(3), 362–365. https://doi.org/10.1177/02614294211046324
Skinner, E. A., & Belmont, M. J. (1993). Motivation in the classroom: Reciprocal effects of teacher behavior and student engagement across the school year. *Journal of Educational Psychology*, *85*(4), 571–581. https://doi.org/10.1037/0022-0663.85.4.571
Smith, A. (1761). *The theory of moral sentiments* (2nd ed.). Andrew Millar.

Snyder, K. E., & Adelson, J. L. (2017). The development and validation of the perceived academic underachievement scale. *The Journal of Experimental Education*, *85*(4), 614–628. https://doi.org/10.1080/00220973.2016.1268087

Snyder, K. E., Carrig, M. M., & Linnenbrink-Garcia, L. (2021). Developmental pathways in underachievement. *Applied Developmental Science*, *25*(2), 114–132. https://doi.org/10.1080/10888691.2018.1543028

Snyder, K. E., & Linnenbrink-Garcia, L. (2013). A developmental, person-centered approach to exploring multiple motivational pathways in gifted underachievement. *Educational Psychologist*, *48*(4), 209–228. https://doi.org/10.1080/00461520.2013.835597

Snyder, K. E., Malin, J. L., Dent, A. L., & Linnenbrink-Garcia, L. (2014). The message matters: The role of implicit beliefs about giftedness and failure experiences in academic self-handicapping. *Journal of Educational Psychology*, *106*(1), 230–241. https://doi.org/10.1037/a0034553

Solomon, R. C. (1988). *Continental philosophy since 1750: The rise and fall of the self* (Vol. 63). Oxford University Press.

Spearman, C. (1904). 'General intelligence', objectively determined and measured. *American Journal of Psychology*, *15*, 201–293. https://doi.org/10.2307/1412107

Steenbergen-Hu, S., Olszewski-Kubilius, P., & Calvert, E. (2020). The effectiveness of current interventions to reverse the underachievement of gifted students: Findings of a meta-analysis and systematic review. *Gifted Child Quarterly*, *64*(2), 132–165. https://doi.org/10.1177/0016986220908601

Stern, W. (1912). *Die psychologischen Methoden der Intelligenzprüfung und deren Anwendung an Schuldkindern*. Johann Ambrosius Barth.

Sternberg, R. J. (2007a). Cultural concepts of giftedness. *Roeper Review*, *29*(3), 160–165. https://doi.org/10.1080/02783190709554404

Sternberg, R. J. (2007b). Intelligence and culture. In S. Kitiyama & D. Cohen (Eds.), *Hanfbook of cultural psychology*. Guilford Press.

Sternberg, R. J. (2010). Assessment of gifted students for identification purposes: New techniques for a new millennium. *Learning and Individual Differences*, *20*(4), 327–336. https://doi.org/10.1016/j.lindif.2009.08.003

Sternberg, R. J. (2017). ACCEL: A new model for identifying the gifted. *Roeper Review*, *39*(3), 152–196. https://doi.org/10.1080/02783193.2017.1318658

Sternberg, R. J. (2018). 21 ideas: A 42 years search to understand the nature of giftedness. *Rooper Review*, *40*(1), 7–20. https://doi.org/10.1080/02783193.2018.1393609

Sternberg, R. J. (2022a). Giftedness as trait vs. state. *Roeper Review*, *44*(3), 135–143. https://doi.org/10.1080/02783193.2022.2071365

Sternberg, R. J. (2022b). Personal talent curation in the lifetime realization of gifted potential: The role of adaptive intelligence. *Gifted Education International*, *38*(2), 161–173. https://doi.org/10.1177/02614294221086505

Sternberg, R. J., & Desmet, O. (2022). Introduction to terminological controversies in gifted education. *Gifted Education International*, *38*(3), 345–353. https://doi.org/10.1177/02614294221117096

Sternberg, R. J., & Karami, S. (2021). Gifted for whom? Individualism, dyadism, and collectivism in the definition of giftedness. *Gifted Education International*. https://doi.org/10.1177/02614294211052393

Stoeger, H., Balestrini, D. P., & Ziegler, A. (2018). International perspectives and trends in research on giftedness and talent development. In S. Pfeiffer, M. Foley-Nicpon, & E. Shaunessy-Dedrick (Eds.), *APA handbook of giftedness and talent* (pp. 25–39). American Psychological Association.

Stryker, S. (1957). Role-taking accuracy and adjustment. *Sociometry*, *20*(4), 286–296. https://doi.org/10.2307/2785981

Südkamp, A., Kaiser, J., & Möller, J. (2012). Accuracy of teachers' judgments of students' academic achievement: A m eta-analysis. *Journal of Educational Psychology*, *104*(3), 743–762. https://doi.org/10.1037/a0027627

Tannenbaum, F. (1938). *Crime and community*. Columbia University Press.

Tannenbaum, A. J. (1983). *Gifted children: Psychological and educational perspectives*. MacMillan.

Tercan, H., & Yıldız-Bıçakçı, M. (2022). Exploring the link between Turkish gifted children's perceptions of the gifted label and emotional intelligence competencies. *Scientific Reports*, *12*(1), 13742. https://doi.org/10.1038/s41598-022-17966-7

The Royal Swedish Academy of Sciences. (2022). *The Nobel Prize in Physics 2022* [Press Release]. https://www.nobelprize.org/uploads/2022/10/press-physicsprize2022-2.pdf

Thomas, W. I., & Thomas, D. S. (1928). *The child in America: Behavior problems and programs*. Knopf.

Tsai, K., & Fu, G. (2016). Underachievement in gifted students: A case study of three college physics students in Taiwan. *Universal Journal of Educational Research*, *4*(4), 688–695. https://doi.org/10.13189/ujer.2016.040405

Valsiner, J. (2019). Living through generalizing: Psychology of desire for becoming. In C. Højholt & E. Schraube (Eds.), *Subjectivity and knowledge: Generalization in the psychological study of everyday life* (pp. v–vii). Springer. https://doi.org/10.1007/978-3-030-29977-4

Van Boxtel, H. W., & Mönks, F. J. (1992). General, social, and academic self-concepts of gifted adolescents. *Journal of Youth and Adolescence*, *21*(2), 169–186. https://doi.org/10.1007/BF01537335

Veas, A., Gilar, R., Miñano, P., & Castejón, J. L. (2016). Estimation of the proportion of underachieving students in compulsory secondary education in Spain: An application of the Rasch model. *Frontiers in Psychology*, *7*(March), 303. https://doi.org/10.3389/fpsyg.2016.00303

Vialle, W., & Ziegler, A. (2015). Gifted education in modern Asia: Analyses from a systemic perspective. In D. Y. Dai & C. C. Kuo (Eds.), *Gifted education in Asia: Problems and prospects* (pp. 273–291). Information Age Publishing.

von Bertalanffy, L. (1968). *General systems theory*. George Braziller.

Wagner, C., Singer, P., Strohmaier, M., & Huberman, B. (2014). Semantic stability and implicit consensus in social tagging streams. *IEEE Transactions on Computational Social Systems*, *1*(1), 108–120. https://doi.org/10.1109/TCSS.2014.2307455

White, S. L. J., Graham, L. J., & Blaas, S. (2018). Why do we know so little about the factors associated with gifted underachievement? A systematic literature review. *Educational Research Review*, *24*, 55–66. https://doi.org/10.1016/j.edurev.2018.03.001

Whitmore, J. R. (1980). *Giftedness, conflict and underachievement*. Allyn & Bacon.

Wiley, K. R. (2020). The social and emotional world of gifted students: Moving beyond the label. *Psychology in the Schools*, *57*(10), 1528–1541. https://doi.org/10.1002/pits.22340

Winzer, M. (1996). *Children with exceptionalities in Canadian classrooms* (4th ed.). Allyn & Bacon Canada.

Wittgenstein, L. (1953). *Philosophical investigations* (G. Anscambe, Trans.). Basil Blackwell.

Zaitseva, L. V., Mayorova, I. M., Fedorenko, M. V., Hakki, A. M., & Zubarzyat, I. A. (2018). Gifted students' personal features comparative analysis depending on style preferences in painting. *Helix*, *8*(1), 2858–2862. https://doi.org/10.29042/2018-2858-2862

Zeidner, M., & Shani-Zinovich, I. (2011). Do academically gifted and nongifted students differ on the Big-Five and adaptive status? Some recent data and conclusions. *Personality and Individual Differences*, *51*(5), 566–570. https://doi.org/10.1016/j.paid.2011.05.007

Ziegler, A. (2005). The actiotope model of giftedness. In *Conceptions of giftedness* (2nd ed., pp. 411–436). Cambridge University Press. https://doi.org/10.1017/CBO9780511610455.024

Ziegler, A., Balestrini, D. P., & Stoeger, H. (2018). An international view on gifted education: Incorporating the macro-systemic perspective. In S. I. Pfeiffer (Ed.), *Handbook of giftedness in children: Psychoeducational theory, research and best practices* (2nd ed., pp. 15–28). Springer. https://doi.org/10.1007/978-3-319-77004-8_2

Ziegler, A., & Bicakci, M. (2023). *Labeling the gifted: An overview of four core challenges [Keynote address]*. Gifted Students: Nomen est Omen, Univerzita Tomáše Bati ve Zliné, Zlin, Czechia.

Ziegler, A., Chandler, K. L., Vialle, W., & Stoeger, H. (2017). Exogenous and endogenous learning resources in the Actiotope Model of Giftedness and its significance for gifted education. *Journal for the Education of the Gifted*, *40*(4), 310–333. https://doi.org/10.1177/0162353217734376

Ziegler, A., & Phillipson, S. N. (2012). Towards a systemic theory of gifted education. *High Ability Studies*, *23*(1), 3–30. https://doi.org/10.1080/13598139.2012.679085

Ziegler, A., & Stoeger, H. (2010). How fine motor skills influence the assessment of high abilities and underachievement in Math. *Journal for the Education of the Gifted, 34*(2), 195–219. https://www.scopus.com/inward/record.uri?eid=2-s2.0-79551499845&partnerID=40&md5=b486076a9f65c8fce93f8a16d8004418

Ziegler, A., & Stoeger, H. (2012). Shortcomings of the IQ-based construct of underachievement. *Roeper Review, 34*(2), 123. http://search.ebscohost.com/login.aspx?direct=true&db=edb&AN=73909769&lang=tr&site=eds-live&authtype=uid

Ziegler, A., & Stoeger, H. (2017). Systemic gifted education: A theoretical introduction. *Gifted Child Quarterly, 61*(3), 183–193. https://doi.org/10.1177/0016986217705713

Ziegler, A., Stoeger, H., & Vialle, W. (2012). Giftedness and gifted education: The need for a paradigm change. *Gifted Child Quarterly, 56*(4), 194–197. https://doi.org/10.1177/0016986212456070

Ziegler, A., & Stöger, H. (2004). Identification based on ENTER within the conceptual frame of the Actiotope model of giftedness. *Psychology Science, 46*, 324–341.

Ziegler, A., Vialle, W., & Wimmer, B. (2013). The actiotope model of giftedness: A short introduction to some central theoretical assumptions. In S. Phillipson, H. Stoeger, & A. Ziegler (Eds.), *Exceptionality in East Asia: Explorations in the actiotope model of giftedness* (pp. 1–17). Routletge.

Ziegler, A., Ziegler, A., & Stoeger, H. (2012). Shortcomings of the IQ-Basedconstruct of underachievement. *Roeper Review, 34*(2), 123–132. https://doi.org/10.1080/02783193.2012.660726

Zimmerman, E. (1985). Toward a theory of labeling artistically talented students. *Studies in Art Education, 27*(1), 31–42. https://doi.org/10.2307/1320388

THE CONTINUING SIGNIFICANCE OF VOCABULARIES OF MOTIVE FOR SYMBOLIC INTERACTIONIST THOUGHT

Eric O. Silva

Georgia Southern University, USA

ABSTRACT

The literature on the vocabularies of motive and associated concepts of accounts, neutralizations, and aligning actions has been exceptionally productive in documenting how actors mitigate the threat of stigmatization in a variety of circumstances. This paper reviews this literature that has been published since the last major reviews of this literature. It identifies two recent developments in the study of vocabularies of motive: account giving in situations of cultural ambiguity and in times of conflict. Taken together, this work yields several insights into how actors use motives to advance their goals. Finally, the chapter argues that the insights from this burgeoning body of work should be applied to the study of the culture wars. Such scholarship would help to further establish the importance of interactionist thought by correcting some of the limitations in current approaches to the study of cultural conflict that provides reified and overdetermined explanations.

Keywords: Vocabularies of motive; accounts; neutralizations; aligning actions; culture wars; stigma

INTRODUCTION

The concept of vocabularies of motive (and associated concepts of accounts, neutralizations, and aligning actions) are among the most important in the interactionist tool kit. These concepts get to the heart of Blumer's (1969) vision of symbolic interaction. They provide a scheme for identifying how actors actively

Essential Issues in Symbolic Interaction
Studies in Symbolic Interaction, Volume 59, 69–87

Published under exclusive licence by Emerald Publishing Limited
ISSN: 0163-2396/doi:10.1108/S0163-239620240000059004

and dialogically define reality in several circumstances. Motives are a sensitizing concept that allows us to capture how "joint actions" are negotiated (Blumer, 1969). Moreover, this line of research avoids pitfalls that can take us away from traditional interactionist approaches. Namely, it calls for a focus on the empirically verifiable meanings that can be found in various settings and away from the unverifiable attempts to attribute motive to actors or provide moral evaluations of meanings. This chapter will advocate for the continuing utility of the research on "vocabularies of motive" (Mills, 1940) and the attendant concept of accounts (Scott & Lyman, 1968), neutralizations (Sykes & Matza, 1957), and aligning activity (Stokes & Hewitt, 1976). Not only will it make the case for the utility of this line of research but it will also update the reviews provided by Albas and Albas (2003), Hunter (1984), and Orbuch (1997).

After an overview of the concepts, the chapter will outline how this line of research has been extremely productive in documenting how actors mitigate stigma by redefining ostensibly problematic conduct. In this section, I will discuss some of the noteworthy research on the subject and how it represents an important contribution of symbolic interactionism but also the social sciences more generally. In the next section, I review two fruitful developments in this tradition: account giving under conditions of cultural ambiguity and in settings where actors are trying to dominate others. In the final section, I argue that interactionists can offer a particular contribution to sociology and scholarship more generally by continuing to study how actors employ motives in their culture wars work. This type of research can help academics and the public to better understand the competing worldviews that are engaged in contemporary culture wars. Such analysis also allows symbolic interactionists to demonstrate how the agentic manipulation of meaning can have structural consequences.

MOTIVES AND ASSOCIATED CONCEPTS

Motives are a deeply rooted concept within symbolic interactionist thought (Albas & Albas, 2003). Mills (1940), draws on Kenneth Burke, to conceptualize vocabularies of motive as the stated reasons people give to explain their conduct. This conceptualization of motives pushes scholars away from the psychological and subjectivist explanations of human action that seek to locate the internal "spring" that pushes people to act and toward the role that interaction and culture play in constructing reality. This conceptualization fits with the interactionist concern for groundedness. We do not have empirical access to whatever combination of elements move an actor in a particular direction. We can, however, observe the statements that people make to explain their actions. Such explanations are drawn from a cultural "vocabulary" that provides individuals with acceptable explanations for their actions. In turn, these vocabularies are influenced by their cultural and institutional context (Perinbanayagam, 1977).

Scott and Lyman's (1968) notion of accounts is similar to Mills' concept of motives. Both accounts and motives conceptualize how actors draw on cultural scripts to justify conduct. The notion of the account moves past the etymologically confusing use of the term motives offered by Mills (see Albas & Albas, 2003). Moreover, Scott and Lyman identify two broad logics used in explaining oneself: justifications and excuses. In the former, one claims that one has acted properly despite accusations to the contrary. In the latter, one accepts that one has acted unfortunately, but one is not morally culpable because one was not in control.

Accounts, as formulated by Scott and Lyman (1968), have a retrospective character, but, as with motives, it is also possible that one's decision-making might be informed by what one thinks they will be able to account for in the future (Murphy, 2004). Moreover, accounts given at one point in time can serve to facilitate future conduct (Winchester & Green, 2019). Another element of the temporality of accounts is that actors indexically reference the constructed past to assign motives (Katovich & Wieting, 2000). Such a past can inform the "background expectancies" (Scott & Lyman, 1968) that actors draw on when evaluating an account. Past interactions are particularly salient in the contexts of social relationships where actors situate themselves, in part, by appealing to a shared or common past (Katovich & Couch, 1992), which includes emotions (Mattely, 2002). For example, in the film *Million Dollar Baby*, Maggie justifies her request for euthanasia from her former trainer on the past that she shares with him (Katovich, 2011). His willingness to disrupt his life and risk legal jeopardy was certainly influenced by the emotional salience of this bond (see Mattely, 2002). Within a group, the issuance and honoring of accounts can plausibly influence accounting processes in the future. For example, the irregular regular members of a bar observed by Katovich and Reese II (1987) would account for their absence. Upon acceptance of the account, they would regain their status as privileged members of the community. One might speculate that recurring absences from the bar might become part of a patron's identity and thus give them the confidence that future accounts of prolonged absences will be accepted and their favored status preserved. Additionally, Lutfiyya and Miller (1986) have argued that in ongoing relationships, future-oriented accounts serve as bank accounts that can be drawn upon when predicted disjunctures do come to pass.

Given the concern interactionists have with producing astructural scholarship (Musolf, 2016), motives and accounts are particularly important concepts. Vocabularies of motive operate at the nexus of structure, culture, and agency. For Blumer, society is organized around the "joint act." Joint actions, however, are often so habitualized that it would seem that outcomes are predetermined. It is only when joint action becomes problematic that attributing and presenting motives becomes salient. Accordingly, the study of motives has guided much theorization on the relationship between cognition, culture, interactions, and institutions.

Ethnomethodologists have also identified motive giving is a foundational way by which structure is produced in social interaction (Housley & Fitzgerald, 2008). Blum and McHugh (1971) criticize interactionist approaches to motives and accounts as focusing on "surface phenomena" and missing deeper processes. For their part, they define motives as rules of relevance that allow members to make sense of others' conduct. Moreover, assigning motives serves to produce identities.

For example, Loseke and Cahill (1984) explain that when experts assign motives to women who remain in abusive relationships, they are constructing the discredited category of the battered woman who lacks agency. Such stereotypes then influence the type of treatment given by service providers. Blum and McHugh's concern that sociologists should not treat accounts as providing insight into subjective processes is similar to Mills' (1940) criticism of motive mongering (see also Backman, 2011). Blum and McHugh open the study of motives not merely to problematic situations but to all times where actors must accomplish social order. It also pushes scholars to move beyond surface level recitation of the content and logic of the arguments that actors make. While these are important points, I argue that there is value in documenting how actors use cultural logics to explain their conduct and defend themselves against stigmatization.

There are two concepts, neutralization and aligning activity, that have documented how motives are implicated in the maintenance of structural patterns. Sykes and Matza's (1957) concept of neutralizations has been highly influential in criminology (Maruna & Copes, 2005). Although Sykes and Matza (1957) do not cite Mills (1940), their notion of neutralization "run[s] parallel to the concerns expressed in the early work on accounts" (Orbuch, 1997, p. 463). Scott and Lyman (1968) drew explicitly on the types of neutralizations identified by Sykes and Matza in constructing their typology of accounts. This typology includes the denial of responsibility, denial of injury, denial of the victim, condemnation of the condemners and appeals to higher loyalties. Neutralizations are "justifications for deviance" (Sykes & Matza, 1957, p. 666), which is essentially similar to the concept of motives and accounts. The concept of neutralization is a component of the drift theory of deviance which argues that juvenile delinquents belong to mainstream culture, but the use of neutralizations allows them to drift into deviance (Maruna & Copes, 2005). While the drift theory of deviance, of which neutralizations are a component, moves away from the classic concerns of motives/accounts scholarship, much of the actual research using this concept is very similar to the work done on accounts and motives. Variations notwithstanding, this work tends to identify a case of deviance and then document the reasons actors provide to mitigate stigmatization or guilt. Regarding temporality, naturalizations can be said to precede an act and accounts to follow it. In their study of shoplifters, however, Cromwell and Thurman (2003, 547–548) convincingly argue that "accounts, neutralizations, and rationalizations are essentially the same behavior at different stages in the criminal event."

Aligning actions provide a broader, albeit less influential, conceptualization of the role that motives play in maintaining social relationships and action. Stokes and Hewitt (1976) in their classic theorization of the relationship between culture and interaction tied these overlapping research traditions together under the concept of aligning activity. Regardless of the numbers of actors involved, disagreement about what should occur undermines actors' ability to engage in joint action (Blumer, 1969; Stokes & Hewitt, 1976). They (p. 838) define "aligning actions" as the "largely verbal efforts to restore or assure meaningful interaction in the face of problematic situations of one kind or another." Actors communicate with each other to align their conduct with cultural standards and each other. Aligning actions are arguments for redefining situations that have become problematic due to "discrepancies between what is actually taking place in a given situation and what is thought to be typical, normatively expected, probable, desirable or, in other respects, more in accord with what is culturally normal" (p. 843). Although this concept has not been used as often as motives, accounts, or neutralizations, it provides an important elaboration on these ideas.

Vocabularies of motive and associated concepts are particularly important in symbolic interactionist thought. First, accounts are bound up in the construction of self and identity. Strauss (1997), in his foundational interactionist work, *Mirrors and Masks*, identifies the discernment of interactants' motives as an integral component of the identity construction process that occurs during social interaction. The issuance of motives is also an integral part of the process of self-presentation, particularly in situations where individuals face condemnation for violating social norms (see also Scott, 2015). Second, methodologically, these concepts facilitate groundedness by providing generic processes that can serve as sensitizing concepts across multiple cases and by discouraging researchers from taking large speculative leaps into the unconsciousness of their subjects. Third, and relatedly, the concept of motives allows scholars to capture meaning making in a (relatively) neutral manner. Because the focus is on what people say and not necessarily what they *really* mean or *why* they are doing it scholars can focus on vocabularies of motive allowing sociologists to avoid unfalsifiable speculative leaps or reifying theoretical constructs. Fourth, motives help to manage the paradox that although conduct is meaningful people may not be fully aware of the meanings of their conduct. It reminds scholars that their subjects may be honest about or even certain of the actual subjective processes that caused them to make a given choice. This approach thus provides a way to examine culture and the construction of generalized other. Although scholars do not have direct access to whatever it is that motivates a person to act in a particular way, their subjects' description of their conduct does tell something about a particular culture (Hewitt, 2016; Mills, 1940).

Given the utility of these concepts, it is not surprising that sociologists have employed motives, accounts, neutralizations, and aligning activity in a tremendous amount of research (Albas & Albas, 2003; Orbuch, 1997). I will now turn to a summarization of the empirical literature on motives. I argue that while the main thrust of this literature has focused on the experiences of isolated actors who defend themselves against the stigmatization that stems from having violated hegemonically supported norms, there has also been development of research on how accounts and motives are offered during times of uncertainty and on behalf of variably empowered actors and collectivities.

DEFENDING THE SELF AGAINST STIGMATIZATION

The past 20 years have seen continued examination of the processes by which individuals who stand accused of violating widely held social norms seek to defend their selves by redefining their conduct in culturally acceptable ways.

These studies have shown actors using motives, accounts, or neutralizations to manage the stigmatization that might come from a variety of actions such as patronizing a bar in the morning (Skjælaaen, 2016), homeschooling one's children (Lois, 2009), shoplifting (Cromwell & Thurman, 2003), sex doll ownership (Hanson, 2022); early termination of breastfeeding (Murphy, 2004); having been incarcerated for a gun related crime (Pogrebin et al., 2006); managing negative stereotypes of professional athletes' marriages (Simonetto, 2019); failure to comply with diabetes care (Allen, 2013) or a healthy diet (Harris, 2017); assaulting incarcerated child molesters (Trammell & Chenault, 2009); not reporting sexual assault (Weiss, 2011); having body integrity identity disorder (Davis, 2014); not recycling (Markle, 2014); being of Middle Eastern descent in the aftermath of 9/11 (Marvasti, 2005); committing serial murder (James & Gossett, 2018); and genocide (Bryant et al., 2018). While these studies examine a variety of contexts, there are also basic similarities. Ultimately, they show us how actors try to construct favorable realities in difficult situations.

While this work has generally not addressed all of Blum and McHugh (1971) critiques of this literature, these studies collectively make several important contributions to literature. First, substantively, they provide documentation of the worldviews of actors in a variety of situations. Of course, one's stated motives are not necessarily their actual motives (Mills, 1940). Nevertheless, this work provides evidence of the types of claims that the accused seem to believe will improve their circumstances. This tells us something about the logics of various types of actors. It also shows us something about how people use culture as these studies are grounded in empirical observations and do not depend on reified theoretical concepts (e.g. governmentality).

Second, on a theoretical level, they provide empirical support for important elements of the symbolic interactionist perspective. It demonstrates the importance of the self. That the self is socially constructed. It is not simply a given that a label will operate in a particular way. Moreover, the existence of varieties of constructions shows that people have some agency when building a sense of self. That others' opinions are indeed highly important – even to the most marginalized and irredeemable.

Third, many of these studies are especially accessible. Because they do not require prior knowledge of complex statistical procedures or arcane theoretical constructions, they can be assigned to students. As interactionists warily ponder their relevance (Fine & Tavory, 2019), it is worth remembering that our widest audience is likely to be students. Work that can be assigned to students has the potential to maintain the interactionist perspective. These studies work well in the classroom. They provide empathy and also document important sociological concepts. They show how individual thinking is bound up with structural and cultural context. For the nonexpert, such research can efficiently demonstrate the limitations of individualistic or psychological understandings of people.

Fourth, this set of concepts facilitates empirical grounding. It provides means for analyzing qualitative data that are readily measurable. The study of motives and accounts does not require what Mills referred to as "motive mongering."

Such concern for empirical grounding is at the heart of interactionist scholarship and, frankly, distinguishes interactionism from other approaches to social science.

The above review shows that these concepts have been exceptionally useful for documenting situations where marginalized actors who have been accused of breaking widely accepted informal norms or laws defend themselves against stigmatization by defining their conduct as some type of exception. Despite its tremendous productivity, there is still much that has not been covered in the literature on motives. As Nichols (1990) explained three decades ago, there are multiple dimensions along which this research could develop. Of these, this paper will consider how research on motives has developed in two areas identified by Nichols: the relative degree of unity of the audience and the levels of stratification of the audience.

ACCOUNTING FOR DISAGREEMENT AND DOMINATION

As the above section demonstrates, the research on motives and associated concepts has been exceptionally productive. Nonetheless, there is still unrealized potential. There are two dimensions along which research on aligning activity has expanded: situations where there is disagreement about which norms should prevail and situations where actors pursue domination rather than accord. Of course, conditions of cultural ambiguity and conflict can and often do coincide with each other. However, because they are analytically distinct, I believe it makes sense to discuss each in turn.

Cultural Ambiguity

The typical study of motives and aligning activity shows how actors who stand accused of the violation of uncontroversial norms defend their identities. I believe that the above review shows that the study of motives has, like much social science (Prus, 1997), tended to over assume the unity of culture. The concept of vocabularies of motives, however, can be useful for discovering the subcultural themes within a society. Campbell (1991) has argued convincingly that Mills' interest in the vocabularies of motive that exist in a particular context has been ignored in place of the study of how people in particular circumstances explain their own deviance. The necessity of understanding account making under conditions of divided moral expectations is increasingly necessary. Globalization means that people of different backgrounds are going to be in contact with each other. Also, the rise of the internet has resulted in greater capacity for moral disagreement than might have happened in the past.

Accordingly, there have been an increasing number of studies that have examined how actors use vocabularies of motive when there is widespread normative disagreement. Situations of motive talk under conditions of cultural uncertainty or disagreement have been taken up in the study of victims of domestic abuse (Dunn, 2005; Sharp, 2009); athletic team's use of Native

American symbolism (Silva, 2007), teaching alternatives to evolutionary theory in public schools (Silva, 2014); support for Donald Trump and the policies of his administration (Dignam et al., 2021; Silva, 2019a; Silva & Flynn, 2020a, 2020b), Christians who enjoy mixed martial arts (Borer & Schafer, 2011), practicing midwifery in states where it is illegal (Suarez & Bolton, 2018), and neutralizing the condemnations of pharmaceutical and agricultural corporations (Silva et al., 2023).

These studies highlight several features of the function of motives and aligning activity in the absence of moral unity. These findings include the presence of strong justifications and accounts of authority, motives as a tool for reconciling cultural contradictions, constructing collective identities to mitigate stigmatization, and importance of social media. It also provides further empirical support for important components of interactionist thought such as the principles of human agency and interactive determination (Snow, 2001).

First, in situations of cultural disagreement, actors are free to use stronger and more encompassing justifications than those identified in the literature on accounting under conditions of moral consensus. By a strong justification, I mean the actor claims that a category of activity is *always* acceptable as opposed to a weak justification where the actor defends a specific act as an *exception* to an agreed-on rule. For example, Silva (2007) found that many mascot defenders do not recognize Native American mascots as "impermissible" and are not trying to define the contested practice as an exception. Instead, they often argue, without qualification, that the imagery is either harmless ("denial of injury") or beneficial ("assertion of consequence") to society. Likewise, midwives in prohibition states offer unqualified justifications of the public good they provide (Suarez & Bolton, 2018).

Similarly, when actors know that there is widespread disagreement over the definition of the situation, such fragmentation leads to debates over who is qualified to render a judgment. That is, actors will not only justify conduct but they also justify their voice. For example, in Silva's (2007) study of mascot controversy, some actors would justify their ability to define the situation by claiming to be Native American. Such "claims of authority" seem to be absent from the literature on accounts of individual behavior. Perhaps this absence is because those who defend personal conduct have comparatively fewer supporters and hence feel as though they have less opportunity to assert their authority (Silva, 2007). For another example, Suarez and Bolton (2018) show that midwives who practice in the few states where it is illegal draw on public support and legality in other states to justify themselves.

Second, motive talk can also be a means of reconciling competing cultural expectations. For example, Sharp (2009) shows how conservative Christian wives use vocabularies of motive to leave abusive marriages without sacrificing their identities that otherwise proscribe divorce. Furthermore, Borer and Schafer (2011) examine the accounts given by Christian fans of mixed martial arts in online forums. These fans are caught between two moral orders. As they account for their seemingly contradictory enjoyment of organized violence, they forge tangible identity boundaries in the public sphere.

Third, actors in cases of cultural discord use motives to create collective identities that minimize stigmatization. Dunn (2005) examines how activists and scholars produce a vocabulary of motives for women who remain in physically abusive relationships. In this case, there is disagreement over how much culpability should be given to victims. The victim as survivor characterization stems from collective attribution of motives given by scholars and activists under this situation of cultural disagreement. Additionally, the accounts provided by the subjects of Borer and Schafer's (2011) research produce cultural boundaries from which identities can be constructed. The existence of multiple others making a similar claim can thus empower actors to mitigate stigma with a collective identity.

Fourth, this research demonstrates the importance of social media in dramatizing and concretizing cultural differences. Silva and Flynn (2020a) show how countervailing alignments serve to produce a liminal stigma for both critics and defenders of Trump's family separation program. This liminal stigma would likely be impossible in face-to-face conversation where individuals are less likely to spend time around others who are unlike themselves (McPherson et al., 2001) or to express unpopular opinions (Eliasoph, 1997). Likewise, Borer and Schafer (2011) demonstrate how accounting behavior that occurs online can allow conflicted individuals to try out and practice certain accounts.

Fifth, this literature further establishes the role of agency in the construction of reality (Snow, 2001). Silva (2014) shows how those who oppose the uncontested teaching of evolutionary theory in public schools use several arguments that contradict the messages favored by leadership of the intelligent design movement. The difficulty leaders had in preventing other creationists from casting intelligent design as religiously motivated reveals the agency that individuals possess. Moreover, agency is demonstrated by the multiple ways that Trump supporters responded to Trump's offensive characterization of unauthorized immigrants at the commencement of his presidential campaign (Silva, 2019a). His comments about Mexicans "not sending their best" (Ye Hee Lee, 2015) was variably ignored, celebrated, and refocused. These multiple responses to the same obdurate reality indicate the relative freedom they possess to interpret their world.

Sixth, these studies also support the principle of interactive determination (Snow, 2001) as adversaries each coinfluence the definition of the situation. For example, both Trump supporters and opponents contributed to the same boundaries. Many of Trump's critics and supporters cast Trump as expressing conservative opinion more generally. Moreover, Silva et al.'s (2023) examinations of the ways that online commenters attempt to neutralize the stigmatization of vaccines and genetically modified organisms often had the effect of reinforcing elements of their opponents' definition of the situation. Attempts to neutralize antivaccine arguments would sometimes include acknowledgment of vaccine opponent's condemnation of pharmaceutical companies.

The recent exploration of how motives and associated concepts are used in times of cultural disunity yields several insights and furthers empirical support of interactionist principles (Snow, 2001). This literature has also recently expanded into the study of domination and conflict.

Conflict and Domination

Just as the study of motives has tended to assume cultural unity, it has also tended to assume that actors wish to pursue alignment rather than disalignment. This tendency is a function of empirical work that has focused on marginalized individuals who seek to protect themselves against stigmatization. This inclination has been challenged in the literature on motives specifically (Dellwing, 2012, 2015) and interactionism more generally (Athens, 2007, 2013; Musolf, 2016).

Radical interactionists have called for interactionist analysis into conflict and inequality (Athens, 2007, 2013; Musolf, 2016). Athens has argued that interactionists have failed to sufficiently center the role of domination and conflict in everyday life. Athens (2007, 2013) has called for a radical interactionism that keeps many of the central tenets of symbolic interactionism but maintains that domination is a central feature of group life that must always be accounted for. Gougherty and Hallett (2013) agree that radical interactionism addresses long-standing criticisms of symbolic interaction by placing more emphasis on conflict and domination. Through a reanalysis of the ethnographic classic, *Learning to Labor*, they show how the apolitical and functionalist Goffmanian concepts of deference and demeanor can be repurposed "in a way that accounts more explicitly for the broad role of symbols in domination" (pp. 30–31). In similar fashion, the literature on motives is positioned to demonstrate how domination is exercised in situations of conflict and domination. Dellwing (2015) relates that the literature on aligning activity unduly presumed that actors desire peaceful resolutions. He contends, "Those whose behavior is challenged, 'called out', need not align their actions; they can resist others' challenges and make counter challenges, leading to sustained conflicts over alignment" (p. 160). Moreover, in many cases one must make a mutually exclusive choice about which faction one will be aligned with (Dellwing, 2012). Accordingly, research on motives has begun to yield some insights about how motive talk is leveraged in the pursuit of domination. This work has included studies of motives used by the powerful to justify the domination of others including: dishonest professional practices (Shulman, 2000), corporate crime (Leasure, 2017), the US invasion of Afghanistan and Iraq (Husting & Orr, 2007), leaders in the Executive Branch of the US government justifying the "Enhanced Interrogation" program used by the CIA in the 2000s (Balfe, 2023), police accounts of actions captured by body cameras (Schneider, 2023), and young cisgender women's motives for problematizing hypothetical transgender partners and children (Sumerau & Holway, 2022). These studies demonstrate several features of accounting of the powerful including cumulative power, a greater capacity to engage in character attacks, the ability of actors to persist in the face of fierce criticism, and the unstated premises that the comparatively powerful draw on when defining reality.

First, this literature has uncovered the cumulative power that can accrue from organized account giving. Shulman (2000) shows how professional communities can provide members with explanations for apparent malfeasance. Within the collective practice of organizations, these repeated accounts take on a cumulative power that goes beyond mitigating the stigma of an individual and toward the repetition of institutionalized conduct. For private detectives their accounts of deception allow them to take "advantage over unwilling targets of work-related deceptions. Second, they help to obscure any potential harm that results from using work-related deceptions" (p. 276). Likewise, Silva (2007) documents how the public accounts offered in defense of Native American imagery in team sports take on a cumulative power that continued (for many decades, at least) to allow teams to use imagery regarded by many as racist. Leasure (2017) do not reference the concept of cumulative power, nonetheless, they show how accounts of domination can be built into organizational practice.

Second, it demonstrates how empowered actors can attempt to dominate through character attacks. For example, there are important differences between situations where actors defend their personal actions (e.g. shoplifting or sex doll use) and situations where actors contribute to a public debate over the acceptability of an institutional practice (e.g. athletic teams' use of Native American symbolism) – organizational inertia and numerous likeminded allies (Silva, 2007). Power derives from not needing to convince others to accept a definition of the situation. The powerful simply need to convince others to ignore the claimants. These differences expand the rhetorical options of account-givers. Condemnation of the condemners is a classic justification for deviance (Sykes & Matza, 1957). But it is far less potent in the hands of a shoplifter than the spokesperson of a well-resourced organization. Silva (2007) found that this structural advantage results in new types of aligning activity, the rejection of challenge, where one "call [s] for the dismissal of the challenge or the challengers" (p. 256). These rejections undercut the authority of one's adversaries without *necessarily* even having to address their claims. Additionally, Husting and Orr (2007) argue that the label of "conspiracy theorist" operates as a discursive mechanism to not provide an account of one's conduct. The label moves the discussion from the topic at hand to an assault on the legitimacy of those who are so labeled. For example, in the aftermath of the 9/11 attacks the Bush administration and sympathetic press dismissed US Representative Cynthia McKinney's calls for accounting for intelligence failures and war profiteering as merely being conspiracy theories.

Third, this research demonstrates *how* oppression can be enacted in the face of criticism. Silva and Flynn's (2020a, 2020b) previously mentioned study of the neutralizations of the Trump administration's short-lived policy of separating child migrants from their parents is another instance of motive talk being used to exact domination. In this case, the liminal stigma faced by supporters of the policy could plausibly justify their own sense of victimhood. Accordingly, their need to defend their own character might lessen any potential guilt stemming from support for the policy. Again, in Silva's (2019a) aforementioned study of the neutralization of Trump's 2019 characterization of unauthorized immigration there were ultimately a number of laminations (Goffman, 1974) offered in the defense of Trump. Each lamination is its own level of defense. In many cases of domination, the offending party does not need to convince others that they are acting properly. They merely need to convince them to stop criticizing the practice. As discussions on the acceptability of a practice divide into multiple debates, each debate distracts from the other making a resolution less feasible.

Fourth, it captures the moments where otherwise taken for granted hegemonic or elite definitions of the situation are constructed. Schneider (2023) outlines the accounts used by police to explain actions recorded with body-worn cameras. Importantly, these accounts show the level of violence that police believe to be acceptable and the fact that police sometimes decline to explain their conduct. Sumerau and Holway (2022) show how young cisgender women use anticipatory vocabularies of exemption and difficulty in their considerations of hypothetical transgender partners and children which contributes to the stigmatization of transgender people.

CULTURE WARS WORK AND THE VOCABULARIES OF MOTIVE

In this final section, I will consider how recent work on motives should be further applied to our understandings of the cultural tiffs variably referred to as cultural wars (Hunter, 1991), status politics (Gusfield, 1963), or stigma contests (Schur, 1980). The recent wave of right-wing political victories such as Donald Trump's electoral victory and Great Britain's exit from the European Union has increased both scholarly and popular focus on these phenomena. The recent advances in the study of motives have the potential to yield important insights by demonstrating the culture wars work (Borer & Murphree, 2008; Borer & Schafer, 2011; Silva, 2014) that goes into these competing constructions of reality. Culture wars work refers to the social construction of reality in struggles over cultural matters (Borer & Murphree, 2008, p. 110, n. 13). The concept of motives is a useful tool for describing culture wars work.

Especially with the rise of Trump, much work seeks to understand the worldviews of conservatives. Campbell (2016) identifies the number of Americans who are moderate has declined, while the ranks of liberals and conservatives have grown and that ideological positions predict policy preferences. Mason (2018) argues that the growth of partisan identities drives policy disagreement between liberals and conservatives. Accordingly, much recent scholarship has sought to divine the worldviews of conservatives and (less frequently) liberals. It follows the classic mold of seeking to dowse the internal springs to action that push participants in the culture wars. This work, however, could benefit from recent developments in the literature on vocabularies of motive.

A common thrust of these studies is that Trump supporters who support conservative ends are *motivated* by a sense that their status has been threatened (Silva, 2019b). Hochschild (2018) in her ethnographic study of conservatives in Louisiana identifies a deep story they ascribe to that holds that while they have been waiting in line patiently for the American Dream, minorities, facilitated by the federal government, have been allowed to cut in line in front of them. Moreover, Hochschild (2019) concludes that Trump has actively manipulated the shame of his followers. She observes that during his presidency, Trump routinely performed a "de-shaming ritual" wherein "a) He does or says something transgressive. b) Public commentators rebuke him for it. c) He defiantly rails against the rebukers – a gesture which symbolically eliminates shame – and which his followers find cathartic" (p. 12). Lamont (2018) and colleagues (Lamont et al., 2017) argue that the US is marked by affronts to self-worth resulting from decades of neoliberal precarity. One manifestation of this crisis of recognition gaps are the emotive and polarized politics marked by the career of Trump. Others identify the white nationalism of Trump's base. McVeigh and Estep (2019) compare the rise of Trump in 2016 to the reemergence of the Ku Klux Klan in the 1920s. This research, of course, takes liberals' definitions of the situation for granted.

This lacuna is partially addressed by scholarship that seeks to identify the basic differences between liberals and conservatives with the inevitable consequence of oversimplification. Existing literature on cultural conflict has tended to offer an oversimplified vision of the types of identities and boundaries that emerge. Much work posits a dichotomous conflict between liberals and conservatives and then seeks to decipher the worldviews of these competing groups. Hunter (1991) famously argued that while there are many fronts to the culture war, they are connected in that each disparate battle – be it funding for the arts, gay marriage, drug legalization, prostitution, or creationism – fall under the common heading of the "struggle to define America" by shaping its public culture (Hunter, 1991). He elaborates that while each side espouses "freedom and justice," they have different understandings of the concepts. "Where *cultural conservatives* tend to *define freedom economically* (as individual economic initiative) and *justice socially* (as righteous living), *progressives* tend to *define freedom socially* (as individual rights) and *justice economically* (as equity)" (emphasis in original, p. 115). Importantly, each camp has contrasting moral visions which lead to intractable political disputes. Similarly, Lakoff (2002) claims that liberals and conservatives have incommensurable moral visions that stem from their differing ways of analogizing the nation to a family. Conservatives believe in a strict father morality in which children/citizens must respect authority and become self-disciplined to survive a dangerous world. While liberals hold a nurturant parent morality where children/citizens should be empathetic and protect those in need. Similarly, Hetherington and Weiler (2018) identify the fixed worldviews of conservatives who oppose social change, do not trust outsiders, drive pick-up trucks, enjoy meatloaf, and country music. Correspondingly, liberals have a fluid worldview that embraces novelty and outsiders, drive Priuses and enjoy chicken curry. They also acknowledge a mixed perspective that is torn between the poles of fixed and fluid. Finally, Whitehead and Perry (2020, p. 10) identify Christian nationalism (which "includes assumptions of nativism, white supremacy, patriarchy, and heteronormativity, along with divine sanction for authoritarian control and militarism") as an ideological fault line in the US. They then take a more nuanced approach than the preceding scholars by identifying four orientations – rejectors, resistors, accommodators, and ambassadors.

While this scholarship identifies important aspects of cultural conflicts, the above review of recent developments in the study of vocabularies of motive suggest problems with these attempts to understand cultural conflicts and also offer a means of addressing these deficiencies. One problem with these approaches is that they ignore the complexity of the construction of reality. Of course, some degree of simplification is necessary. But this approach unnecessarily misses important aspects of how actors understand their worlds. Agreement that exists between these factions (Alexander & Smith, 1993; Brown, 2000; Thomson, 2010) and intrafactional conflict (Benford, 1993; Borer & Murphree, 2008; Silva, 2018; Thomson, 2010) goes unacknowledged. A second problem with such reification is that it promotes an overdetermined picture of cultural conflict. Actors are pushed by their shame or racism. It neglects the agency of actors in defining these unclear situations or the dialogic ways that opponents influence each other. The results of these problems are not simply moot. Any applicable value of this research (e.g. empathy) will be diminished by an incomplete picture.

Fortunately, the above reviewed advances in the study of motives under conditions of cultural ambiguity and efforts to dominate are poised to address these shortcomings. Participants in the culture wars are very much engaged with the attribution motives. In election debates, social media, and Thanksgiving dinners, actors find themselves in situations where they need to account for why their definition of reality should dominate. For each topic discussed, there are an array of competing claims about what is happening and what should happen. The interactionist study of motives in these stigma contests should provide a level of conceptual detail that is often missing from other approaches to the study of cultural conflict and disagreement.

An analysis of culture wars work that draws on the literature outlined in the preceding section would help to solve these problems within the existing literature by providing greater clarity about the construction of reality in the culture wars. The research reviewed above has shown how collective identities are actively (Borer & Schafer, 2011; Dunn, 2005) and dialogically constructed (Silva, 2019a) constructed to mitigate stigma. It suggests that participants in culture wars are not simply playing out internalized scripts into which they were socialized but are actively negotiating the countervailing narratives in US culture (Borer & Schafer, 2011; Sharp, 2009). It demonstrates how multiple laminations or levels of debate can impede resolution (Silva 2019a, Silva & Flynn, 2020b); and how seemingly cruel or offensive practices can be maintained in the face of fierce criticism (Husting & Orr, 2007; Silva, 2007; Silva & Flynn, 2020a, 2020b). Finally, the above research can examine meaning making without trying to delve into (the empirically inaccessible) psyches of actors. Thus far, these qualities of cultural conflicts have only been demonstrated in a limited range of cases. With further research on how motives are used in cultural disagreements in a greater number of topics, however, interactionists would be able to provide scholars and the wider public with a picture of cultural conflict that better reflects the dynamism and nuances of the obdurate world.

Addressing these concerns could demonstrate the usefulness of an interactionist approach not only to scholars but to general audiences, as well. I will conclude with some consideration of how such an approach to the study of cultural conflict could be useful to nonacademic audiences (and, thus, help to address the perennial concern that interactionists have with our marginality to academia, much less society (Fine, 1993; Fine & Tavory, 2019; Maines, 2001). By identifying the processes by which actors draw on motives in the culture wars, this line of research could continue to guide readers to gain a greater understanding of the various ways that these topics can be defined. Such a careful summation of the variety of ways of thinking about these contested issues can have several benefits: First, it can promote empathy and, perhaps, mutual respect (see Lamont, 2018). Allowing readers access the rationales, if not worldviews, of others might show that other people can interpret reality differently without being stupid or immoral. From a point of mutual respect for the rationality of adversaries, we might hope that steps toward resolution or compromise can be taken. Second, it can facilitate the avoidance of statements that are more controversial than one realizes. Beyond the lofty goal of reaching a consensus is the practical need to be able to work with others without alienating them. This research would allow a reader to see that their own common sense is a point of contention for others. Third, it can help to avoid simplistic mischaracterizations and the disaffection that can stem from such mischaracterizations. Likewise, a fourth potential benefit is that can facilitate the persuasion of others by allowing one to anticipate the actual criticisms of their position and thus make stronger cases.

CONCLUSION

This paper has shown how the literature on motives and associated concepts has moved beyond the examination of how actors massage the definition of the situation to mitigate their own stigma in the face of moral consensus to consider situations where there is little cultural agreement and those where actors are seeking to dominate others. This research has demonstrated how key elements of interactionist thought (interactive determination, the importance of human agency) are supported by this scholarship. It has also provided some insights into culture and conflict – the strong justifications, claims of authority, and character attacks found in such cases – how motives serve as a tool for reconciling cultural contradictions, the importance of social media, the cumulative power of accounts given by organized collectives, the persistence of powerful actors' conduct in the face of criticism, and the otherwise hidden logic of elite worldviews. It is argued that this literature can fruitfully build on these developments by further examining how actors use motives in their culture wars work. Doing so will not only attend to concerns of the interactionist community but also further establish the usefulness of explicitly symbolic interactionist thought in mainstream sociology and beyond.

ACKNOWLEDGMENT

Thanks to an anonymous reviewer who offered insightful comments on these points.

REFERENCES

Albas, C. A., & Albas, D. C. (2003). Motives. In L. T. Reynolds & N. J. Herman-Kinney (Eds.), *Handbook of symbolic interactionism* (pp. 349–366). Rowman Altamira.

Alexander, J. C., & Smith, P. (1993). The discourse of American civil society: A new proposal for cultural studies. *Theory and Society*, *22*(2), 151–207.

Allen, D. (2013). "Just a typical teenager": The social ecology of "normal adolescence"—Insights from diabetes care. *Symbolic Interaction, 36*(1), 40–59.

Athens, L. (2007). Radical interactionism: Going beyond Mead. *Journal for the Theory of Social Behavior, 37*(2), 137–165.

Athens, L. (2013). "Radical" and "symbolic interactionism": Demarcating their borders. In L. Athens & N. K. Denzin (Eds.), *Radical interactionism on the rise (Studies in symbolic interactionism)* (pp. 1–24). Emerald Publishing Limited.

Backman, C. (2011). Vocabularies of motive among employers conducting criminal background checks. *Acta Sociologica, 54*(1), 27–44.

Balfe, M. (2023). Accounting for enhanced interrogation: Elite perspectives. *Deviant Behavior, 44*(3), 421–437.

Benford, R. D. (1993). Frame disputes within the nuclear disarmament movement. *Social Forces, 71*(3), 677-701.

Blum, A. F., & McHugh, P. (1971). The social ascription of motives. *American Sociological Review, 36*(1), 98–109.

Blumer, H. (1969). *Symbolic interactionism: Perspective and method.* University of California Press.

Borer, M. I., & Murphree, A. (2008). Framing Catholicism: Jack Chick's anti-Catholic cartoons and the flexible boundaries of the culture wars. *Religion and American Culture: A Journal of Interpretation, 18*(1), 95–112. https://doi.org/10.1525/rac.2008.18.1.95

Borer, M. I., & Schafer, T. S. (2011). Culture war confessionals: Conflicting accounts of Christianity, violence, and mixed martial arts. *Journal of Media and Religion, 10*(4), 165–184. https://doi.org/10.1080/15348423.2011.625262

Brown, S. S. (2000). Popular opinion on homosexuality: The shared moral language of opposing views. *Sociological Inquiry, 70*(4), 446–461.

Bryant, E., Schimke, E. B., Nyseth Brehm, H., & Uggen, C. (2018). Techniques of neutralization and identity work among accused genocide perpetrators. *Social Problems, 65*(4), 584–602.

Campbell, C. (1991). Reexamining Mills on motive: A character vocabulary approach. *Sociological Analysis, 52*(1), 89–97.

Campbell, J. E. (2016). *Polarized: Making sense of a divided America.* Princeton University Press.

Cromwell, P., & Thurman, Q. (2003). The devil made me do it: Use of neutralizations by shoplifters. *Deviant Behavior, 24*(6), 535–550.

Davis, J. L. (2014). Morality work among the transabled. *Deviant Behavior, 35*(6), 433–455.

Dellwing, M. (2012). Little dramas of discomposure: On doing face-work with disaligning actions. *Symbolic Interaction, 35*(2), 146–161.

Dellwing, M. (2015). Resisting alignment: Negotiating alignment, responsibility, and status in everyday life. In T. Müller (Ed.), *Contributions from European symbolic interactionists: Conflict and cooperation, studies in symbolic interaction* (Vol. 45, pp. 159–176). Emerald Publishing Limited.

Dignam, P., Schrock, D., Erichsen, K., & Dowd-Arrow, B. (2021). Valorizing Trump's masculine self: Constructing political allegiance during the 2016 presidential election. *Men and Masculinities, 24*(3), 367–392.

Dunn, J. L. (2005). "Victims" and "survivors": Emerging vocabularies of motive for "battered women who stay". *Sociological Inquiry, 75*(1), 1–30.

Eliasoph, N. (1997). 'Close to home': The work of avoiding politics. *Theory and Society, 26*(5), 605–647.

Fine, G. A. (1993). The sad demise, mysterious disappearance, and glorious triumph of symbolic interactionism. *Annual Review of Sociology, 19*(1), 61–87.

Fine, G. A., & Tavory, I. (2019). Interactionism in the twenty-first century: A letter on being-in-a-meaningful-world. *Symbolic Interaction, 42*(3), 457–467.

Goffman, E. (1974). *Frame analysis: An essay on the organization of experience.* Harvard University Press.

Gougherty, M., & Hallett, T. (2013). Revisiting learning to labor: Interaction, domination, resistance and the "grind. In L. Athens & N. K. Denzin (Eds.), *Radical interactionism on the rise (Studies in symbolic interactionism)* (pp. 123–159). Emerald Publishing Limited.

Gusfield, J. R. (1963). *Symbolic crusade: Status politics and the American temperance movement.* University of Illinois Press.
Hanson, K. R. (2022). The silicone self: Examining sexual selfhood and stigma within the love and sex doll community. *Symbolic Interaction*, *45*(2), 189–210.
Harris, D. A. (2017). Just the "Typical College Diet": How college students use life stages to account for unhealthy eating. *Symbolic Interaction*, *40*(4), 523–540.
Hetherington, M., & Weiler, J. (2018). *Prius or pickup?: How the answers to four simple questions explain America's great divide.* Houghton Mifflin.
Hewitt, J. P. (2016). Dramaturgy and motivation: Motive talk, accounts, and disclaimers. In C. Edgley (Ed.), *The drama of social life* (pp. 109–122). Routledge.
Hochschild, A. R. (2018). *Strangers in their own land: Anger and mourning on the American right.* The New Press.
Hochschild, A. R. (2019). Emotions and society. *Emotions and Society*, *1*(1), 9–13.
Housley, W., & Fitzgerald, R. (2008). Motives and social organization: Sociological amnesia, psychological description and the analysis of accounts. *Qualitative Research*, *8*(2), 237–256.
Hunter, C. (1984). Aligning actions: Types and social distribution. *Symbolic Interaction*, *7*(2), 155–174.
Hunter, J. D. (1991). *Culture wars: The struggle to define America.* Basic Books.
Husting, G., & Orr, M. (2007). Dangerous machinery: "Conspiracy theorist" as a transpersonal strategy of exclusion. *Symbolic Interaction*, *30*(2), 127–150.
James, V., & Gossett, J. (2018). Of monsters and men: Exploring serial murderers' discourses of neutralization. *Deviant Behavior*, *39*(9), 1120–1139.
Katovich, M. A. (2011). Death becomes mead: Toward a radical interactionist reading of million dollar Baby. In N. K. Denzin, L. Athens, & T. Faust (Eds.), *Blue ribbon papers: Interactionism: The emerging landscape. Studies in symbolic interaction* (Vol. 36, pp. 161–181). Emerald Publishing Limited. https://doi.org/10.1108/S0163-2396(2011)0000036009
Katovich, M. A., & Couch, C. J. (1992). The nature of social pasts and their use as foundations for situated action. *Symbolic Interaction*, *15*(1), 25–47.
Katovich, M. A., & Reese II, W. A. (1987). The regular: Full-time identities and memberships in an urban bar. *Journal of Contemporary Ethnography*, *16*(3), 308–343.
Katovich, M. A., & Wieting, S. G. (2000). Evil as indexical: The implicit objective status of guns and illegal drugs. *Symbolic Interaction*, *23*(2), 161–182.
Lakoff, G. (2002). *Moral politics: How liberals and conservatives think* (2nd ed.). The University of Chicago Press.
Lamont, M. (2018). Addressing recognition gaps: Destigmatization and the reduction of inequality. *American Sociological Review*, *83*(3), 419-444.
Lamont, M., Park, B. Y., & Ayala-Hurtado, E. (2017). Trump's electoral speeches and his appeal to the American white working class. *British Journal of Sociology*, *68*, S153–S180.
Leasure, P. (2017). Neutralizations in retail banking: A qualitative analysis. *Deviant Behavior*, *38*(4), 448–460.
Lois, J. (2009). Emotionally layered accounts: Homeschoolers' justifications for maternal deviance. *Deviant Behavior*, *30*(2), 201-234.
Loseke, D. R., & Cahill, S. P. (1984). The social construction of deviance: Experts on battered women. *Social Problems*, *31*(3), 298–310.
Lutfiyya, N. M., & Miller, D. E. (1986). Disjunctures and the process of interpersonal accounting. In C. J. Couch, S. L. Saxton, & M. A. Katovich (Eds.), *Studies in symbolic interaction, supplement 2: The Iowa school (part A)* (pp. 131–147). JAI Press.
Maines, D. (2001). *The faultline of consciousness: A view of interactionism in sociology.* Aldine de Gruyter.
Markle, G. (2014). Accounting for the performance of environmentally significant behavior: The symbolic significance of recycling. *Symbolic Interaction*, *37*(2), 246–263.
Maruna, S., & Copes, H. (2005). What have we learned from five decades of neutralization research? *Crime and Justice*, *32*, 221–320.
Marvasti, A. (2005). Being Middle Eastern American: Identity negotiation in the context of the war on terror. *Symbolic Interaction*, *28*(4), 525–547.

Mattely, C. (2002). The Temporality of emotion: Constructing past emotions. *Symbolic Interaction, 25*(3), 363–378.
Mason, L. (2018). *Uncivil agreement: How politics became our identity*. University of Chicago Press.
McPherson, M., Smith-Lovin, L., & Cook, J. M. (2001). Birds of a feather: Homophily in social networks. *Annual Review of Sociology, 27*, 415–444.
McVeigh, R., & Estep, K. (2019). *The politics of losing: Trump, the Klan, and the mainstreaming of resentment*. Columbia University Press.
Mills, C. W. (1940). Situated actions and vocabularies of motive. *American Sociological Review, 5*(December), 904–913.
Murphy, E. (2004). Anticipatory accounts. *Symbolic Interaction, 27*(2), 129–154.
Musolf, G. R. (2016). The intellectual origins of the debate over the astructural bias. In *The astructural bias charge: Myth or reality?* (pp. 1–18). Emerald Publishing Limited.
Nichols, L. (1990). Reconceptualizing social accounts: An agenda for theory building and empirical research. *Current Perspectives in Social Theory, 10*, 113–144.
Orbuch, T. L. (1997). People's accounts count: The sociology of accounts. *Annual Review of Sociology, 23*, 455–478.
Perinbanayagam, R. S. (1977). The structure of motives. *Symbolic Interaction, 1*(1), 104–120.
Pogrebin, M., Stretesky, P. B., Prabha Unnithan, N., & Venor, G. (2006). Retrospective accounts of violent events by gun offenders. *Deviant Behavior, 27*(4), 479–501.
Prus, R. C. (1997). *Subcultural mosaics and intersubjective realities: An ethnographic research agenda for pragmatizing the social sciences*. State University of New York Press.
Schneider, C. J. (2023). Police accounts of body-worn camera footage in news media. *Symbolic Interaction, 46*(1), 47–71.
Schur, E. M. (1980). *The politics of deviance: Stigma contests and the uses of power*. Prentice-Hall, Inc.
Scott, S. (2015). *Negotiating identity: Symbolic interactionist approaches to social identity*. John Wiley & Sons.
Scott, M., & Lyman, S. (1968). Accounts. *American Sociological Review, 33*(1), 46–62.
Sharp, S. (2009). Escaping symbolic entrapment, maintaining social identities. *Social Problems, 56*(2), 267-284.
Shulman, D. (2000). Professionals' accounts for work-related deceptions. *Symbolic Interaction, 23*(3), 259–281.
Silva, E. O. (2007). Public accounts: Defending contested practices. *Symbolic Interaction, 30*(2), 245–265.
Silva, E. O. (2014). Neutralizing problematic frames in the culture wars: Anti-evolutionists grapple with religion. *Symbolic Interaction, 37*(2), 226–245.
Silva, E. O. (2018). Stigmatization and validation of atheism, literalism, and non-literalism, in the discourse over evolutionary theory. *Secularism and Nonreligion, 7*(1), 1.
Silva, E. O. (2019a). Accounting for Trump: The neutralization of claims of racism in the early stages of the 2016 presidential campaign. In *The interaction order* (Vol. 50, pp. 197–216). Emerald Publishing Limited.
Silva, E. O. (2019b). Donald Trump's discursive field: A juncture of stigma contests over race, gender, religion, and democracy. *Sociology Compass 13*(12), e12757. https://doi.org/10.1111/soc4.12757
Silva, E. O., Dick, B., & Flynn, M. B. (2023). The evil corporation master frame: The cases of vaccines and genetic modification. *Public Understanding of Science, 32*(3), 340–356.
Silva, E. O., & Flynn, M. B. (2020a). Liminal Stigma and disaligning activity: Online comments about Trump's family separation policy. *Symbolic Interaction, 43*, 126–155.
Silva, E. O., & Flynn, M. B. (2020b). The ideational stigmatization of immigration detainees, their advocates, captors, and their apologists in the commentary section of US newspapers. *Genealogy, 4*(4), 102.
Simonetto, D. (2019). "I was with him before he was anything": The identity talk of football wives. In *The interaction order* (pp. 181–196). Emerald Publishing Limited.
Skjælaaen, Ø. (2016). How to be a good alcoholic. *Symbolic Interaction, 39*(2), 252–267.
Snow, D. A. (2001). Extending and broadening Blumer's conceptualization of symbolic interactionism. *Symbolic Interaction, 24*(3), 367–377.
Stokes, R., & Hewitt, J. P. (1976). Aligning actions. *American Sociological Review, 41*(5), 838–849.

Strauss, A. L. (1997). *Mirrors and masks: The search for identity*. Transaction Publishers.

Suarez, A., & Bolton, M. (2018). Catching babies in prohibition states: Midwives' accounts for an illegal profession. *Symbolic Interaction*, *41*(2), 165–184.

Sumerau, J. E., & Holway, G. V. (2022). Transgender possibilities and the Cisgendering of family among Cisgender women. *Symbolic Interaction*, *45*(2), 167–188.

Sykes, G. M., & Matza, D. (1957). Techniques of neutralization. *American Sociological Review*, *22*(6), 664–670.

Thomson, I. T. (2010). *Culture wars and enduring American dilemmas*. The University of Michigan Press.

Trammell, R., & Chenault, S. (2009). "We have to take these guys out": Motivations for assaulting incarcerated child molesters. *Symbolic Interaction*, *32*(4), 334–350.

Weiss, K. G. (2011). Neutralizing sexual victimization: A typology of victims' non-reporting accounts. *Theoretical Criminology*, *15*(4), 445–467.

Whitehead, A. L., & Perry, S. L. (2020). *Taking America back for god: Christian nationalism in the United States*. Oxford University Press.

Winchester, D., & Green, K. D. (2019). Talking your self into it: How and when accounts shape motivation for action. *Sociological Theory*, *37*(3), 257-281.

Ye Hee Lee, M. (2015, July 8). Donald Trump's false comments connecting Mexican immigrants and crime. *Washington Post*. https://www.washingtonpost.com/news/fact-checker/wp/2015/07/08/donald-trumps-false-comments-connecting-mexican-immigrants-and-crime/

INVESTIGATING THE INTERACTIONIST MINDED SELF

David Schweingruber[a] and David W. Wahl[b]

[a]*Iowa State University, USA*
[b]*McMurry University, USA*

ABSTRACT

The interactionist minded self *(IMS), the package of cognitive processes, including the internal conversation, that the classic pragmatist philosophers and early interactionist sociologists claimed were important for understanding self and action, has been underinvestigated. These conceptions of the self have tended to be treated as a set of hermeneutical devices rather than as testable propositions about how people think. The authors identify several empirical claims about the IMS, discuss the diversity of minded activity (including the claim that some people don't have internal conversations), summarize some of the findings from our research on internal conversations, provide a set of topics related to the IMS that we believe should be researched, and discuss methods for researching these and other topics related to the IMS.*

Keywords: Self; internal conversation; generalized other; reflexivity; symbolic interactionism

Symbolic interactionists have long had an interest in the workings of the human mind. George Herbert Mead focused on the cognitive as the key for understanding both the self and action. According to Mead (1934), "The essence of the self... is cognitive: it lies in the internalized conversation of gestures which constitutes thinking, or in terms of which thought or reflection proceeds" (p. 173). This conception of the self has been challenged by subsequent interactionists, but in this paper, we will argue that it has also been underinvestigated. Mead's claims have tended to be treated as a set of hermeneutical devices rather than as testable propositions about how people think. Interactionists use their concepts to interpret aspects of social life but typically have not conducted research aimed at examining, testing or refining them or establishing their empirical viability.

Essential Issues in Symbolic Interaction
Studies in Symbolic Interaction, Volume 59, 89–104

Published under exclusive licence by Emerald Publishing Limited
ISSN: 0163-2396/doi:10.1108/S0163-239620240000059005

This paper is an extension of our earlier paper, "Whither the Internal Conversation?" (Schweingruber & Wahl, 2019), in which we argue that while interactionists have long claimed that internal conversations were important for understanding the self, we have conducted little research on the topic. Rather we have focused on other levels of analysis. A typical interactionist study, following Blumer's three premises (1969), is attuned to the meaning of things for the people being studied, how they learn these meanings, and how they may modify these meanings. This type of analysis doesn't require looking in detail at the internal conversations said to be key for understanding the self and action.

We are calling our topic here the interactionist minded self (IMS). By this, we mean the package of cognitive processes, including the internal conversation, that the classic pragmatist philosophers and early interactionist sociologists claimed were important for understanding self and action. We are not going to argue that the IMS is the most important phenomenon interactionists should investigate. Rather, we will argue that we don't have sufficient evidence to know its value for understanding social life. To what extent interactionists should care about the workings of the mind is an open question because we have not paid enough attention to it.

Here is the crux of the matter: If interactionists were to investigate the claims of the classical pragmatists and early interactionist sociologists about the IMS (and which continue to be made today despite a paucity of evidence), would our findings increase our understanding of social life? Or can we safely ignore this level of analysis? Our own ongoing research has attempted to explore this question. Based on this research, some of which we describe below, we believe that understanding the internal processes by which people construct meaning, negotiate societal expectations, and guide their actions will increase our understanding of social life. This is true whether the findings of this research support or challenge the claims by previous scholars about the IMS.

In this paper, we will (1) identify several empirical claims about the IMS, (2) discuss the diversity of minded activity, (3) summarize some of the findings in our research on internal conversations, (4) provide a set of topics related to the IMS that we believe should be researched, and (5) discuss methods for researching these and other topics related to the IMS.

THE INTERACTIONIST MINDED SELF

A literature review for a paper on the IMS might be expected to cover the claims of the most important characters in its development (e.g. Mead, Peirce, James, Dewey, Cooley, and Blumer), explain how they differed, enter into debates about what they "really meant," and attempt some kind of synthesis (e.g. Wiley, 1994, 2016). However, our position is that not enough research has been conducted on the internal conversation and other aspects of the IMS and that "more research is required before more productive theorizing can occur" (Schweingruber & Wahl, 2019). Instead, we are going to state some specific empirical claims from this body of work that should be subject to empirical scrutiny.

First, humans engage in internal conversation. This seemed to be assumed by the scholars listed above – and by many of us who experience having an almost continuous internal conversation. It is also demonstrated by empirical research within the symbolic interactionist tradition, including Athens' (1974, 1977, 1992, 1997) research on violent criminals and Schweingruber's (2006a, 2006b; Schweingruber & Berns, 2003, 2005, 2010) research on door-to-door salespersons, and research outside the interactionist tradition (e.g. Archer, 2003; Caetano, 2017; Edwards et al., 1988, 1989; Heavey & Hurlburt, 2007; Honeycutt, 2003, 2010; Honeycutt et al., 2015; Honeycutt et al., 1990; Hurlburt, 2011; Hurlburt & Akhter, 2006; Morin et al., 2018; Morin & Uttl, 2013; Morin et al., 2011). However, as we'll see below, research indicates that the internal conversation is just one of multiple minded processes that people engage in. Also, some people claim not to engage in internal conversation at all. So, while Mead and others may assume that everyone has internal conversations, perhaps only some people do.

Second, the internal conversation allows people to construct lines of action. It allows them to make decisions about what action to pursue, to plan action, and to guide that action. As Norbert Wiley (2016) puts it, "inner speech seems to be a necessary condition for agency... In one sense, it is the whole self that decides and acts. But in a more localized or pinpointed sense, action is the work of the dialogical self conversing with itself in the arena of inner speech" (p. 75).

Third, the internal conversation is used to deal with the problems and troubles people encounter. This claim, an extension of the idea that the internal conversation is used to construct lines of action, is supported by research by Archer (2003) and Caetano (2017). This ability becomes especially important when action is not habitual but involves dealing with problems.

Fourth, the internal conversation allows people to be affected by society and to negotiate it. The concept of internalizing society is not unique to symbolic interactionism. Berger and Luckman use the concept of internalization to describe "the reappropriation by [humans] of this same reality, transforming it once again from structures of the objective world into structures of the subjective consciousness" (Berger, 1967; cf. Berger & Luckmann, 1966). People learn to think using the concepts of their culture and language. However, the interactionist contribution is to view this internalization as dialectical. According to this view, through the internal conversation, society enters into a dialogue with the self. Society can talk back to the self, evaluating the self's impulses and plans. The self can talk back to society, mulling over, challenging, and possibly rejecting its dictates. "The internalization in our experience of the external conversations of gestures which we carry on with other individuals in the social process is the essence of thinking" (Mead, 1934, p. 47). Or as Manford Kuhn put it, "Thinking, for all the symbolic interactionists, is an internal conversation among the self and internalized others" (Kuhn, 1964, p. 7). The influence of society is also evident in Cooley's (1902) "looking-glass self," wherein the imagined perceptions of others take centerstage in internalized self-development.

Fifth, individuals may interact internally with some representation of some community or group, what Mead calls the "generalized other." This is one way that people are affected by and negotiate society. According to Mead: "The organized community or social group which gives to the individual his unity of self may be called 'the generalized other.' The attitude of the generalized other is the attitude of the whole community" (cf. Athens, 1994; Mead, 1934, p. 154). The concept of the generalized other is a key illustration of the question of whether Mead's concepts are meant to be testable propositions or general hermeneutical principles? Can we find the generalized other in someone's mental processes? Or is it just a way of thinking about how people may orient themselves toward the attitudes of other people in their community? In our own ongoing research, which we describe below, we have attempted to find instances of individuals taking the attitude of the generalized other. One of the anonymous referees reviewing one of our papers told us this effort was misguided since:

> The presence of others and of the generalised [*sic*] other does not necessarily have to be personified or consciously acknowledged by individuals. The underlying concerns of their internal conversations reflect the role of values, norms, relationships, contexts and resources. The social is an integral part of inner life (Anonymous reviewer, personal communication, March 29, 2021).

In this quote is the attitude that the generalized other is a hermeneutical principle, not an empirically available process.

Sixth, individuals can interact with specific internalized individuals in their internal conversations. This is another way that people are affected by and negotiate society. In this process, people engage in internalized interaction with specific individuals rather than the generalized other. The internalization of individuals is especially important to Cooley (1902), who highlights the role of "imaginary conversation." Likewise, Athens (1994, p. 525) suggests that people converse with "*phantom others*, who are not present, but whose impact upon us is no less than the people who are present during our social experiences."

Seventh, the internal conversation involves different "phases" of the self. Various pragmatists and interactionists make this claim but disagree about what these phases are. For instance, Mead (1934) calls these phases the "I" and the "me." For Mead, "I" is the impulse or desire that solicits action from the "me," or social self, that recognizes and understands the norms and demands of society. The "I" and "me" are also conceptualized as representing the self as subject and the self as object or the present self and the past self. Another pragmatist philosopher, Peirce (1958) conceptualizes the phases of self as the "I" and the "you." The "I," for Peirce, as for Mead, represents the active, present-state consciousness of the self that encompasses one's beliefs, intentions, and desires. However, Peirce connects the ongoing internal dialogue of the "I" to the "you," a future representation of self, as opposed to Mead's past representation of "me." The "you" internalizes others from the external social environment. "You" refers to individuals with whom we interact in everyday life. As noted by Wiley (2016), the "you" allows "for visitors to the internal conversation" (p. 152). In the rehearsal of a future event, "you" is the internal representation of the other. It is through the "you" that the "I" acquires meaning and significance. In isolation, the "I" could not comprehend or define itself – it requires the "you." Wiley (2016) suggests that Mead's *past-to-present-to understand the future* ongoing communication and Peirce's *future-to-present-to understand the past* internal interaction can be combined in a more efficient manner. Wiley presents an I–you–me model of phases of selfhood. This configuration of the internal conversation involves "the I, or present self, talking to the you, or future self, about the me, or past self" (p. 153).

In addition to these specific empirical claims that should be explored, a conceptual question hangs over our project: Can we operationalize the internal conversation of the IMS as the words people say to themselves? During this project, we have encountered the objection that we are being too literal. As we argue in our earlier paper, there has been little interactionist research on the contents of internal conversations, i.e. words people say to themselves. Indeed, most theorizing, and even most empirical research, by interactionists or others does not involve analysis of specific internal conversations (Schweingruber & Wahl, 2019). Interactionist concepts like the generalized other and the phases of the self are treated as hermeneutical principles rather than testable claims. In addition, there is also an empirical challenge to the IMS: some people claim to not have internal conversations.

THE DIVERSITY OF MINDED ACTIVITY

Many people, including the authors, experience having a running conversation with themselves. Presumably so did Mead and Peirce – as their analysis of minded behavior isn't based on research on other people's mental processes and doesn't include any examples of it (Archer, 2003). However, recent research and anecdotal evidence indicate that there is variety in people's mental processes and that some people don't seem to experience having an internal conversation. This represents a challenge to the IMS.

Russell Hurlburt and his colleagues (Hurlburt, 2011; Hurlburt & Akhter, 2006) have used descriptive experience sampling (DES) to study what they call "pristine inner experience." Their research subjects carry beepers, which sound randomly to indicate to the subjects that they should make a record of their inner experience. This is called "pristine" because it is not affected by experimental manipulation or by a request to engage in introspection. Subjects are then interviewed by a researcher in an attempt to produce a detailed description of their mental experience. Their method does reveal instances of what they call "inner speech," but it is not found in a majority of samples.

In Heavey and Hurlburt's (2007) article based on 300 moments of pristine experience collected from 30 college students, the most common type is inner seeing (34%), followed by inner speech (26%), feeling (26%), unsymbolized thinking (22%) and sensory awareness (22%). The researchers report that "DES shows repeatedly that many, if not most, people who have unsymbolized thinking (the experience of thinking without words or other symbols) will at first report such thinking to be in words. Only after repeated training as they iteratively confront the apprehension of their own experience do they come to recognize their presupposition of words as being false" (p. 805–806).

Some people report not having internal conversations. For instance, the animal scientist Temple Grandin (1995), who writes about her experience as an autistic person, claimed,

> I think in pictures. Words are a second language to me. I translate both spoken and written words into full-color movies, complete with sound, which run like a VCR tape in my head. When someone speaks to me, his words are instantly translated into pictures (p. 3).

Another claim about not having an internal conversation was the subject of a Reddit conversation in 2020 when a person using the screen name Vadermaulkylo (2020) posted the following:

> Today, I told my mom that I have no internal monologue and she stared at me like I have three heads. Is having one common?
>
> I sincerely thought it was a fictional concept that "Dexter" made up. It shocks me beyond belief to know that people may have one.
>
> How do you do it? I can't imagine doing that.

The subsequent discussion revealed that some people were surprised that anyone had internal conversations, while others were shocked that anyone didn't since for them an internal conversation was synonymous with "thinking." One person gave the following description of how he thought without engaging in internal conversation:

> I think like op [original poster]. Thinking is visualizing and searching out my intuitions and feelings, in short. I think about how it fits in my value system, how it makes me feel, how it may make others feel.
>
> There is no discernible voice. My mind wanders to locations and predicts what could happen, almost as a simulation, or recalls relevant past events for me to mull over. It's a soup of feelings, visualizations, and flashes of inspiration that give me relevant data that I then process until an answer resonates with me.
>
> Answers just "come" to me and it's right 99% of the time, and when it's wrong it's usually due to a misunderstanding on my part. (Carc, 2020)

Hinwar and Lambert (2021) coined the term *anauralia* to describe the condition of not having what they call auditory imaginary and equate with inner speech.

The existence of people who claim to have no internal conversation presents a challenge to a model that views internal conversation as essential to the self. It also reminds us of the key question of whether the concepts of the IMS are meant to be empirically available or just hermeneutical principles. If one person can report an internal conversation about how they arrived at their decision, while another person reaches the same decision via a "soup of feelings, visualizations, and flashes of inspiration that give me relevant data that I then process until an answer resonates with me," does this suggest that we can safely ignore the internal conversation? Or is the internal conversation the verbal version that gives us insight about the nonverbal decision making?

WHAT WE'VE LEARNED ABOUT THE MINDED SELF

Our current research project has involved collecting and analyzing accounts of internal conversations from students in an introduction of sociology class (Schweingruber, Wahl, Beeman, et al., 2023). We asked students to make a written record of one internal conversation of their choosing. We defined internal conversations as "conversations people have with themselves, either aloud (when they are alone) or silently. Sometimes, but not always, they involve imagining or rehearsing conversations with other people" (p. 5).

Our analyses are based on a collection of 1,000 of these records. We used the practices of grounded theory to develop categories and relationships between them that are grounded in these data. Here, we summarize some of our findings from our published work (Schweingruber, Wahl, Beeman, et al., 2023), conference presentations (Beeman et al., 2019; Schweingruber, Wahl, Linhart, et al., 2023; Weston et al., 2017) and research in progress.

Do People Have Internal Conversations?

The first empirical claim we listed above is that people have internal conversations. Our research, as well as other studies of internal conversation cited above indicate that at least some people have internal conversations. However, we need to be aware that, as Heavey and Hurlburt (2007) found, some of our subjects may be translating unsymbolized thinking or some other form of inner experience into words. In fact, although we asked students to record an internal conversation, around a quarter of them instead described one (without quoting any part of it). We need different research methods to better examine the diversity of mental activity.

Do People Use Internal Conversations to Guide Action?

As we stated above, interactionists (and others who have studied or theorized about the internal conversation) have highlighted its role in planning, choosing, and guiding action. We investigated this issue by creating a typology of the uses of internal conversations (Schweingruber, Wahl, Beeman, et al., 2023). We found that around three-quarters of internal conversations in our collection had a use that prepared for action. These uses included *decision making*, *self-direction*, *to-do lists* and *rehearsals*. Around a quarter involved uses that don't prepare for action (at least no immediate action). These include *complaining*, *worrying*, and *wondering*. Our findings support the contention that the internal conversation is often used to prepare for action.

Is the Internal Conversation Used to Deal With Problems?

Similarly, research and theory on the internal conversation has suggested the internal conversation is often used to deal with problems and troubles that people encounter. Our research supports this claim as a majority of internal conversations focused on "problematic and negative aspects of social life." These include internal conversations that make decisions about action as well as worrying and complaining.

Does the Internal Conversation Allow People to Be Influenced by Society?

Another key claim about the internal conversation is that it is a mechanism that allows people to be influenced by and to negotiate society. One way that we studied this was by recording which individuals show up in internal conversations and whether they spoke. Other people appeared in over two-thirds of internal conversations; they spoke in fewer than a fifth of them. The most common people to appear were friends, parents, and boy/girlfriends. These internalized people exert influence in a variety of ways. People may engage in rehearsals with other people, may engage in explicit role-taking, where they attempt to view a situation from the perspective of another person, and may attempt to anticipate someone else's actions. Other ways that people bring internalized others into their internal conversation include making plans to meet with another person, planning to make a desired impression on another person, planning to follow instructions given by another person, planning to seek aid or advice from another person, taking into account the effect on another person of some decision, or comparing oneself to another person.

Are People Influenced by a "Generalized Other"?

Another way that society may influence people is through what Mead (1934) referred to as the generalized other. Just as individuals can take the attitude of individual other people, they can take the attitude of the generalized other, "[t]he organized community or social group which gives to the individual his unity of self" (p. 154). In our ongoing research on the generalized other in internal conversations, we operationalize the generalized other as any way that the attitudes of some community or group influence the self (Schweingruber, Wahl, Linhart, et al., 2023). We use the term *implicit generalized other* to refer to the fact that internal conversations rely on the language, concepts, and assumptions of some community. In this respect, the generalized other is a hermeneutical device that can be applied to every part of an internal conversation. However, this implicit generalized other is not dialogical. We use the term *explicit generalized other* to refer to how the attitudes of the community enter into internal conversation. One example of this is individuals anticipating the response or judgment of a community. For instance:

> Hm, what should I wear tonight? I want to wear something that looks nice, but if I overdo it people will laugh at me.
>
> I hope my friends don't think I'm lame if I stay in.

People may also make reference to what is "normal" or "expected" in a community or refer to emotions related to judgments of the community, like embarrassment or shame, among other ways that the generalized other can enter into internal conversations.

What Are the Phases of the Self?

We have not systematically investigated "phases" of the self in internal conversation to see how closely internal conversations conform to some pattern proposed by other scholars. Rather, we have attempted to develop categories that are grounded in our data. One typology, which we call *discourse type*, involves who is speaking to whom in internal conversations (Schweingruber, Wahl, Beeman, et al., 2023). Seventeen percent of the internal conversations in our study were *dialogues* in which both the self and some internalized other spoke. These dialogue included *rehearsals*, which involved planning for the future, *retrospective internal interactions*, which took place in the past, and *imaginary internal interactions* where people engaged in dialogues that were unlikely to occur, such as conversations with celebrities or dead loved ones. Eight percent of the internal conversations were *monologues* to others in which the self spoke to an internalized other person who did not respond. One percent were *monologues* by others to the self – all involved people imagining relatives speaking to them.

Seventy-three percent of the internal conversations were *soliloquys* – the self spoke to the self. However, these came in a variety forms. Some seemed to involve two phases of the self speaking back and forth, as in this example:

> Do you like the way you look?
>
> No
>
> Are you ever going to do anything about it?
>
> Yes
>
> What are you gonna do to change?
>
> Workout and eat healthier
>
> When?
>
> Soon

However, others involved a pattern described by Archer (2003) where a segment of internal conversation at time-1 becomes an object for the segment at time-2, and so on. For instance,

> It's Sunday and that means I work tomorrow night.
>
> I wonder if I could somehow get off work so I can use that time to study for finals.
>
> I could text Anthony and see if he could cover my shift, but he will probably say no because he doesn't like staying out that late. Maybe I could ask around tomorrow before my shift to see if anyone can pick it up.
>
> Or I could just call in sick.
>
> I could call in and tell the managers I am sick, and didn't go to class on Monday either.
>
> Okay first I am going to text Anthony, and if he says no, which he probably will, then I'm going to call in sick so I don't have to go to work.

Other internal conversations involve some segments commenting on another segment while others just change topics. Internal conversations take a variety of forms.

THE FUTURE OF INTERACTIONIST MINDED SELF RESEARCH: RESEARCH TOPICS

In the next sections of this paper, we will identify what we believe are some of the most important issues for future investigation of the IMS – some of which arise from issues we have discussed above and some additional ones – and how to research them. Interactionists should be attempting to test and refine claims made by Mead, such as about the phases of the self and the ways society influences people through the generalized other; to make connections to other aspects of the self studied by interactionists, like emotions and identities; and to build on insights from non-interactionist social scientists, such as about phenomenological aspects of internal conversations and the relationship between internal conversations and other forms of reflexivity.

The Diversity of Minded Experiences

We need research that investigates the diversity of minded experiences. This research may require in-depth interviewing that would explore all the ways that people think, visualize, imagine and so on and how they work (or don't work) together. This research would aim to uncover different strategies and different styles of mental activity. Expanding beyond the cognitive aspects of the internal conversation would involve asking phenomenological questions like how do the "voices" in internal conversations sound. This line of research would also focus on how different types of minded activity are used in different situations. It would also attempt to compare different populations of people. An overarching question for this research is how people use the different minded strategies available to them to navigate social life.

Phases or Capacities of the Self

A focus on diversity is also important for understanding phases of the self. One of the problems of studying the phases as posited by the classical pragmatist philosophers and interactionist theorists is operationalizing them. The segments of internal conversations in our study aren't easily categorized into "I," "me," and "you." These phases are idealizations of how people might think rather than categories derived from analysis of data. Another issue is the unit of analysis. Should we be looking for these phases in specific internal conversation segments or in someone's entire pattern of internal conversation? How can we determine whether Mead, Peirce or Wiley has the most accurate description of phases? (An objection to this line of argument, of course, is that we are taking these theorists too literally.)

It may be better to view the styles of thinking described as "phases" as capacities or abilities. People develop the ability to treat themselves as objects, to call to mind past, present, and future versions of themselves and to communicate between them, and so on. Research ought to focus on what sort of capacities people use in internal conversations and how these may be strung together in the flow of thought. The goal should not be to discover some universal pattern but rather to find patterns or styles of how people use these capacities. This approach is along the same lines as Archer's (2003) research but with a much closer focus on the details of internal conversations.

Society's Influence Through the Internal Conversation

As indicated above, we have explored the questions of how individuals and society (the generalized other) influence selves in internal conversation. Both of these questions need much more investigation. Regarding internalized individuals, we need to understand which individuals enter into people's internal conversations, what they do or say, and the different ways they may shape the behavior of the self. We also need to understand the different ways that communities or groups enter into internal conversations, including which communities or groups appear in internal conversations and the different ways they shape behavior, such as through imagining reactions toward different lines of behavior, thinking about what is "normal" or "expected," or calling to mind the moral values or standard recipes of action of some community.

Emotions in Internal Conversations

The IMS is mainly cognitive. However, some interactionist research has challenged the lack of focus on emotions for understanding the self. Athens (1994, p. 525), for instance, argues that internal conversations transform "our raw, bodily sensations into emotions." Especially notable is Francis et al.'s (2020) study of dementia, which showed that as dementia patients lose their ability to access shared definitions and reflected appraisals," their self perseveres in "the established self-sentiments developed over a lifetime of interaction" (p. 170). This raises the question of the relationship between the cognitive and the emotional parts of the self and how we develop self-sentiments that may continue even after the cognitive self is gone. We need to understand more about how emotions enter into internal conversations, including how people experience, interpret and navigate emotions.

Identities in Internal Conversations

Identities, both of the self and of others, are found throughout internal conversations (Schweingruber, Wahl, Beeman, et al., 2023). We need to learn more about how people select identities, enact identities, seek to have identities verified by others, and respond to challenges to identities, as well as how they interpret and act toward other people's identities. Research along these lines should also be useful for connecting processual interactionism, which has viewed the internal conversation as the driver of action, with structural symbolic interactionism, which has emphasized the causal efficacy of identities (Burke, 1991, 2004; Stryker & Burke, 2000). Research on internal conversations offers a way of possibly connecting these two interactionist perspectives.

The Understanding Uses of Internal Conversations

We also need a better understanding of specific uses of the internal conversation. For instance, one common use of the internal conversation in our research is *self-direction*, which involves telling oneself to do something (not deciding what to do) (Schweingruber, Wahl, Beeman, et al., 2023). People do this with different strategies, like self-motivation, self-convincing, self-instruction, justification, self-reward, and self-flagellation. Another common use is *rehearsals*, some of which consist of dialogue between the self and imagined others (often job interviewers) and some of which consists only of practicing speech before an imagined audience. Some rehearsals picture worst-case scenarios, some imagine best-case scenarios, and some include more than one scenario (Weston et al., 2017). Again, gaining a better understanding of particular uses of internal conversation is important for understanding how people use them in their lives.

The Internal Conversation and Other Forms of Reflexivity

One of the reasons interactionists are interested in the internal conversation is because it allows people to engage in reflexivity. However, noninteractionist researchers, like Archer and Caetano, have done more to connect the reflexivity of the internal conversation to the other ways that people exercise reflexivity. We need more research on how people connect their internal conversations to conversations with other people, to diaries, and to other ways that people communicate with themselves. Again, this should be part of an investigation of how different people use reflexivity to navigate social life.

The Phenomenological Aspects of Internal Conversations

Interactionists have focused on the cognitive aspects of internal conversations while ignoring phenomenological aspects highlighted by Hurlbert. For instance, we need to explore what the "voices" in internal conversations sound like and how this may shape people's use of and experience with them. Another potentially fruitful topic is silent reading. When an individual is reading to themself, do they have a voice that is sounding in their head? If so, what is that voice? Is it the voice of the reader or fictionalized voices constructed in the mind for the reader? Perhaps these are voices assigned to characters by the reader based on their imagining of the character or intimate others in their social sphere that inspire the character's depiction in the reader's mind.

THE FUTURE OF INTERACTIONIST MINDED SELF RESEARCH: RESEARCH METHODS

A particular challenge that faces any researcher fashioning a research design involving internal conversations lies in the method by which internal conversations are recorded for analysis. Direct access to internal conversations is not within our technological capacity. If all we have at our disposal is to direct individuals to recall their internal conversations, that is a problematic endeavor. If our memories are subject to being reshaped and transformed over time, what chance do recalled internal conversations have of being authentic? However, as we note elsewhere (Schweingruber & Wahl, 2019), a similar difficulty can be applied to meanings. We do not have direct access to the inner mechanisms of meaning formation and application. And yet, sociologists delve into studies of internalized meanings with valid research designs all the time. Tackling the difficulties of internal conversations should be no different.

In the aforementioned research projects conducted by Hurlburt (2011), Hurlburt and Akhter (2006), and Schweingruber, Wahl, Beeman, et al. (2023), research participants were asked to record recalled internal conversations. With Hurlbert, participants recorded their inner experience when a beeper sounded. For Schweingruber et al.'s student participants, a class assignment motivated them to write down an internal conversation of their choosing. In both cases, participants relied on the memory of an inner conversation. Wahl (2022) largely derived internal conversations from transcribed narratives of research participants providing their sexual histories. Wahl noted, during the grounded theory analysis of the transcripts, that participants had been injecting internal conversations into their narratives. Wahl claims this to be a more organic provision of internal conversations, as the inner dialogue comes from the natural flow of the narrative. Still, the conversation is recalled by the storyteller and, perhaps in some cases, is a tool for adding more theatrical effect to the narrative. Hurlbert, Schweingruber, Wahl, and their colleagues were able to successfully research internal conversations and justify their research design.

Questions of recall have been considered in other empirical work on internal conversations. Holt-Reynolds (1991) believed employing three mediums would be effective in collecting the inner dialogues of teachers: (a) through biographical writing, (b) through discussion, and (c) through an exploration of analytical course assignments they create. Hung and Appleton (2016) explored the internal conversations of persons transitioning from state care. Using Archer's (2003) interview framework, the concept of internal conversations was explained to participants, and they were asked if they had used internal conversations and how they had used internal conversations. In much the same way, Barratt et al. (2020) interviewed participants about their experience with internal conversations before asking broader questions. The researchers reported that participants were "able to relate to the concept and understood what was being referred to" (p. 874).

Schweingruber and Wahl (2019) asked researchers to consider a variety of research avenues to investigate the inner dialogue, including (1) conducting ethnographies in locations where internal conversations are examined, discussed, and debated, (2) incorporating questions of internal conversation into other research projects, and (3) direct interviewing of participants about their internal conversations. Other design strategies may include having individuals record their internal conversation in journals and employing surveys as a recording technique.

In their research design, sociological investigators should be mindful to work with different populations and individuals with different styles of cognition. Working with different populations may reveal if there are differences regarding internal conversations that are based on culture, gender, race or ethnicity, social class, or religious faith. The examination of different styles of cognition is imperative as the inner nature of the internal conversation is not a fixed experience for all. For instance, those who claim to not experience internal dialogues must be approached differently than those who can relay an inner conversation. There are many questions to investigate when it comes to those who claim to not have an inner voice. For instance, is their lack of an inner voice merely an absence of a conscious voice, when, in fact, the internal conversation is taking place in a subconscious realm? When asked about their internal conversations, do they have an understood definition of what an internal conversation is, one that is shared with the researcher? If some individuals experience internal conversations, while others do not, there are seemingly endless paths a researcher can take.

The most effective way to record and collect internal conversations may be beyond the reach of our capabilities currently. But just as there is a call, in this work, for researchers in sociology, and particularly symbolic interactionists, to take up the empirically under-served topic of the IMS, there is equally an appeal for researchers to divine new and more effective method for collecting and analyzing inner dialogues. There is also an essential need for researchers to continue approaching untouched avenues for study on the topic.

CONCLUSION

The internal conversation and the other minded processes we discuss in this article are worth studying. If meanings are important, it is worthwhile to examine how people develop, reconstruct, and negotiate them in their mental processes even though we cannot predict to what extent this will illuminate our understanding of social life. We owe a great debt to Mead and other early scholars who helped develop the package of concepts we call the IMS. However, our obligation is not merely to use their concepts as principles for interpreting social life. Rather, it is to develop more accurate understandings of the minded self through research using a variety of appropriate methods.

REFERENCES

Archer, M. (2003). *Structure, agency and the internal conversation*. Cambridge University Press.

Athens, L. (1974). The self and the violent criminal act. *Urban Life and Culture*, *3*(1), 98–112.

Athens, L. (1977). Violent crime: A symbolic interactionist study. *Symbolic Interaction*, *1*(1), 56–70.

Athens, L. (1992). *The creation of violent criminals*. University of Illinois Press.

Athens, L. (1994). The self as a soliloquy. *The Sociological Quarterly*, *35*(3), 521–532.

Athens, L. (1997). *Violent criminal acts and actors revisited*. University of Illinois Press.

Barratt, C., Appleton, P., & Pearson, M. (2020). Exploring internal conversations to understand the experience of young adults transitioning out of care. *Journal of Youth Studies*, *23*(7), 869–885.

Beeman, S., Schweingruber, D., & Wahl, D. W. (2019). Self processes in internal conversations [Conference session]. In *Annual Meeting of the Society for the Study of Symbolic Interaction*. New York City, NY, United States.

Berger, P. (1967). *The sacred canopy*. Doubleday & Company.

Berger, P., & Luckmann, T. (1966). *The social construction of reality*. Anchor Books.

Blumer, H. (1969). The methodological position of symbolic interactionism. *Symbolic Interaction*, *1*(1), 1–60.
Burke, P. J. (2004). Identities and social structure: The 2003 Cooley-Mead award address. *Social Psychology Quarterly*, *67*(1), 5–15.
Caetano, A. (2017). Coping with life: A typology of personal reflexivity. *The Sociological Quarterly*, *58*(1), 32–50.
Carc. (2020, February 1). Reddit. https://www.reddit.com/r/NoStupidQuestions/comments/exan65/comment/fg7zi52/
Cooley, C. H. (1902). *Human nature and the social order*. Charles Scribner's Sons.
Edwards, R., Honeycutt, J. M., & Zagacki, K. S. (1988). Imagined interaction as an element of social cognition. *Western Journal of Speech Communication*, *52*, 23–45.
Edwards, R., Honeycutt, J. M., & Zagacki, K. S. (1989). Sex differences in imagined interactions. *Sex Roles*, *21*(3/4), 263–272.
Grandin, T. (1995). *Thinking in pictures: My life with autism*. Vintage Books.
Heavey, C. L., & Hurlburt, R. T. (2007). The phenomena of inner experience. *Consciousness and Cognition*, *17*, 798–810.
Hinwar, R. P., & Lambert, A. J. (2021). Anauralia: The silent mind and its association with aphantasia. *Frontiers in Psychology*, *12*, 1–7.
Holt-Reynolds, D. (1991). *The dialogues of teacher education: Entering and influencing preservice teachers' internal conversations* (Vol. 91, No. 4). National Center for Research on Teacher Learning.
Honeycutt, J. M. (2003). *Imagined interactions: Daydreaming about communication*. Hampton Press.
Honeycutt, J. M. (Ed.). (2010). *Imagine that: Studies in imagined interactions*. Hampton Press.
Honeycutt, J. M., Vickery, A. J., & Hatcher, L. C. (2015). The daily use of imagined interaction features. *Communication Monographs*, *82*(2), 201–223.
Honeycutt, J. M., Zagacki, K. S., & Edwards, R. (1990). Imagined interaction and interpersonal communication. *Communication Reports*, *3*(1), 1–8.
Hung, I., & Appleton, P. (2016). To plan or not to plan: The internal conversations of young people leaving care. *Qualitative Social Work*, *15*(1), 35–54.
Hurlburt, R. T. (2011). *Investigating pristine inner experience*. Cambridge University Press.
Hurlburt, R. T., & Akhter, S. A. (2006). The descriptive experience sampling method. *Phenomenology and the Cognitive Sciences*, *5*(3–4), 271–301.
Kuhn, M. (1964). The reference group reconsidered. *The Sociological Quarterly*, *5*(1), 5–21.
Mead, G. H. (1934). *Mind, self & society from the standpoint of a social behavioralist*. University of Chicago Press.
Morin, A., Duhnych, C., & Racy, F. (2018). Self-reported inner speech use in university students. *Applied Cognitive Psychology*, *32*, 376–382.
Morin, A., & Uttl, B. (2013). Inner speech: A window into consciousness. *The Neuropsychotherapist*. https://doi.org/10.12744/tnpt.14.04.2013.01
Morin, A., Uttl, B., & Hamper, B. (2011). Self-reported frequency, content, and functions of inner speech. *Procedia – Social and Behavioral Sciences*, *30*, 1714–1718.
Peirce, C. S. (1958). *Collected papers of C.S. Peirce: Vol. I-VIII* (C. Hartshorne, P. Weiss, & A. Burks, Eds.). Harvard University Press.
Schweingruber, D. (2006a). Success through a positive mental attitude? The role of positive thinking in door-to-door sales. *The Sociological Quarterly*, *47*(1), 41–68.
Schweingruber, D. (2006b). The why, what and how of selling door-to-door: Levels of purpose and perception in a sales company. In K. McClelland & T. Fararo (Eds.), *Perception, meaning, and action: Control systems theories in sociology*. Palgrave Macmillan.
Schweingruber, D., & Berns, N. (2003). Doing money work in a door-to-door sales organization. *Symbolic Interaction*, *26*(3), 447–471.
Schweingruber, D., & Berns, N. (2005). Shaping the selves of young salespeople through emotion management. *Journal of Contemporary Ethnography*, *34*(6), 679–706.
Schweingruber, D., & Berns, N. (2010). Organizing door-to-door sales: A symbolic interactionist analysis. In P. Kivisto (Ed.), *Illuminating social life* (5th ed.). Sage.

Schweingruber, D., & Wahl, D. W. (2019). Whither the internal conversation. *Symbolic Interaction, 42*(3), 351–373.

Schweingruber, D., Wahl, D. W., Beeman, S., Burns, D., Weston, G., & Haroldson, R. (2023). Voices in and uses of internal conversations. *Social Currents, 10*(3), 286–307.

Schweingruber, D., Wahl, D. W., Linhart, L., Weston, G. H., & Beeman, S. (2023). Identifying the generalized other in internal conversations [Conference session]. In *Annual Meeting of the Midwest Sociological Society*. Minneapolis, MN, United States.

Stryker, S., & Burke, P. J. (2000). The past, present, and future of an identity theory. *Social Psychology Quarterly, 63*(4), 284–297.

Vadermaulkylo. (2020, February 1). Today, I told my mom that I have no internal monologue and she stared at me like I have three heads. Is having one common? *Reddit*. https://www.reddit.com/r/NoStupidQuestions/comments/exan65/today_i_told_my_mom_that_i_have_no_internal/

Wahl, D. W. (2022). Carnal voices: Internal conversations in sexual self-development. *Sexuality & Culture, 26*(1), 1274–1297.

Weston, G., Schweingruber, D., Beeman, S., Burns, D., & Haroldson, R. (2017). All the world's a stage: The role of rehearsal in internal conversations [Conference session]. In *Couch-Stone Symposium/Annual Meeting of the Midwest Sociological Society*. WI, United States: Milwaukee.

Wiley, N. (1994). *The semiotic self*. University of Chicago Press.

Wiley, N. (2016). *Inner speech and the dialogical self*. Temple University Press.

PHENOMENOLOGICAL AND INTERACTIONAL INTERPRETATIONS OF CORPORALITY AND INTERSUBJECTIVITY IN HATHA YOGA

Krzysztof T. Konecki

University of Lodz, Poland

ABSTRACT

The author presents the author's experiences of the body in hatha yoga practice using Maurice Merleau-Ponty's phenomenological concepts and perspective to understand the feelings about the body, thoughts, and emotions. The author interprets the corporeality and intersubjectivity of hatha yoga practice in light of the author's theory. The author gives some examples of embodied perception from the author's practice. The examples the author's give are based on the author's experience in yoga practice and self-observations that the author have done during the research project on experiencing hatha yoga practice and knowledge transfer.

Keywords: Experiencing the body; knowledge transfer; hatha yoga; intersubjectivity; intercorporality

INTRODUCTION

I will present Maurice Merleau-Ponty's possible interpretation of hatha yoga practice in this paper. I try to interpret the corporeality and intersubjectivity of hatha yoga practice in light of his theory. I had a lot of self-observations while

Essential Issues in Symbolic Interaction
Studies in Symbolic Interaction, Volume 59, 105–124

Published under exclusive licence by Emerald Publishing Limited
ISSN: 0163-2396/doi:10.1108/S0163-239620240000059006

practicing hatha yoga and experienced embodied perception. The examples given in the paper are based on my experience in yoga practice and self-observations.[1]

According to Merleau-Ponty, it cannot be said that access to an individual's mind is only possible for the individual himself. In body-to-body interactions, a mind–body relationship is formed not only in the situation of the individual who initiates the interaction but also with the interaction partner. The mind is formed in the interaction between the "I" and the environment, which is reminiscent of George Herbert Mead's concept. The difference is that in Merleau-Ponty's case, it is mainly the body that is involved in this interaction. Relationships with the surrounding environment are also interactions with other entities that have a body, with objects, and with inanimate nature. Interactions with others are interbodily in nature, which suggests that meanings, definitions of situations, and self-definitions are formed in interactions between at least two bodies. One could summarize the symbolic–interactionist vision of intercorporality (Mead, 1934; Blumer, 1969; Strauss, 1969) as consciously undertaken interactions and negotiations of meanings and definitions of situations and selves.

However, in light of Merleau-Ponty's (2005) phenomenological theory, we experience the world through the body, often prereflectively, reacting with gestures without consciously recognizing their meaning; meaning is embodied in them prereflexively before linguistic naming and reflection occur. A sad face may be a reaction to the sad face of another, and a laugh expressing joy may be a direct reaction to the laughter of an interaction partner. Similarly, we can react to signals from our own body; pain can be felt before we name it, and we can even function with it in everyday life by unconsciously shifting it to the background of our perception. It then exists in the background of our daily activities.[2]

The sensation of the taste of food being eaten occurs immediately before we name what we are feeling, and often we don't even name it or reflect on it; the body keeps the sensation to itself. The touch of another living being evokes an immediate reaction in our body; the body knows whether the touch is friendly or hostile, authentic or artificial (Konecki, 2005, 2008). These gestures can be "implicitly purposeful" (Churchill, 2022, p. 57). The touch of companion animals is a way of communicating with them; we do not always subject what we feel then to reflection, and the sensation of friendship, for example, appears in the body and remains there. The consequence can be the production of psychological as well as social bonds (Konecki, 2008). Although the context of our body's reaction to environmental signals is essential, it is not often subject to conscious reflection in the abovementioned situations.

In this article, I will discuss the practice of yoga, in which a practitioner interacts with his/her body, the body of the yoga teacher, and with the bodies of others in the same space. We will see how one can communicate with the body and how bodily intersubjectivity arises. The theme of prereflexive response to the movements of others' bodies and interbody communication in hatha yoga practice will also be addressed, i.e. how bodies are interpreted and what meanings are ascribed to them (the body as subject and object).

***

According to Merleau-Ponty, it is possible to return to things in themselves through the body and the description of experience and, thus, what precedes our reflective knowledge:

"To return to things themselves is to return to that world which precedes knowledge, of which knowledge always speaks, and in relation to which every scientific schematization is an abstract and derivative sign-language, as is geography in relation to the country-side in which we have learnt beforehand what a forest, a prairie or a river is" (Merleau-Ponty, 2005, pp. IX–X)

We do not consider causal explanations; we are interested in what is revealed to us, what "haunts" us, as it were, without psychological or scientific classification. Our primary relationship with the world is bodily and preconscious. We prereflectively know the world and others through bodily relations with them. Therefore, one can say after Merleau-Ponty, "We do not know what we see" (Van Manen, 2016, p. 128). The perception of the world is prereflective; it has the character of the actual existence of us in the world, presence through the body thrown into the world, into the situation of the here and now. Thus, I can say that "I was already here before I thought of it." The distinction between the body and the outside world and the division of mind and body disappear (Morley, 2001). Even though our speech has an embodied character, language and words are gestures. "The word is the thought's body," (Van Manen, 2016, p. 129). Thought is the other side of the word. Things also speak to us, language is the expression of the meanings they convey to us, and this is especially true of the "pathic," or vocative, poetic, emotional language that is often expressed by artists in art (Van Manen, 2016, p. 130).

I PRACTICE HATHA YOGA IN YOGA SESSION: SELF-REPORT WITH CONTEMPLATIVE REFLECTION

I watch the yoga teacher, look at him, listen to his instructions, and repeat his movements; out of the corner of my eye, I watch others practicing beside me. I imitate the teacher, but sometimes I don't because I know what he will do in a moment, what the next move or position should be. My body knows I don't have time to reflect; I do what I should and can do. But he is there, and I, a professor of sociology at the University of Lodz, am his student. He is there himself, spatially isolated, showing me what to do. He has power over me, he is the teacher, and I am the student. I follow him.

I perform the bridge pose. Suddenly, I see him approaching me; he wants to correct something in my body positioning; I don't like it; I know well that my body knows what it can do and how it can perform the position! The body was frightened.

What does he want from me? He is a Hindu and probably doesn't understand our culture. Or I don't know who I am? Why is he going to teach me? He probably wants to show control of the situation here and now. How will it look to him that I can't and don't know how to? I have done so much to present myself well and what? And nothing?

I must abandon these assumptions; here, only the body works; I must concentrate; the rest are illusions, and I must reduce them. Only the body, mine and his. Oh, HE touches, corrects, grabs my hips, pulls my body up, and supports me momentarily! Shoulders straighten, a little pain, dizziness.

But in the end, I am grateful to him. He was right; I no longer feel discomfort in the position. I feel that I am fully here and now with him. My body and his body needed to merge momentarily; otherwise, how could I be here with him?

Thrown into the boundlessness of being, wanting to understand Other, I observed my own body and his during the practice and felt the space between our bodies; when we were close, we were close; when we were far, we were far away. Distance is measured with our bodies, but also with glances, hand gestures, gestures of greeting, or threatening. When body movements occurred, the length was measured by the meaning of those gestures. You are distant or close to me, hostile or friendly. You are watching me; you are curious. But I realized that later, not while those intermovements were happening.

I feel his body as it appears in my space. He is here, and I am here; we are together, and our relationship is narrowed down to a possible commonality. I am not fully aware of it; but he is, and I am here; it is evident we are together. Why wonder about motives? The intentionality of consciousness? What if I am unaware of his gestures but feel them repeating mechanically?

I am standing in the mountain position (*tadasana*). I concentrate on my feet, the hard floor, and the mat sticking precisely to it; out of the corner of my eye, I see that he (Other) next to me is wobbling; I am also swaying, and I can feel it. We are rocking, both of us. And at the same time, we regain our balance, here and now. I close my eyes, but he is next to me. Is he wobbling? I can't see. I'm rocking, so he's probably swaying, too; I don't need to know; I can feel it.

The muscles of my body drape over my bones, my muscles tense, and I feel the fascias even though I shouldn't feel them. And he probably feels them too; here, we are together in our bodies, not identical, but shared, in the same space. His feet and my feet touch the same surface, the same gravity, the same smell around and in him, and in me, the same light, the same touch of my own body, the same sounds, and the same breaths. We are together in this mood of unification and sameness of movement, smell and light, and the vastness of this space. It is my body that is in this all-encompassing mood.

Standing on my forearms (*salamba sirsasana*), I feel pain in my shoulders; he is standing next to me, but I don't know if he feels this pain, the same as I feel. There is a definite possibility that he feels identical; there is a potency of feeling identical pain. I sympathize with him if he is in pain, just as I sympathize with myself.

Muscles, bones, and tendons are similar, although they have a different history. We developed our bodies differently. We have different habits, limitations, and bodily habitus; hatha yoga enables us to recognize these barriers. I can recognize the world through my body and he through his, we recognize together through our bodies in the same space, together we identify ourselves, but at the same time, we recognize Other – a common perspective on the world, the same movement, the same position, and the same being. We stand on our forearms, legs up, head down, legs wobbling. I tense my thigh muscles, try to maintain balance, and not move. I sense the stability and immobility of the inverted world. I cannot fall to the side because HIS space is there; I cannot violate it; my mat is my home; I can move and respect the home of another. My movement and my stability should express respect for Others.

He leaves the position, but I persist. Something makes us different; I exit the position identically after a while, and something connects us.

We both touch our foreheads to the mats. The touch with our foreheads is relaxing; there is satisfaction and the smell of mats and sweat. Silence all around. I do not observe others; I immerse myself in my self, and others do not observe me. I know they are next to me. I know what they are doing without looking. I know, they know-we-know – a commonality, shared by a common space, connecting space and the bodies in it. There are bodies and something between them. What is it?

INTERPRETATION

There Is No Body Without Space and No Space Without a Body

According to Merleau-Ponty, it cannot be said that access to an individual's mind is only possible for the individual himself. In body-to-body interactions, a mind–body relationship is formed not only in the situation of the individual initiating the interaction but also with the interaction partner. The mind is formed, as it were, in the interaction between the "I" and the environment, which is reminiscent of George Herbert Mead's concept, except that in Merleau-Ponty's case; it is mainly the body that is involved in this interaction rather than the mind being separated explicitly from the body. Relationships with the surrounding environment are also interactions with other entities that have a body and with objects and inanimate nature. Interactions with others are interbody, suggesting that meanings, definitions of situations, and self-definitions are formed in interactions between at least two bodies.

By perceiving other bodies, we connect with them. They are part of our existential situation; we are no longer the same people we were alone seeing another person. Whatever the other does, and I see it, feel it, experience it here and now, in the same space; it affects the practitioner as in the session of yoga described in the example above.[3] And vice versa. We become a pair.[4] We can perceive the other's intentions prereflectively as soon as the gesture of the other appears. It is not necessary to cognitively adopt the other's perspective (reciprocity of perspectives); here, something happens beforehand that ensures mutual matching of actions in the interaction.[5]

Of course, reflection and categorization may come later. But the intention is shared intersubjectively earlier, such as when yawning or pretending to bite a child's finger, as in the example given by Merleau-Ponty. For Merleau-Ponty, intercorporeality is "carnal intersubjectivity" (Tanaka, 2014, p. 268). Intersubjectivity here is understood as a communicative connection between two-minded bodies, not just minds. Understanding another is done through interaction related to one's actions and the actions of another. "Our basic ability to understand others is perceptual, sensorimotor, and nonconceptual" (Tanaka, 2014, p. 269). To know the world is to act in the world: "To perceive is first and foremost to act – perception is a reflection of the body's possible actions toward objects, and objects are the poles of this action" (Maciejczak, 2001, p. 17).

Intercorporeality has two basic properties: **behavior matching** and **interaction synchrony**. Intercorporeality can be understood as **behavior matching**. We can observe this as early as infancy; hearing others cry, an infant usually starts crying itself. Another example is the imitation of facial expressions noticed in interaction partners, such as a grimace of pain or a smile. We can notice it in yoga practice when I see a grimace or smile on the face of Other (e.g., a teacher). I smile and feel the smile, not reflecting on it. ("I feel his body as it appears in my space").[6] Even if we don't mimic someone else exactly, there is the potency of matching our gestures to those of another (potential behavior matching, Tanaka, 2014, pp. 269–270). This is not emotional contagion because contagion implies a one-sided relationship, whereas what happens in behavior matching is about mutual adjustments and merging into a "we" relationship. This property of an inter-relationship is precisely the basis for the emergence of empathy.

Intercorporeality is also about **interactional synchronicity**. If someone is speaking quietly, I lean toward him to hear him better or try to focus on his mouth to reconstruct better-spoken words. If someone babbles, I also try to respond quickly. An infant also adapts its body movements to the speed of the caregiver speaking (Tanaka, 2014, p. 273). In hatha yoga, we try to perform all actions at one pace. We are self-adjusting our rate to that of others, as it were ("I see that he (Other) next to me is wobbling; I am also swaying, and I can feel it. We are rocking, both of us.") Communication thus appears as an interaction between two or more bodies rather than two or more Cartesian minds. Minds are not private and hidden from interaction partners; they are available intersubjectively precisely in interbody interactions. Here we have **a resonance** between bodies; of course, this only happens when we are open enough to another person and, at the same time, closed enough to be ourselves constantly and distinct from another (Rosa, 2020, p. 162).

Rhythmic synchronization in the form of behavior is especially possible in dance or an orchestra playing music but also in the practice of hatha yoga. The interaction of bodies can be synchronized but also transformative. Interaction is a distinct dimension in which we transform ourselves as a result of receiving specific signals from the other body and continuously responding to those signals (as to the signals from the master, see paragraph "**I practice hatha yoga in yoga session. Self-report with contemplative reflection.**"). In hatha yoga, we transform ourselves by being with others in a given position; those others can be our predecessors, contemporaries, or future (imagined) interaction partners. Predecessors are all masters and their disciples who performed yoga postures similarly in the past; I unite with them as I do with contemporary practice partners in the here and now. In the future, there will be others who will perform yoga postures as I do it now.

This property of intercorporeality is the basis for the emergence of a **certain mood** in a given interaction. Meetings with other interaction partners occur in a specific and often familiar environment. For example, when meeting others in the

Yoga Practice Room, I associate this space with stretching the body, concentrating on performing certain postures and specific body movements, and ultimately relaxing the body and mind. A mood of calmness appears in this space. When I enter the room, I activate a specific body pattern. The space resonates with my body and mind ("The touch with our foreheads is relaxing; there is satisfaction and the smell of mats and sweat. Silence all around."). My mood of haste and practical matters from the lifeworld changes to slow and impractical physical actions, movements leading to the performance of hatha yoga postures.

The mood changes are always connected with the feelings of the body, and the **"body schema"** matters: "[Body] schema is a system of sensory-motor capacities that function without awareness or the necessity of perceptual monitoring" (Gallagher, 2005, p. 24; quoted in Tanaka 2018a:224). The body schema adapts itself to space and objects. Still, it has the same possibilities of modification depending on the environment, so the transformation comes together with the feelings and emotions, which also can change. The perception comes from body schema: "It also adjusts the whole bodily action in correspondence to the ongoing environmental changes (which implies that the body schema is also operating as a perceptual system). And thus, as a body-as-subject, "I" appears in the world with the mode of "I can" before "I think"" (Tanaka, 2018a, p. 224).

In yoga exercises, my mat determines my movement space, I interact with it, and I do not go beyond the mat. The pattern of my body is such that to keep my balance, I can grab onto objects next to me, jump on one foot outside of my space (in this case, the mat), and stay standing. However, my "mat space" does not allow this; I have to manage inside this rectangle; I cannot violate this space because I can also enter the other's space. His mat space is not for me; his body is there; it fills his rectangle; it is not MY space. ("I cannot fall to the side because HIS space is there; I cannot violate it; my mat is my home.") My body pattern changes; I can do many movements and maintain stability in a small space. I do not have to prop myself up and appropriate the space of Other.

Interactions have an embodied character; we infer intentions from gestures. This happens even in interactions with animals. If my cat is looking in a specific direction and looks back at me, I notice it and will follow that direction. The movement of her body (head) indicates to me what to do. I often do this outside of consciousness. I know that I should go in the direction she suggests. She moves forward because she sees that I see what she is doing. We synchronize our movements and ultimately match our actions. Our intentions, based on intercorporeal interaction, become mutual. After a brief stroking ritual, the cat leads me to the bowl and gets food from me. The interactional context, the elements that were recognized in the distant past, delineates, together with our matching movements, the meanings of our actions. We understand the actions of others through our sensorimotority in a nonconceptual way, and thus mainly through the body rather than the mind.

The interaction between the two bodies becomes a separate entity. It becomes autonomous from the outside world and has unique characteristics. The goal is achieved by adjusting the body's movements. Intentionality arises between (in-between) bodies (Tanaka, 2017, p. 342). In between bodies, the self is also formed. Tanaka cites Kimura (see also Tanaka, 2018b, p. 277), who emphasizes the reality of the "in-between" (Japanese *aida*), which is not distance in the metric sense, but a space of interaction and adjustment between at least two people. This is the case in an orchestra, where there is a specific space between the playing of one musician and another and, further, the other musicians. Anticipation of the following sounds is created. There is an adjustment of body movements, both of the musicians and the audience (Tanaka, 2017, pp. 334–335). This space gains a certain autonomy; the subjectivity of one musician enters the realm of intersubjectivity. Eventually, a particular mood is created, and the individual self emerges in this ontological space. In the practice of yoga, knowing the sequence of movements in a particular pose or series of postures, like in the sun salutation, for example, I anticipate what the practice leader or my neighbor will do; I know what will happen to all of us, and he/she/they also know this and move as we all do.

However, the autonomy of this space of specific activities has rules. Certain behaviors are more expected and acceptable, considered natural to facilitate interactions, while others are the opposite (Tanaka, 2017, p. 348). A painful corrective touch on the instructor's part in hatha yoga practice is not acceptable, while a gentle but explicit touch is accepted. An aching body is unlikely to be taken in yoga practice. Rules develop according to what we bring and agree on during practice, and agreements occur mainly in the interaction between bodies, e.g. corrective touching of another body, and the practitioner's reaction is precisely the interbody interaction regulated by norms.

Intercorporeality in Hatha Yoga Practice

Intercorporeality occurs in hatha yoga, based on bodywork and working with the body in an interactional context. We have already partially mentioned this in the previous paragraph. Practitioners' bodies **match each other** in movement, achieving a specific position (behavior matching). More specifically, interpersonal matching would refer to imitating and matching the body movements of a practitioner's subject to the body movements of Other, in this case, the hatha yoga instructor and other practitioners, and matching between practitioners.

On the other hand, **synchronization**, the second aspect of intercorporeality, would involve adjusting the practitioner's rate of executing positions after receiving instruction, verbal or bodily, from the yoga teacher. Anselm Strauss' term for matching ("articulation") could be used here (Strauss, 1988). Interactional sociological theory can also be helpful. We adjust our actions and schedules by arranging to go to a restaurant for dinner, scheduling business meetings with others, or arranging a date. But aligning ourselves with others also involves micro phenomena, such as coordinating our body movements with those of another. In hatha yoga, we coordinate the moves even when not looking at the teacher and close practitioners; we feel their pace of movement.

In the transmission of knowledge in the practice of yoga, we are not dealing with passive imitation of body movements (although the element of imitation exists). Instead, as the interaction develops, the practitioner adapts to the movements of the teacher's body, as well as the image of the yoga postures to be achieved, so performing movements similar to those presented by the interaction partner, in this case, mainly the hatha yoga instructor. The instructor often stops his movements while watching others to show his movements exactly, which are the model to follow at that moment. This momentary stop and the students' gaze directed at the teacher's body is that space in which intersubjectivity and understanding between bodies are created. Stopping in motion is a moment in the movement of the body. The student becomes aware of his limitations and the possibilities in his body by being in front of the teacher's body. Thus, his "I" can stand out; the student can be himself and be a student in this situation. However, without the teacher and other practitioners, this could not happen. Our subjective self is formed through the interdependence of being (in yoga practice) with others (Tanaka, 2018b, p. 280). Focusing on the same object, the position (its shape) of hatha yoga allows us to be with others at the exact moment ("We are together in this mood of unification and sameness of movement, smell and light, and the vastness of this space.") And this happens regardless of the cultural conditioning of individual practitioners. The essence of forming the self in bodily interactions is universal.

In the practice of hatha yoga in pairs, it is essential to adjust the bodies of the two people (behavior matching; see Fig. 1 from the mentioned research project, see footnote 1). The photo shows an example of performing a Warrior II pose. It is a matter of matching each other's arm and leg positions to look the same according to the teacher's instruction and how he demonstrates movements and positions. So, we have the matching of the teacher's body position and each other's body positions as a pair. In Fig. 1, the left arms are synchronized perfectly, with no adjustment to the right arms. But there is such potency. The yoga teacher will make sure the alignment happens. The feet are aligned. We also see similar facial expressions; the couple smiles without seeing each other. All this is done gradually, with slight movement adjustments by both people when each person responds to the partner's movement so that both people are aligned with each other (articulation). The space between the partners is filled with intersubjective intention to articulate the body's position with body movements. In this space, the intersubjective agreement is created; there is mutual observation out of the corner of the eye and feeling the movements of the other (if we can't see the person). The final adjustment of the position evokes joy; what we can call positive emotional energy is created, derived from engaging in a given interaction ritual (Collins, 2004).[7]

The performance of postures is just such a microritual within the broader pattern of hatha yoga practice sessions. In the session, the practitioners' body movements and postures are aligned and performed simultaneously and in the same space; the movements are repetitive, and sometimes the practice outwardly resembles a slow group ballet dance. From the faces in Fig. 1, one can see that a joyful body appears; joy is visible in the body and is expressed with the body. It is the objectified body at the moment it is presented to another body; the Other sees it, and the subject no longer influences how he or she perceives it. So, the body presented to others in the interaction, here to the photographer (the interaction with the camera and the photographer), is also relevant to the final interpretation of what intentions the body expresses (showing joy). I (the photographer) am the one who interprets them that way. My concentrated gazing and disciplined

Fig. 1. Matching Positions (Behavior Matching) in Hatha Yoga Practice in Pairs, Warrior II Position. *Source:* Photo by the author.

fascination (Churchill, 2022:54–55) allow me to arrive at the meanings contained in the movements, especially since I can empathize as an eyewitness to the event and as a yoga practitioner who can empathize with the position being performed.

In Fig. 2, we see body matching and concentrated faces – the students follow the teacher's instructions. They try to imitate his moves and the pose, and "concentrate on one point in front of them," which they can choose according to the instruction. The female student at the front of the group wants to check if she is matching the pose correctly; we see it from her glances. Generally, the bodies are still and focused; the eyes, faces, and poses show that, and then we can feel it.

Transformation of the Body Schema

In hatha yoga, we experience body resistance when performing specific postures. This is especially the case at the beginning of the practice; sometimes, resistance to certain positions is due to the body schema developed during various life events. For example, this schema can refer to situations that we describe

Fig. 2. Body Matching. *Source:* Photo by Kamil Glowacki.

verbally, but their essence is contained in body movement habits. Here are descriptions of these habits: one does not stand on one's head, one stands on one's feet; bending the body backward is harmful, it can damage the spine, one cannot bend backward so much; one cannot stand still, one must act and move, the body is never stationary. These patterns are embodied, which is about perceiving the body as an entity that "can't" do something although we also have the perception of "I can" do it.

Body schema is a holistic and unconscious predisposition to perform particular movements and body positions in a specific physical space and environment: "Body schema is a system of sensory-motor capacities that function without awareness or the necessity of perceptual monitoring" (Gallagher, 2005, p. 24; quoted in Tanaka 2018a, p. 224). The body schema is subject to change. Additionally, it takes place in the prereflective mode, when we acquire certain habits:

> Since the body schema is a certain system open to the world, a correlate of the world, the acquisition of habits must be understood as its expansion, filling and concretization. The body schema is the scaffolding on which mastery, the world's inhabitation, is supported. The body's acquired knowledge of the world and itself, made possible by the body schema providing the general structures of all possible experiences, continuously expand it. This knowledge is available only through the body's efforts and cannot be reached through intellectual reflection. (Maciejczak, 2001, pp. 46–47)

Performing inverted postures, for example, is not usually part of the body schema for beginners in hatha yoga. In this case, the individual may feel resistance to performing specific movements and inverted postures when the head is down and the legs are up (See Fig. 3). The body schema can explain a lot regarding so-called obstacles in the practice of hatha yoga. These obstacles mainly appear in beginner practitioners. However, it is not just resistance inherent in the mind that causes an individual not to want to perform specific postures; it is also the lack of a particular body schema to enable them to be performed that causes this resistance. Overcoming it involves transforming the body schema for different movements and positions. The lived body interacting with the physical body converts the physical body and brings out particular abilities that exist in the body to perform new movements. The lived-body

Fig. 3. Standing on the Forearms (*salamba sirsasana*). An inverted position is not usually part of our body scheme. *Source:* Photo by Kamil Glowacki.

experience changes as the body adjusts to being able to do something it didn't do before. Its range of motion expands.

A similar transformation of the body schema can be accomplished by becoming aware of your feet touching the mat in a standing position, such as the mountain position (*tadasana*, see Fig. 4). This may happen when the instructor says, "feel your feet, feel the touch of your skin to the mat, feel the connection to the floor, then the connection to the earth, then feel the connection to the whole world." The foot touching the mat allows me to connect with a physical object through the touch of the skin and the feeling of resistance in the toes; I feel the physical object, the mat, and the hard floor or ground beneath it. The mat is warm or cool, rough or smooth. It speaks to me. Then I feel that touch on my skin as I become aware of that place and what is happening there. This touch is inside me; I am the one who feels it and singles myself out as the subject of this touch. There is, after all, some space between my body and the mat; the mat is not me, I am not the mat, but I am not quite sure about that. And at the same time, I am connected to the materiality of this world. My body schema has been transformed; in this context, I feel my body wider outside, but my inside feeling of this connection is widened. I become "bigger" and "deeper." I reach farther because the body's sensations changed, followed only later by the reflective mind ("The muscles of my body drape over my bones, my muscles tense, and I feel the fascias even though I shouldn't feel them.")

Fig. 4. Mountain Pose (*tadasana*). Standing still allows one to feel muscles and fascias and to notice the balance of the body and connect with the physical ground, interacting with the mat and the hardness and surface of the mat base. *Source:* Photo by Kamil Glowacki.

Moreover, standing still, I can feel my body wobbling. I am standing still, stable, and struggling to maintain my balance. Paradox. I can feel this by concentrating on my feet and the ground of my feet. I feel the body wobble, and, therefore, some of my micromovement during the stability of the whole body. The body's schema of "moving-not-moving relationships" changes. The micromovement of my entire body provides the immobility of the standing position. Later, there is a reflection on what it means to be immobile. What does immobility mean in general? Reflective "I" is based on the pre-reflective movement of the body.

The Body as Subject and Object

There are interactional situations in which the body passes interchangeably from the subject role to the object role and vice versa; this happens, for example, in an erotic encounter. "The erotic experience is one that most poignantly reveals to human beings their ambiguous condition; they experience it as flesh and spirit, as the other and subject" (De Beauvoir, 2010, p. 416). This interchangeability shows the referentiality of the body's roles and the ambivalence of subjectivity and objectivity. Moreover, we can gain acceptance for our own body and the body of the Other; this frees us from external definitions of roles, norms, and limitations. In such an encounter, "freedom" haunts us.

My body in yoga practice also appears interchangeably as subject and object (Tanaka, 2018a; Tarasiuk, 2023). There is a constant dynamic of subject–object interchangeability here. Ambivalence emerges. I feel it when, as the subject, I want to perform a difficult hatha yoga pose, and I can't do it. I want to, and by that, my body strives to perform the position, so the body appears here as an object. But on the other hand, the resisting body is a subject. I (the subject) act toward it (the object); I want to force it to perform the yoga position, but at a certain point, the subject does not express this desire:

> I entered the pose very quickly, and nothing distracted me. I was thinking only about my body, not about what others think about me. **I followed the teacher's voice**. My **body obeyed me until I performed the side plank pose** – *Vasisthasana*. When I leaned on my right hand, I kept my balance and **wondered when others had a problem with it** (then, for the first time, my attention was distracted, and despite focusing on the position, I **watched what was happening around me**). When we changed arm to the left and started to perform this position, I was terrified . . . The left arm swayed in all possible directions. It behaved like a piece of rubber or a thin stick that bent under the influence of weight and could break at any moment. It did not cause me physical pain but fear. I didn't know what was happening because I had no control over it – my left hand was a foreign body. I felt angry with it; I wanted to tame my hand somehow, so I stopped the position and tried to do it again. However, the efforts did not bring results, and the "bending of the hand to all sides" continued. I found that it did not make sense, and I stopped trying again. I was surprised and scared. (self-report, woman exerciser, research collaborator)

In the description, we have an example of alternating perspectives of the body as subject and object. "My body obeyed me," i.e. it was an object, an obedient executor of the practitioner's commands although not precisely a practitioner because "I followed the teacher's voice," i.e. the teacher's voice materialized in her body and her movements. In addition, the practitioner observes others to see if other bodies have the same problem performing the pose. At a certain point, the body takes control of the mind; when it is not able to perform the pose, it gives a signal by rocking to all sides, fear appears, a feeling of lack of control; the body is Other, not me. "I" cannot handle it; eventually, "I" gives up. It has decided that I will not perform the pose at this moment. I feel the body's subjectivity, and "I" is its object, feeling surprised and fearful.

It can sometimes happen that the body directs our attention; when the body feels discomfort, our attention goes automatically there. To these points, the mind wants to check what is happening there. But the body decides about the work of the mind at that moment: "Please come to me, to this point, I feel discomfort here." We can paraphrase the signals from the body:

> In positions that did not involve discomfort, I directed my attention to the stretched body element - arms, legs, etc. Positions involving discomfort (e.g., those that demand significant effort, such as planks and later *chaturanga dandasana*, i.e., going down with hands on the mat

> and remaining horizontal 5 cm above the ground) absorbed my attention. They did it because of this discomfort. (man, exerciser, research participant)

> During the practice, I had a lot of control over my breathing, and I consciously used it to perform the postures better and hold them longer. Especially in the warrior sequence, I was always breathing deeply and thinking about my breath. The breath absorbed me so much that I could not think about anything else; I focused, and nothing distracted me. The greater the fatigue, the greater the focus. I was in a trance; I reacted instinctively to commands; I felt just like a warrior. (woman, exerciser, research collaborator)

In yoga, we experience intersubjectivity when, among other things, the teacher touches our body. Generally, I AM the owner of my body and the subject who can act. However, at the moment of the touch of the Other, I am only the owner of my own body, which can read the intention of the Other. But "I" does not know the intentions of the Other and cannot recognize them mentally. Touch can be interpreted as purely technical and instructional, but it can also be taken as an intrusion into my privacy and corporeality; it can threaten my integrity, the integrity of my body, and my self. The body as an object is vulnerable. One can even unconsciously violate its integrity and cross the privacy barrier. But the body knows what touch means before I give it an interpretation. Interpretations can change, just as touch can be perceived differently by the body, and the body can initially react differently to this touch. It reacts internally beforehand to what reaches it from the outside, for example, through explanations from the teacher.

This is why yoga teachers prepare the recipient for possible touch; they pay a lot of attention to what they want their touch to look like or how it will be received. Before they touch, they ask permission to do it. Here they take up the perspective of another (interchangeability of viewpoints, Schütz, 1970, 1972). One can differentiate how a touch is received due to body patterns shaped in the individual's past biography (memory is in the body, Samudra, 2008). They can even be culturally shaped. For a traditional yoga teacher using the original Hindu school and practice, touch poses no problem. Touching seems normalized and natural, with no motives other than technically improving a pose or maximizing body stretch.

In contrast, a Western practitioner tends to have a body schema in which the boundaries of the body are delineated, and the privacy and even the degree of the delicacy of touch are very clearly defined (see my description of the response to touch in this article). A touch that is too delicate may not fulfill the technical purpose imagined in the student (the ascribed motive of the other) and may evoke associations from a different situational context in the recipient of the touch (e.g., an erotic touch or a touch that shows power or superiority). It is also the intention of the toucher not to violate the boundary of pain, but the recipient may read this intention differently. Therefore, there may be a clash of two body schemas here, incompatible intentionalities.

Seen Through Other

Often, hatha yoga is an opportunity for self-presentation (Tarasiuk, 2023). When I wish to present myself to others in hatha yoga, I become an object to them. But by seeing/knowing (realizing) how I am perceived, I am also an object to myself because of *ME*:

> External perception and the perception of one's own body vary in conjunction because they are the two facets of one and the same act. (Merleau-Ponty, 2005, p. 237)

My being is corporeal, as Merleau-Ponty would say (Fontana & Van De Water, 1977, p. 126). When I concentrate on performing a position perfectly, I want the teacher to notice this, and perhaps other practitioners and the audience to accept me as a competent practitioner. A silent negotiation of my self with the help of my body takes place here. My body is the subject of persuasion and image creation, but the moment I make it the object of others' perceptions, I contribute to its objectification. The perceptions of others clash with my perceptions of their interpretations, which is the basis of my self-definition, my "I," which at this moment is in yoga practice with others and becomes "me." Without juxtaposing my ideas about my bodily potentials expressed through my body with the gaze of others, I would not be able to be myself; I would not know who I am, here and now, for myself. ("He is a Hindu and probably doesn't understand our culture. Or I don't know who I am? Why is he going to teach me? He probably wants to show control of the situation here and now. How will it look to him that I can't and don't know how to?") Am, I a competent practitioner worthy of acceptance and even admiration? Or do I still need to practice a lot to reach acceptance in the eyes of the teacher and other practitioners? Others enable me to define myself and even separate myself from my own closed and seemingly inaccessible subjectivity to others.

Connection With My Own Body

Even when perceiving my body as an object, I perceive it reflectively, without introspection; **it is mine**, although as if external ("My body knows I don't have time to reflect; I do what I should and can do.") I constantly retain a sense of agency and a feeling that I am the one acting (mineness; Tanaka, 2018c, p. 248). The body is mine, I do not experience depersonalization, but I ignore it as an object worthy of attention. The fact that I own my body does not evoke any feelings or emotions in me. Hatha yoga allows us to return to the body when we lose the connection. We are thinking here of the practice of yoga as an experimental situation, not therapeutic or in a religious context.

The body is absent from our daily lives (Van Manen, 2015, p. 49). This is for two reasons: Firstly, the body is a given; it gives us the possession of a so-called minimal self, that is, it is in the background, but through it, we move and carry out daily projects. We do not focus on it, but we know it is there.

We are in contact with it although this contact is not realized at every moment; even if it is, it is not the most crucial focus of our attention. Second, when dealing with practical matters, we lose contact with the body; we ignore it because we are usually in a hurry, have specific things to do, are making a career, and are running away from the here and now (Leder, 1990). We ignore it even when the body signals something (pain, discomfort). We have developed a specific habitus of overlooking the body in our lives. We live mainly in the mind.[8] In addition to managing the body, we can be alienated from it by feeling foreign, false, or hostile (Rosa, 2020, p. 202).

When we practice hatha yoga, the minimal self about feeling the body becomes the point of concentration. I am here in practice, with my body moving in a certain way and striving to perform a particular position. The body, or I, performs these movements and positions. Paying attention to other bodies is also related to the attention focused on my body. The body returns to favor; I become friends with it; it is mine because I feel it fully, in pain, stretching, limitations, pushing the limits, and achieving the unattainable a moment ago. I become aware that it is no longer an absent body with a so-called "minimal self."

CONCLUSIONS

According to Merleau-Ponty's philosophy, the mind of our interaction partners is not hidden and inaccessible to us. It is observable and accessible to us through the actions of the Other, and it exists "between" our body and our interaction partner. Mutual understanding in hatha yoga is made possible by this interaction of bodies and my reflexive I. This interaction is also made possible by the body giving me signs of possibilities for action and performing specific actions to others. What we could see at the beginning of the paper in my description of responses to bodily practice in hatha yoga. Therefore, we can expand the interpretation of bodily interactions by Merleau-Ponty by adding our input on the contemplation of practice that starts with the self-observations we proposed in our research. The pre-reflective reactions could be followed by post-reactive reflections that became active and still bodily interpretations of what happened just before when we had reacted spontaneously without minded aware focus on the moves of our body. We can see it thanks to the research through self-observations and self-reporting, and contemplative memos on self-reports. Our reflection can influence the future reactions of our body to the bodies of the Others, so the prereflective could also become a reflective dimension (Legrand, 2007). It could also be the conscious background of changing our body schema and, at the same time, our interpretation of the events in the lifeworld, of selves and of Others. We can see it thanks to the research by self-observations and self-reporting and contemplative memos on self-reports (Konecki, 2022a).[9]

The transformation of the perspective of the world is changed through changing the body schema. The hatha yoga space could become a resonance space when we react to the other and meet the other to create an authentic intersubjective space of understanding "I" and "Me" in society (Rosa, 2020). Contemplating it becomes the basis of reflective transformation (Rehoric & Bentz, 2008).

Intersubjectivity arises when bodies interact. Intersubjectivity in hatha yoga is possible through resonant space (Rosa, 2020, p. 196); we respond to another body while still being ourselves because we are in contact with our body. I draw on the theoretical and sociological findings of Hartmut Rosa. He talks about the search for resonant spaces that would enable us to move away from the social idea of continuous growth and modes of dynamic stability that are filled with competition and are in a constant state of accelerating production, new technologies, and lifestyle changes, all of which lead to depression and burnout (see also Han, 2015). This resonance would allow us to avoid alienation, obtain the much-desired recognition in the eyes of others, and enter into a resonance mode with others, including the natural world. It can happen in many bodily practices, including yoga, meditation, and contemplation in walking, running, hiking, climbing, and cycling, among others. Let us add the following to Hartmut Rosa's conclusion: the categories of bodily interaction, the recognition of our pre-reflective perception of the body, reflection on the body and its use as an object for oneself and others, and being a bodily object for others when this perception does not influence us. This would allow us to be fully and consciously in the world, or instead, one should write, "to be toward the world" (Maciejczak, 2001, p. 73), where history, language, and culture, together with the body, have a role in getting to know the world and the self and understanding others.

NOTES

1. It is based on my research experience in an investigation conducted within the framework of the project sponsored by Narodowe Centrum Nauki (NCN; National Science Center) project Opus 15, number 2018/29/B/HS6/00513: "Experiencing the body and gestures in the social world of hatha yoga. Meanings and transmission of knowledge in bodily practice" (see further paragraphs: Intercorporeality in hatha yoga practice; Transformation of the body schema; Body as subject and object). Generally, I do not present the data from this project; they are extensively presented in other publications, where the transfer of knowledge and interactions with teachers are described in detail (Konecki, 2022b; Konecki et al., 2023; Tarasiuk, 2023).
2. "In an effort to elude the a priori tendencies of Husserl's concept of absolute consciousness, Merleau-Ponty took the notion of gestalt as his starting point, suggesting that man receives meaning from his world in addition to giving it. Meaning is both conferred upon the world and derived from it. The origin or genesis of meaning is to be sought by uncovering, as it were, the vertically constituted world – the world as experientially derived meaning. Meaning is not simply the product of a transcendental consciousness that maintains a distance between itself and its world of intended objects; it is a product of our experience, an experience that is prior to the idealistic dichotomization of subject and object" (Fontana & Van der Water 1977, p. 122; see also Moustakas, 1994; Van Manen, 2015).
3. "… the space experienced through the intermediary of my body is space 'lived through' (*éspace vécu*, as Merleau-Ponty calls it); that is, it is the open field of my possible locomotions" (Schütz, 2011, p. 194).
4. "…the observations do not constitute the perception. A baby of 15 months opens its mouth if I playfully take one of its fingers between my teeth and pretend to bite it. And yet it has scarcely looked at its face in a glass, and its teeth are not in any case like mine. The fact is that its own mouth and teeth, as it feels them from the inside, are immediately, for it, an apparatus to bite with, and my jaw, as the baby sees it from the outside, is immediately, for it, capable of the same intentions. 'Biting' has immediately, for it, an intersubjective significance. It perceives its intentions in its body, and my body with its own, and thereby my intentions in its own body" (Merleau-Ponty: 410).
5. Alfred Schütz assumed such a version of cognitive intersubjectivity: "In the first place, by the reciprocity of perspectives, one assumes that the other person and oneself see things with the same typicality and that differences in relevances are irrelevant for the purposes at hand" (Barber, 2002, p. 419). Schütz assumes collaboration in a common understanding of the situational aspects of the interaction. It is a clean type of reciprocity without any contextual disturbances.

6. Quotations in the bracket are the excerpt from my self-report presented earlier in the paper.

7. The practice of hatha yoga becomes a resonant sphere, as it were (in the sense of Hartmut Rosa, 2020, p. 171), both horizontally (resonating with the yoga teacher and the values he presents) and vertically, when we resonate with our practice partner(s) in our exchange of gestures. And this is where the recharging of emotional energy takes place. Practicing hatha yoga during a retreat can be considered a "pure resonant oasis." According to Rosa, in this oasis there is a lack of self-effectiveness; there is a calming down, and there is no stirring that can lead to the transformation of the individual. However, one can't fully agree with this. Resonance oases can prepare someone for action; meditation retreat centers are precisely the place to transform the individual, which is the basis for transformative action in resonance with others outside these centers. It is not that these oases close down and isolate individuals from the world forever. The situation is similar to reading books, when I immerse myself in reading and am isolated from the lifeworld. However, after a while, I return to the reality of everyday life, not the one I was reading about, but the practical one, and I am still under the influence of the book I immersed myself in. I may already see the world differently, thanks to reading this book.

8. As Rosa (2020, p. 93) wrote, this type of lifestyle is a consequence of "acceleration," which is based on a forcibly competitive socio-economic system.

9. The body schema could change by consciously concentrating on the breathing, for example:

"During the practice, I noticed that I have more strength, and the positions that require it turned out much better than last week. I tried to use as much conscious breathing as possible. As soon as my attention slipped away, some exercises became more difficult. It seemed I was already exhausting myself; I quickly returned to my breath consciousness and tried to adjust it to the asana. As soon as I started to breathe consciously, I noticed that my body fit better, and the body was gaining a new energy supply" (woman, exerciser, research collaborator).

REFERENCES

Barber, M. (2002). Alfred Schutz: Reciprocity, alterity, and participative citizenry. In *Phenomenological approaches to moral philosophy. Contributions to phenomenology* (Vol. 47). Springer. https://doi.org/10.1007/978-94-015-9924-5_21

Blumer, H. (1969). Symbolic interactionism. Perspective and method. University of California Press.

Churchill, S. D. (2022). *Essentials of existential phenomenological research*. American Psychological Association.

Collins, R. (2004). *Interaction ritual chains*. Princeton University Press.

De Beauvoir, S. (2010). *The second sex* (C. Borde and S. Malovany-Chevallier (trans.)). Alfred A. Knopf. Beauvoir.

Fontana, A., & Van De Water, R. (1977). The existential thought of Jean-Paul Sartre and Maurice Merleau-Ponty. In J. Douglas & J. M. Johnson (Eds.), *Existential sociology* (pp. 100–129). Cambridge University Press.

Gallagher, S. (2005). *How the body shapes the mind*. Oxford University Press.

Han, B.-C. (2015). *Burnout society*. Stanford University Press.

Konecki, K. T. (2005). The problem of symbolic interaction and of constructing self. *Qualitative Sociology Review*, *1*(1), 68–89.

Konecki, K. T. (2008). Touching and gesture exchange as an element of emotional bond construction. Application of visual sociology in the research on interaction between humans and animals (93 paragraphs). *Forum Qualitative Sozialforschung/Forum: Qualitative Social Research*, *9*(3), 33. http://nbn-resolving.de/urn:nbn:de:0114-fqs0803337

Konecki, K. T. (2022a). *The meaning of contemplation for social qualitative research. Applications and examples*. Routledge.

Konecki, K. T. (2022b). Who Am I when I Am teaching? Self in yoga practice. *The Qualitative Report*, *27*(11), 2623–2658. https://doi.org/10.46743/2160-3715/2022.5469

Konecki, K. T., Płaczek, A., & Tarasiuk, D. (2023). *Experiencing the body in yoga practice. Meanings and knowledge transfer*. Routledge.

Leder, D. (1990). *The absent body*. University of Chicago Press.

Legrand, D. (2007). Pre-reflective self-consciousness. On being bodily in the world. *Janus Head*, *9*(2), 493–519.

Maciejczak, M. (2001). *Świat według ciała w fenomenologii percepcji M. Merleau-Ponty'ego*. IFiS PAN.

Mead, G. H. (1934). *Mind self and society from the standpoint of a social behaviorist* (Edited by C. W. Morris). University of Chicago.

Merleau-Ponty, M. (2005). *Phenomenology of perception*. Routledge.

Morley, J. (2001). Inspiration and expiration: Yoga practice through Merleau-Ponty's phenomenology of the body. *Philosophy East & West*, *51*(1), 73–82.

Moustakas, C. (1994). *Phenomenological research methods*. Sage.

Rehoric, D. A., & Bentz, V. M. (2008). *Transformative phenomenology. Changing ourselves, lifeworlds, and professional practice*. Lexington Books.

Rosa, H.. (2020) *Przyspieszenie, wyobcowanie, rezonans. Projekt krytycznej teorii późnonowoczesnej czasowości* (Beschleunigung und Entfremdung. Entwurf einer Kritischen Theorie spätmoderner Zeitlichkeit – Translation from German to Polish by Jakub Duraj, Jacek Kołtun). Europejskie Centrum Solidarności.

Samudra, J. K. (2008). Memory in our body: Thick participation and the translation of kinesthetic experience. *American Ethnologist*, *35*(4), 665–681.

Schütz, A.. (2011) *Collected papers V. Phenomenology and the social sciences* (Edited by E. Lester). Springer.

Schütz, A. (1970). *On phenomenology and social relations: Selected writings* (Edited by H. Wagner). University of Chicago Press.

Schütz, A. (1972/1932). *The phenomenology of the social world*. Heinemann.

Strauss, A. L. (1969). *Mirrors and masks*. The Sociology Press.

Strauss, A. (1988). The articulation of project work: An organizational process. *The Sociological Quarterly*, *29*(2), 163–178. http://www.jstor.org/stable/4121474

Tanaka, S. (2014). Creation between two minded-bodies Intercorporeality and social cognition. *Kvarter*, *9*, 265–276.

Tanaka, S. (2017). Intercorporeality and Aida: Developing an interaction theory of social cognition. *Theory & Psychology*, *27*(3), 337–353. https://doi.org/10.1177/0959354317702543

Tanaka, S. (2018a). Bodily basis of the diverse modes of the self. *Human Arenas*, *1*, 223–230. https://doi.org/10.1007/s42087-018-0030-x

Tanaka, S. (2018b). The self in Japanese culture from an embodied perspective. In G. Jovanović, L. Allolio-Näcke, & C. Ratner (Eds.), *Challenges in cultural psychology, historical legacies and future responsibilities*. Routledge.

Tanaka, S. (2018c). What is it like to be disconnected from the body? A phenomenological account of disembodiment in depersonalization/derealization disorder. *Journal of Consciousness Studies*, *25*(5–6), 239–262.

Tarasiuk, D. (2023). *Ciało doświadczane i ciało doświadczające. Socjologiczna analiza praktyki hatha-jogi* [*The experienced body and the experiencing body. A sociological analysis of hatha-yoga practice. Ph.D. Thesis*]. Rozprawa doktorska. Łódź: Uniwersytet Łódzki.

Van Manen, M. (2015). *Researching lived experience. Human science for an action sensitive pedagogy*. Routledge.

Van Manen, M. (2016). *Phenomenology of practice. Meaning giving methods in phenomenological research and practice*. Routledge.

THE GRAMMAR OF IDENTITY

Robert Perinbanayagam

Hunter College of the City University of New York, USA

ABSTRACT

The selves of individuals abhor vacuums and find themselves constituting identities with which to fill them. Such identities are either conferred by others or chosen by the agents themselves and cultivated and processed and presented. The processing of identities is best described by using Kenneth Burke's dramatistic grammar. He asked, "What is involved when we ask what a man is doing and why he is doing it?" and he answered that the individual will be performing an act *as an* agent *by using one* agency *or another in defined* scenes *while displaying one* attitude *or another, in order to fulfill one* purpose *or another. In the current essay, these Burkean arguments are applied to the constitution; the processing (that is, choosing one among the multiple identities that an agent bears); and the performing of an identity. It is claimed that identities are constituted in one way or another and performed by processing them according to the Burkean grammar. Identities are not ways of being but ways of doing, by taking one road rather than another.*

Keywords: Dramatism; reflexion and reflection; differentiation of identities; types of identity; roads taken and not taken; performing and processing identities

INTRODUCTION

In seeking to understand the interactional life of human agents, many sociologists draw from the monumental work and vision of G. H. Mead. However, the work of Mead can fruitfully be supplemented by the work of other scholars – Charles Sanders Peirce, Kenneth Burke, and Mikhail Bakhtin, for instance who have made significant contributions toward the understanding of human interactions – nay, of human existence itself. I will take the central idea from Burke's major work on the grammar of motives, the *pentad*, expand it with Burke's conversion of it into a hexad, apply it to given areas in social life, and seek to show that the

Essential Issues in Symbolic Interaction
Studies in Symbolic Interaction, Volume 59, 125–144

Published under exclusive licence by Emerald Publishing Limited
ISSN: 0163-2396/doi:10.1108/S0163-239620240000059007

Burkean grammar manifests itself in the constitution of identity by human individuals.

Burke in his major work, described as the "grammar of motives," asked, "What is involved when we ask, 'What are people doing and why they are doing it?'" and he answered that they will become agents who perform acts by using one agency or another in defined scenes in order to fulfill one purpose or another (1945/1969a). Later, citing the work of Mead, he added the *attitude* that agents will announce as they do their acts as another element in his grammar (1968, p. 445). Any attempt to explain ordinary human conduct as completely as possible must truly approach it with Burke's question and answers. This is certainly the case if one wants to explore the constitution and presentation and processing of an identity by an individual.

THE CONSTITUTION OF IDENTITY

The Grammatical Processing

I begin with a quotation from George Herbert Mead:

> A multiple personality is in a certain sense normal.... There is usually an organization of the whole self with reference to the community to which we belong, and the situation in which we find ourselves. What the society is, whether we are living with people of the present, people of our own imaginations, people of the past, varies, of course, with different individuals. (1934, pp. 142–143)

What exactly is Mead's "multiple personality"? And how is it related to his version of the "self"? Clearly, it is possible to have a self and also to have many "personalities." One way of relating these two concepts as features of an individual's being is to propose that what Mead calls "personality" as a feature of the self is analogous to what has been described as identity. Indeed, it can be said that the self of human agents abhors a vacuum, and agents take steps to construct various identities or accept ones conferred by others to fill it. Such an identity can be a convenient one, handy and readily available, or even one that is sought assiduously and cultivated, such as athlete or lawyer or sociologist or communist or Nazi and so on and so forth, and is integrated as a feature of their respective selves. Finally, if the identity is thrust upon one by force, it could be something like convict or conscript or if by circumstances outside one's control, victim of a terrible disease or a violent attack.

The methods by which the selves of human agents are constituted, and identities defined, can be best described as *reflexivity* and *reflectivity*. Here is a statement on these processes:

> The constitution of the self is accomplished by means of processes that can be described as *reflexion* and *reflection*. Reflexion will refer to the process by which others send messages to an individual that he or she may or may not take into account in the constitution of his or her self. The implicit metaphor here is that of a source of light being reflected onto another object. One dictionary puts it this way: "the return of light, heat, sound, etc., after striking a surface."

> Reflection, on the other hand, signifies the inner dialogue, as a "stream of consciousness" that an agent conducts with himself or herself. (Perinbanayagam, 2023, p. 63)

Insofar as *reflexions* and *reflections* lead to agents incorporating a number of varying identities as features of their respective selves, agents have to process them further to give them a presence in social situations. Such processing is accomplished by adopting the dramatistic grammar described by Kenneth Burke. He asked, "What is involved when we say what people are doing and why they are doing it?" And he answered that "we will use five key terms as generating principles of our investigation. They are *act, scene, agent, agency,* and *purpose*" (1945/1969a). In a later publication he added *attitude*, citing the work of G. H. Mead, to this pentad, making it a hexad (1968). Burke called these elements "the grammar of motives." This grammar is used by individuals to constitute and to process their conduct in everyday life. Each of them thereby becomes an agent in charge of their acts in given situations and defined scenes and thus able to indicate their attitudes and purposes. One answer to Burke's opening question, then, about what people are doing and why they are doing it, is that people are *processing* one of their various identities. In processing their individual identities grammatically, they may not use all its features all the time, but certainly most of them will be put into play. Identity then becomes not so much a way of being as a way of doing – doing acts as agents of these acts by using one agency or another in defined scenes, displaying one attitude or another in order to fulfill one purpose or another, as a complete description of instances of human existence.

Processing an identity, then, is the selection and assembling of the particular details that are to be presented to others in given situations. To begin with, a selection must be made about the nature of the agent one is to present: authoritarian or submissive or egalitarian, seductive, indigent, comradely or hostile, interested or indifferent. Next, agents must select the nature of the agency they want to use – verbal or gestural; physical; instrumental such as guns, clubs, knives, or even space; and so on. The scenes in which the said identity is to be presented are already given, but agents can often select them too: office or home; club or living room. The processing of particular identities will also depend on the purposes of the interactions in which the said identity is being presented, and finally, all these elements of the choice of the grammar of identity will determine the choice of the attitude the agent will seek to adopt and display.

The Dialectical Grammar of Identity

In putting the dramatistic grammar into operation, agents, in the process of constituting their identity, do so not only by defining themselves but also *differentiating* themselves from another identity, either implicitly or explicitly, making the identifying process itself a dialectical process. That is, the identity that is constituted will have a certain relationship to another relevant one, leading to what has been called "dialectical opposition." In doing this, the identifying process achieves a dialectical symmetry – for instance Christian versus Jews, Hindu versus Buddhist, American versus Mexican an African American versus a Euro-American and so on.

These differentiations of one identity and the process of giving it a definite presence in social life are accomplished by either implicit or explicit invocation of an opposite identity. So, a Christian in the US or Europe is not merely a Christian but is also not a Jew. If, however, And, further he or she may also more detail: I am a "Roman Catholic" thereby invoking the opposition "Protestant". Christian is also the dialectical opposite, that he or she is not a Buddhist. For a Buddhist in India or Sri Lanka, the claim that a person is a Buddhist is also that they are not a Hindu. A White American is not only White and not Black, and an African American is not only a person of African descent but also not an Anglo–Saxon, and so on. These categories of identification are characterized by being united in opposition: The first dialectical unity is that they are all about religion and the second is about race or ethnicity.

However, these oppositional identities can change. In a different context, the African American is not merely an African American but just an American and not a German and will be motivated to volunteer to join the army, in say, 1943. One can claim to be a White man as opposed to a Black in one context or moment and an American as opposed to a German in another context and moment, the former being united in opposition as ethnic identities while the latter refers to national ones – they are in opposition but united in that they are both identify as patriots. Indeed it could be said that one invokes and processes these specific identities in order to reject the oppositional identity when a particular situation calls for it.

Such a dialectical apprehension of one's identity gives it a certain clarity and precise definition and can, often enough, provide the locational ambience and motives for one's acts. However, it must be acknowledged that the oppositional identity can vary over time and situation, and an agent may choose one such at one time and another at a different time. These identifications and oppositions are processed by using one or more of the features of dramatistic grammar.[1]

IDENTITY AND MOTIVES

The acknowledgment and acceptance of one's many identities, however, is not just a passive state of affairs but a dynamic one and is the foundation from which one draws the rhetoric of motives that leads to the selected acts of the agent. It is featured in the reflection that the self has as it prepares an act and is given expression. In a pathfinding essay, Nelson Foote argued that "role theory," or what one may call "interactionist theory," lacks a theory of motivation. He proposed that the concept of identification can answer this problem. He wrote

> We mean by identification, appropriation of and commitment to a particular identity or series of identities. As a process, it proceeds by naming; its products are ever-evolving self-conceptions – with the emphasis on the con, that is, upon ratification by significant others.

Foote then described three implications of such commitment to an identity as follows:

> In most situations our identity is so completely habitual and taken for granted that we virtually ignore its presence or relevance in our reflections, concentrating only upon the stimulating environment. Researchwise, it is strategic to focus observations upon those situations where identity itself is acutely problematic in order to observe its determining effect upon behavior (although study of the opposite type of situation – the teacher who insists she was cut out only for fifth-grade math, the fifth grader who insists he was never cut out for it – is also illuminating). (1951, p. 14)

Encountering reflexions and doing reflections, then, agents constitute identities and process them in everyday interactions. The process by which this happens uses the themes received as reflexions, subjecting them to reflections leads to the constitution of an effective rhetoric of motives. Indeed the motivation process that Foote describes here conforms to the dramatistic grammar: In adopting and processing an identity the individual becomes an agent who will chose one or other instrumentation as agencies to undertake one act or another in the relevant scenes in which he or she finds himself or herself in order to fulfill one purpose or another – while displaying one attitude or another.

THE VISUAL GRAMMAR OF IDENTITY

Long before, agents undertake verbal processing of their respective identities in relating to others, they are *seen,* and their identities are observed and appraised by the other. All human agents, in fact, construct a relevant identity by manipulating their appearance through the clothing they wear, the jewelry they sport, the chosen style for their hair and face, and in some instances, the weapons they carry (Stone, 1970). All the dialogs that follow must take these visual features into account. Manlow and Ferree (2021) put this very succinctly as follows:

> Clothing is a functional covering for the body, protecting it from the elements and from those who may do it harm, but more than that, it serves a social purpose in communicating meanings that fall into a myriad of categories that encompass economic standing (one's class position, for example) and social concerns; membership in religious, cultural, and ethnic identities; political adherence; professional status; age; sexual orientation; gender; marital status.

The act of clothing of the human body to claim an identity is influenced by a variety of institutions – religions that dictate the clothing for nuns and monks, cultures that recommend clothing for gendering or for the presentation of status as well as to indicate "taste" and judgment, conformity, and so on. Claims to masculinity, for example, are expressed by managing clothing so that even one who is biologically a woman can make that claim. In Indian society, widowhood is designated by forcing the bereaved woman to wear only white clothing and forbidding the wearing of any jewelry, just as the caste system dictates the clothing of the various castes though these aspects of Indian society have changed drastically in recent years.

In some societies, the fashion industry dictates the visual identity of the individuals. But all these features, in fact, follow the *dramatistic* grammar. The agents define their identity by the act of choosing the visual agency with which their identity is to be processed. These agencies can manifest as one or another attitude: formal, casual, belligerent, flirtatious, provocative, religious, subordinate, or superordinate. For example, monks and nuns in Catholicism and Buddhism use a visual grammar to present their identities, just as a bawd or strip dancer will present her relevant identity by choosing appropriately. The purpose of these chosen agencies is to indicate not only one's attitude and purpose but also to indicate the scenic appropriateness of the identity that one is dramatizing as clearly as possible so that all subsequent dialogs can proceed readily.[2]

These selected costumes that everyone sports in public, then, are addressive acts directed to others in order to define their identity in the scene in which they are appearing as well as process their presence therein. Indeed, these agents do not wear the same costume in every scene, but select one or another to suit the scene and the attitudes and purposes thereof.

Anecdote I – Women's Clothing[3]

Different institutions have varying codes that must be used in presenting their visual identity, just as different scenes demand different codes. These codes embody the grammar of identity systematically. Here is an example from the practices of the Los Angeles Country Club:

> Women's shirts and blouses must be worn inside slacks or skirts, unless designed to be worn outside.
>
> Women's slacks must be of a tailored nature and must be ankle length or longer.
>
> Skirts must be no shorter than 4" above the knee.
>
> Golf attire is acceptable at all times, in the Locker Room, Grill Room, Bar and their adjacent patios.
>
> After 6:00 p.m., dress: dressy skirt and blouse, suit, tailored pants suit, pants and blazer or evening pants outfit is acceptable following the length guidelines above in all other areas of the Clubhouse unless otherwise specified for an event.
>
> Women may wear brimmed hats, not golf caps, coordinating with their outfits in the Clubhouse.
>
> Hats, caps, and visors are never allowed inside the Clubhouse or on adjacent patios, except as noted above for brimmed hats, and except that hats, caps and visors may be worn (with the bill facing forward in the case of caps and visors) only on the uncovered patio adjacent to the Bar. (Los Angeles Country Club, n.d.)

The woman, defined as an agent, is being encouraged to use varied agencies to present her identity and indicate her attitude, at times decorous and others sporting, in the appropriate scenes with the purpose of claiming her status as a regular and authentic member of the club.

Anecdote II – Ecclesiastical Codes

One can take the costuming of a Benedictine nun to display the meticulous care with which she is clothed to define her identity and present to the world. Here is a fine description from the leader of the order.

At the Benedictine Abbey of St. Walburga in Virginia Dale, the nun's habit consists of a tunic, belt, scapular and veil, which are all black. Under the veil is a white headdress called a coif, which frames the nun's face. Fully professed nuns also wear a white veil under the black one.

"Every piece of garment you have is blessed," said Mother Maria Michel News, 55, the abbess. The beautiful blessings, she added, explain each item's meaning, and help the nun to live her vocation as a bride of Christ.

"The belt reminds us that Christ wore chains," she said, referring to his obedience. "The scapular represents our commitment to conversion – to take on the yoke of the Lord, which is sweet. A yoke is usually carried by two: we carry half and Christ carries the other half." The veil is the sign of the nun's consecration. "You put the veil on and you know you belong to (God)," Mother Maria Michael said. "You are not your own." The veil and coif cover the nun's hair, which the Scriptures call a woman's "adornment," to protect her from vanity and to remind her that she is given fully to God, the abbess said. "You act as you wear," she said. "If people wear jeans and T-shirts, they act differently than if they are dressed up in a suit. There is a certain dignity that goes along with wearing the habit ... a certain nobility you are expected to carry. Clothing does express your heart."

Benedictines wear black tunics, she explained, both as a sign of penitence and because it was the cheapest fabric in the fifth century, when the Italian St. Benedict founded the order, the oldest in the Church. (Denver Catholic, 2015)

Here, then, is a rather complex and systematic use of the grammar of identities. In one sweeping gesture, the founders of the order have programmed the very appearance of the agentic nuns in doing acts of clothing and attendant artifacts to present and process an identity that displays both attitudes of reverence and discipline and a purposive commitment to the religious calling as they inhabit sanctified scenes.

THE GRAMMAR IN OFFICIAL IDENTITIES

Anecdote III – Presidential Identity

During Richard Nixon's presidency, he faced many problems and controversies and had to deal with them in discussions with his subordinates. In these interactions, he and his chosen assistant had to use verbal acts to define their respective identities. Here is one such encounter in which this is accomplished – albeit almost unobtrusively.

PRESIDENT: John, sit down, sit down.

DEAN: Good morning.

PRESIDENT: Well, what is the Dean summary of the day about?

DEAN: John caught me on the way out and asked me about why Gray was holding back on information if that was under instructions from us. And it, uh, it was, and it wasn't. Uh, it was instructions proposed by the Attorney General, consistent with your press conference statement that no further raw data was to be turned over to the....

PRESIDENT: Full committee.

DEAN: ... full committee.

PRESIDENT: Right.

DEAN: And that was the extent of it. And Gray, himself, is the one who reached the conclusion that no more information be turned over; he'd turned over enough. Uh, so this is again Pat Gray making decisions on his own as to how to handle his hearings. He has been

totally unwilling all along to take any guidance, any instruction. We don't know what he is going to do. He is not going to talk about it. He won't review it, uh, and I don't think...
PRESIDENT: Right.
DEAN: . . . he does it to harm you in any way, sir.
PRESIDENT: He's just quite stubborn and – he's quite stubborn; also, he isn't very smart. You know he and I –
DEAN: He's bullheaded.
PRESIDENT: He's smart in his own way, but. . .
DEAN: Yeah.
PRESIDENT: . . . but he's got that typical, "Well, by God, this is right and they're not going to do it."
DEAN: That's why he thinks he'll be confirmed, because he thinks he's being, he's being his own man. He's being forthright, honest. He's feels he has turned over too much and so it's a conscious decision that he is harming the Bureau by doing this and so he's not going to—
PRESIDENT: (Sighs) I hope to God that we can get off (unintelligible) though today, this is because the White House told him to do this and that other thing. And also, I told Ehrlichman, I don't see why our little boys can't make something out of the fact that, God darn it, this is the, this is the, the only responsible decision you could possibly make. The FBI cannot turn over raw files. Has anybody made that point? I've tried. . .
DEAN: Sam Ervin has made that point himself. (Nixon Tapes Transcript, 1973)

In this drama between President Nixon and his assistant John Dean, the acts are addresses and rejoinders between a dominant agent and a subordinate one in an office, and the agency is verbal. Nixon gives permission to Dean to sit down: It is the president's territory, and he must give the necessary permission to the other, and he, in a series of statements and questions, controls the dialog. And Dean obediently provides the answers and at times amplifies them, ending his rejoinders with a "sir." Nixon's verbal acts are characterized by an attitude of control and domination, from the opening greeting by Dean with his "Good morning," which goes without a reciprocal greeting. Dean in turn defines his identity by maintaining an attitude of decorous reverence and respect – though rather subdued – and they are both engaged in using the information that Dean has gathered to fulfill the purpose of taking the next step. The operation of the grammar simultaneously identifies both the president and his subordinate.

Anecdote IV – Office Politics

The following incident happened in an office too but should perhaps be considered something of an exception in its choice of a very forceful agency – though it may be common enough in certain scenes. In this office scene, an irate agent is seeking to chastise another for a perceived misdemeanor and chooses a certain metaphor as his agency to display his attitude and purpose by using the agency sarcastically:

A: Doesn't it make you feel good when you report others for fucking off?

The respondent to this address chooses to use the agency to defend himself in his rejoinder:

B: Fuck you – I am here to work.

This receives another address that uses the same allusion to sex and adds a touch of irony:

A: No, fuck you. You fun-loving son of a bitch. (Seckman & Couch, 1989, pp. 327–344)

The word *fuck* is used routinely in a variety of allusions and hardly ever used in its original meaning in ordinary conversations. Indeed, its use in everyday acts to signify a variety of meanings is legion. It is in fact an agency – one whose forms are used as a verb, adverb, and adjective to indicate attitudes signifying an emotionality of one kind or another and which aid in the processing of a particular identity. In this exchange, the word *fuck* becomes not only an agency with which to express hostility but also to assert each agent's identity as an equal to that of the other. The one being reprimanded with that particular agency uses it himself to show that he is not intimidated and is ready to hit back. It is a very forceful agency that admits to no ambiguity. It is also readily available and does not demand any creative skills and is habitually used without having to search for another. It also can be used to advance a claim to a masculinist and irreverent identity that is not bound by the rules of politesse and decorous discourse.

FAMILIAL IDENTITIES

In a family, in all cases the identities of its members are arranged in structures of hierarchy, with both agencies of interaction and the attitudes manifested toward family members strictly regulated. In every act they process, these elements of the grammar are put into practice, and the identities of each agent are defined.

In Indian society, for example, the relations between not only parents and children but between siblings are very strictly regulated and are manifested in the addressive agency that must be used. The particular agencies that are selected will define the identities of the addressor and that of the recipient as well as the attitude. If, for example, the addressor is a younger person addressing an elder, the terminology chosen will indicate an attitude of respect as well as the acceptance of a particular identity.

I will use examples from Tamil Sri Lanka – my own society – as illustration of where the hierarchical processing of identities is strictly observed. There, the differentiation of identity in terms of hierarchy is accomplished by rituals and is typically undertaken verbally by using the plural form for *you* in addressing a superordinate and the singular form in addressing a subordinate. The rejoinders to these forms of address also follow the same form. The plural is *neengal* and the singular is *nee.* In the family circle as well as in the outside world, these rituals are put into practice in dealing with age and rank: deferential identification with pronouns! I may add a little to this study. In earlier times, in the hierarchy of relationship between a man and his wife, the wife was expected to show respect by never using his name, nickname, or even calling him "my husband." Rather, she would use *avar*, a plural form of *him*. At other times she might refer to her husband as "my son's father." To name was to degrade.

Also, in the Tamil world of India and Sri Lanka, for relations between two different castes, such deferential rituals are used to define one's own identity. Once again, the plural form is used to address the superordinate other, and at times a variation on it, *thangal,* is used. This is an indirect allusion to the addressee and avoids the direct form of *neengal*, which in some relationships may be considered presumptuous. In summary, these words can be translated as *nee*, a simple "you"; *neengal* ("you all" even while addressing only one person); and *thangal*, a third person form that represents a further degree of subordination. It is difficult to find a suitable English equivalent though I did consider *thou* but was not quite satisfied with it since the Quakers used that word to indicate a radical equality – indeed, friendship.

The Grammar of Religious Identity

From the moment a child is born, or at least soon after, it is subject to intense reflexions from the people around it. The child receives them and soon subjects them to reflections and fashions a self with various qualifying identities attached to it. The individual is thus able to embed himself or herself in these narratives. George Herbert Mead put the issue in this way while discussing consciousness and the self:

> Then there is another use of "consciousness" with which we have been particularly occupied, denoting that which we term thinking or reflective intelligence, a use of consciousness which always has, implicitly at least, the reference to an "I" in it. This use of consciousness has no necessary connection with the other... (1934, p. 165)

The "I" that undertakes these intelligent reflections must, at least occasionally, wonder and ponder the following issues: Who am I, really? Where did I come from? What happens when I die? Answers to these questions are given in the complex and intricate narratives that various religious systems provide. For a believer in Christianity, the summary answer is "I am a sinner and in need of redemption." For a believer in Hinduism, the summary answer is "I am a carrier of my karma from earlier incarnations and in need of redemption for my next one." Each narrative, then, specifies various acts (rituals) the believers must perform in order to achieve such redemption. These acts are articulated in accordance with the dramatistic grammar that thereby also defines the agent's identity.

One may take the ritual known as the "confession" as a strategic example in which Catholics periodically go to their priest and describe the sins that they have committed recently. These performances in the confessional are indubitably dramas in which devout agents act in defined scenes with the proper reverential and contrite attitude with the purpose of achieving some degree of redemption, at least for the time being. Here is an example in which the act manifests the relevant attitude very clearly in the appropriate scene to achieve some level of redemption:

as the penitent prays. This prayer expresses true sorrow for the sins confessed. This prayer may be expressed in one's own words or consider the agency that is put into place in a formal prayer of sorrow such as the "Act of Contrition" from the *Rites of Penance:*

> My God,
>
> I am sorry for my sins with all my heart.
>
> In choosing to do wrong
>
> and failing to do good,
>
> I have sinned against you
>
> whom I should love above all things.
>
> I firmly intend, with your help,
>
> to do penance,
>
> to sin no more,
>
> and to avoid whatever leads me to sin.
>
> Our Savior Jesus Christ suffered and died for us.
>
> In his name, my God, have mercy. (United States Conference of Catholic Bishops, n.d.)

In the religion of the Hindus, there are many agencies with which agents can define their identity and seek some form of redemption from the karmic weight they may be carrying. One good example is the ritual known as the *puja.* Here is a summary of this act from *Wikipedia*:

> The word pūjā is Sanskrit and means reverence, honor, homage, adoration and worship. Puja, the loving offering of light, flowers, and water or food to the divine, is the essential ritual of Hinduism. For the worshiper, the divine is visible in the image, and the divinity sees the worshiper. The interaction between human and deity, between human and guru, is called darshan, seeing.

Indeed, how does one come to consider oneself as a Catholic or a Hindu? It is by processing the various features of the Burkean grammar: One must act by using the recommended agencies with the correct attitude with the purpose of reaching a deity, typically in the scenes of church or temple.

HEROIC IDENTITY

Anecdote V – Heroic Identity

Often in ongoing social life, individuals will find themselves transformed into a different identity than the one with which they have been functioning until that moment. From a mundane existence and bearing the identity thereof, one is enabled to claim the identity of a hero or heroine. A homeless panhandler in Manchester, England, was sitting on the street begging for money when a bomb went off near him, injuring some children and adults. Yet in a moment of crisis, he assumed the identity of a selfless human agent and jumped in to save some children and help some adults. Here is the account from *The New York Times* of the transformation of his identity into a hero.

> For Chris Parker, the arena's entrance area might have seemed like a good place to ask people for money. Stephen Jones had found a spot nearby to sleep. Now, the two men, both homeless, are being praised as heroes for helping victims of the Manchester Arena bombing. As Manchester and the rest of Britain were trying to come to terms with the country's deadliest terrorist attack in more than a decade, the two men are being hailed on social media for their selflessness and courage. Mr. Parker, 33, was panhandling when the bomb exploded, according to local news reports. The force of the blast knocked him to the floor, but he was unfazed. Rather than running for safety, he went to the aid of victims, comforting a girl who had lost her legs, wrapping her in a T-shirt, and cradling a dying woman in his arms. . . . "Just because I am homeless doesn't mean I haven't got a heart, or I'm not human still," he told ITV News. "I'd like to think someone would come and help me if I needed the help," he said, adding that he had been overcome by an "instinct" to pitch in. (Bilefsky, 2017)

From the dramatistic standpoint, Chris Parker becomes, on the spur of the moment, a heroic agent and uses the agency of his acts of intervention to meet the purpose of saving the lives of other individuals in a deadly scene with an attitude of both compassion and selflessness. In this case, an ordinary agent transform himself into a hero by one single act that reflects compassion by purposefully jumping into a dangerous scene using his own body as the agency.

THE ETHICS OF IDENTITY

The *Wikipedia* account is one of starkest reality.

Anecdote VI – Unethical Identity

> On May 25, 2020, George Floyd, a 46-year-old black man, was murdered in Minneapolis, Minnesota, U.S., by Derek Chauvin, a 44-year-old white police officer. Floyd had been arrested after a store clerk alleged that Floyd made a purchase using a counterfeit $20 bill. Chauvin knelt on Floyd's neck for over nine minutes while Floyd was handcuffed and lying face-down in a street. Two other police officers, J. Alexander Kueng and Thomas Lane, assisted Chauvin in restraining Floyd. Lane had also pointed a gun at Floyd's head prior to Floyd being put in handcuffs. A fourth police officer, Tou Thao, prevented bystanders from intervening.
>
> Prior to being placed on the ground, Floyd had exhibited signs of anxiety, complaining about having claustrophobia, and being unable to breathe. After being restrained, he became more distressed, still complaining of breathing difficulties, of the knee on his neck, and of fear of imminent death. After several minutes, Floyd stopped speaking. For the last few minutes, he lay motionless and Officer Kueng found no pulse when urged to check. Despite this, Chauvin ignored pleas from bystanders to lift his knee from Floyd's neck.

Derek Chauvin had one of two choices: to stop throttling Floyd, not only under the principles of ordinary ethics but also in response to the pleas of the bystanders, or keep throttling Floyd till he died. He chose to keep throttling Floyd, acting to kill him by choosing an often-lethal agency with strong attitudes of hostility, thereby defining his identity that provided him the motives for his acts. That is, his identity moved his acts, just as his acts nourished his identity further.

If the Floyd case is an example of the processing of what would be considered an unethical identity, here is an example of the easy and seemingly routine processing of an ethical identity. The incident received international publicity.

Anecdote VII – Ethical Identity

The group of 10 travelers – which included nine tourists from South Korea – were making their way to Niagara Falls from Washington, DC, when they found themselves in the middle of a blizzard. Two men in the group decided to knock on a door to ask for shovels to try to get their van out of a ditch. They ended up with a place to stay until they could be picked up on Sunday after the storm cleared…

Alex Campagna, a dentist, said on Facebook that at about 2 p.m. on Friday, during "the worst blizzard I've experienced," he heard a "frantic knock on the door." Campagna and his wife ended up inviting the 10 people in, putting them up on couches, in sleeping bags, on an air mattress, and in a spare bedroom, The Times reported. Campagna told the newspaper he didn't want to let the group back out on the roads, adding that he knew, "as a Buffalonian, this is on another level, the Darth Vader of storms."

Choi Yoseob, a member of the tour group that Campagna hosted, told The Times it was "kind of like fate" that they'd ended up at the home of a hospitable family with a full pantry.

"We have enjoyed this so much," Choi said, describing the experience as unforgettable and a "unique blessing."

The group spent Friday and Saturday swapping stories and cooking with their hosts. The Times report said they watched an NFL game on Christmas Eve and made several Korean meals, adding that Campagna and his wife are fans of Korean food themselves and had ingredients needed to make jeyuk bokkeum, stir-fried pork, and dakdori tang, a spicy chicken stew. If the travelers had stayed for Christmas dinner on Sunday, the group likely would have made bulgogi, the report said.

Drivers picked up the tourists on Sunday when roads were cleared and brought them back to New York City, the report said. Choi said he and his wife planned to stay for New Year's Eve. The others are scheduled to fly back to South Korea this week. (Askinasi & Teh, 2022)

Mr. Campagna, to all appearances, did not hesitate to offer sanctuary to people in distress and even continuing hospitality to people in dire need, thereby becoming an ethical agent performing exemplary acts of kindness, displaying attitudes of compassion and understanding in a scene that badly needed these aspects, and constituting, grammatically speaking, an ethical identity.

RECKLESS IDENTITIES

Often individuals present and process identities with reckless indifference to either immediate or long-term consequences to their selves. Such acts are typically animated by attitudes of extreme emotions of either hatred or love. Such moves involve agents who perform acts using both verbal and material agencies to display the relevant attitudes with the purpose of hurting the other, or winning their attention and affection, or making a claim about oneself or a situation.

Anecdote VIII – Reckless Identity: Hatred

Wikipedia provides an account of the acts of Patrick Crusius who, in total disregard of the consequences to the interests of his own self, took a gun and traveled several miles to give vent to his attitude of hatred to people of Mexican origin.

> On August 3, 2019, a terrorist mass shooting occurred at a Walmart store in El Paso, Texas, United States. The gunman, 21-year-old Patrick Wood Crusius, killed 23 people and injured 22 others. The Federal Bureau of Investigation investigated the shooting as an act of domestic terrorism and a hate crime. The shooting has been described as the deadliest attack on Latinos in modern American history.
>
> Crusius was arrested and charged with capital murder in connection with the shooting. He posted a manifesto with white nationalist and anti-immigrant themes, on the imageboard 8chan shortly before the attack. The manifesto cites the Christchurch mosque shootings earlier that year, and the far-right conspiracy theory known as the Great Replacement, as inspiration for the attack. On February 8, 2023, following an announcement that the Department of Justice would not seek the death penalty, Crusius pleaded guilty to 90 federal murder and hate crime charges. On July 7, 2023, Crusius was sentenced to 90 consecutive life sentences, but he is currently pending trial for state charges that would still potentially result in the death penalty under Texas state jurisdiction if found guilty.

Crusius, far from considering his act a criminal one needing to be concealed, made public announcements of his intentions and justifications for his acts and attitudes and even allowed himself to be arrested. Crusius's moves were those of a martyr, ready to face the consequences of his act. Crusius was, in fact, a one-man lynching agent who established his identity by this act of violence, identity as not just a White man but as concerned and politically involved one who was willing to take risky steps to meet its demands. Indeed, the mobs that lynched Black men in the earlier history of the US were doing just that: acting violently to establish their identities as White men, differentiated from Negroes and endowed with inalienable rights and privileges.

Anecdote IX – Reckless Identity: Love

While reckless love is common enough, one that was played out in public is the episode involving King Edward VIII of the UK. He succeeded to the throne on the death of his father, George V, and even from the beginning of his reign he created controversies – for example, speaking in defense of destitute Welsh miners, to the chagrin of the English government. However, it was his love affair with the American Wallis Simpson that indicates reckless love. She was a divorcee, and as such, according to English expectations for their queen, ineligible to marry the King of England. King Edward tried various strategies to marry her nevertheless, but the English government was adamant in its refusal to approve the marriage. King Edward had a number of options at his disposal in handling this conundrum:

- He could have abandoned his quest to marry Wallis Simpson.
- He could have continued his relationship with her and continued to love her without having to marry her.
- He could have accepted a "morganatic" marriage, in which Simpson could be his spouse without being queen.

He rejected them all and insisted that Simpson should be permitted to become a full-fledged queen of the UK, but since that was not forthcoming, he abdicated his throne with a speech (1936) that ended with the following words:

> But you must believe me when I tell you that I have found it impossible to carry the heavy burden of responsibility and to discharge my duties as King as I would wish to do without the help and support of the woman I love.

King Edward abandoned his throne, which entailed not only responsibilities but also enormous privileges, after examining all the consequences of his act to celebrate his attitude of love and regard for a woman to meet the purpose of loyalty and devotion. And he and Wallis Simpson did not really have a happy life. He was often forced to essentially beg the government of the UK for an increase in his official stipend. In the end, he also became an ally of Hitler in the German war against Great Britain on Hitler's promise to restore him to the throne (King, 1936).

RATIOS IN THE GRAMMAR

In practice, then, the grammar of identities is used by an individual to become an agent of his or her own acts and uses one or many agencies – visual, verbal, and gestural – to indicate one purpose or another and to present a selected attitude. The use of the grammar in everyday life is governed by what Burke called "ratios," drawn from the dramatistic grammar. Here is his examination of this issue:

> Insofar as men's actions are to be interpreted in terms of the circumstances in which they are acting, their behavior would fall under the heading of a "scene-act ratio." But insofar as their acts reveal their different characters, their behavior would fall under the heading of an "agent-act ratio." For instance, in a time of great crisis, such a shipwreck, the conduct of all persons involved in that crisis could be expected to manifest in some way the motivating influence of the crisis. Yet, within such a "scene-act ratio," there would be a range of "agent-act ratios," insofar as one man was "proved" to be cowardly, another bold, another resourceful, and so on. (Burke, 1978, pp. 332–333)

These ratios are in operation not only in times of crisis but in ordinary everyday life as well. *Every act an agent constructs and performs typically conforms to the maintenance of these ratios.* Typically, agents will seek to present and process their respective identities by using the grammar and observing the ratios among them. Failure to do so will result at a minimum in the purposes of the act being thwarted, and at a maximum with the agent being labeled with unsavory adjectives or even as a criminal.

In conducting an act, agents will find themselves in a particular scene, and in that scene, the act will typically conform to a scene–act ratio. For example, if the agent wants to address an erotic message to another, this is done, not in the midst of a funeral ceremony or a gathering of professional colleagues or in a crowded subway train, but in a more congenial scene. If in fact an agent violates these scenic constraints, the agent may be said to be violating the demands of the scene-act ratio, and the enterprise may even fail, with the agent's identity being sullied and the label of an eccentric or uncouth or a fool applied. If in a scene such as a funeral, the agent will produce acts that will maintain the ratio of act of sorrow to the scene.

In admonishing one's child, a parent will maintain the agent–act ratio and punish the child, not by whipping or cutting with a sword but by using words, or possibly a gentle admonition. This will also maintain the act–purpose ratio, since the parent wants to both instruct and change the child. And such acts also represent the act–agent agency ratio, since parents will typically use admonishments and perhaps a cane, but not swords, guns, or poison! Here one can see the operation of the act–purpose ratio. Indeed, if these ratios are systematically violated, the agent's identity will probably be defined as criminal or insane. The violation of these ratios in everyday life will play an important role in the definition of the identity of agents, and no doubt will influence the performance and processing of their identity in all the acts that they are seeking to process.

An individual as a candidate for a job while facing an interview in an organization must produce acts that are submissive as opposed to being arrogant, forthcoming as opposed to being secretive and reticent, and decorous as opposed to being uncouth. In doing this, the agent will be maintaining the act-scene-agency ratio. In presenting and processing an identity, agents typically put these ratios into practice at the risk of being a deviant in one way or another. I will present examples of scene and acts and attitude that violate the relevant ratios, with disastrous consequences.

In many societies, men are raised to believe that they have certain rights and privileges in their relations with women. Women must present subordinated identities using one agency or another in their relations with men and be careful about challenging men's authority and rejecting their demands. If in fact a woman does this, she will be subjected to one form of punishment or another. The standard agency of such punishments is beating – indeed, wife-beating is an almost universal agency with which men assert their dominance and their rights. However, sometimes male agents have been known to resort to more telling agencies. Consider a rather tragic event that occurred in New York City some years ago. A fire in a nightclub killed 87 people, and *The New York Times* reported it as follows:

> Eighty-seven people, crammed into an illegal Bronx social club, were asphyxiated or burned to death within minutes in a flash fire early yesterday morning. The police later arrested a man who they said had set the blaze with gasoline after a quarrel there. (Blumenthal, 1990)

And *Wikipedia* gives a telling description of the events preceding the fire (Happy Land fire, Wikipedia, https://en.wikipedia.org/wiki/Happy_Land_fire):

> The evening of the fire, Gonzalez had argued with his former girlfriend, Feliciano, who was a coat check worker at the club, urging her to quit. She said she had had enough of him and did not want anything to do with him anymore. He was ejected by the bouncer around 3:00 a.m. He was heard to scream drunken threats to "shut this place down."

One may ask: What happened to Gonzalez? To begin with, his identity as lover, boyfriend, and companion was rejected and refuted by Lydia Feliciano. Second, he was ejected forcibly by the bouncer, thereby challenging his identity as a man who can take care of himself. Finally, this was done in front of various others, and he was thereby humiliated. Gonzalez's response to these challenges to his identity, aided by alcohol, was an attempt to kill his girlfriend and perhaps the bouncer by an ill-calculated move that killed many but not, ironically, his girlfriend or the bouncer. We have a case where various emotions – jealousy, humiliation, and sorrow – as well as a challenge to the agent's authority, were generated, providing him with a rhetoric with which he was able to activate his identity as a masculinist who takes no shit from a mere woman. The setting of the fire became the agency with which he was seeking to manifest his attitude in the scene in which his identity was challenged and repudiated. All was to no avail, since his girlfriend survived but others got killed. It was clearly a case of inappropriate choice of both agency and scene.

THE GRAMMAR IN THE RHETORIC

In ongoing human relations, agents will seek to persuade the other to accept a point of view or undertake one line of action rather than another. Arguably, every address one makes to another is an attempt to persuade or convince the other to one extent or another. This contingency raises the question of how to do this efficiently with some reasonable chance of success. This issue brings into focus the issue of the uses of rhetoricity in human interactions, and Burke has an answer. He defined the basic function of rhetoric as follows:

> ... the use of words by human agents to form attitudes or to induce actions in other human agents. . . . it is rooted in an essential function of language itself, a function that is wholly realistic, and is continually born anew: the use of language as a symbolic means of inducing cooperation in beings that by nature respond to symbols.

Burke went on to add,

> To consider language as a means of information or knowledge is to consider it epistemologically, semantically, in terms of "science." To consider it as a mode of action is to consider it in terms of "poetry." For a poem is an act, the symbolic act of the poet who made it – an act of such a nature that surviving as a structure or object, it enables us as readers to re-enact it. (1969b, p. 43)

The question that arises, then, is how does one do this? Or rather, how does one fashion the words *efficiently* so that they "form attitudes and induce cooperation in other human agents"? One answer that Burke himself provided is that one uses one's own identity and that of the other or others to construct an efficient rhetorical move by either claiming or showing that there is a "consubtantiality" between one's own identity that of the other – to one degree or other. Here is Burke: "You persuade a man only insofar as you can talk his language by speech, gesture, tonality, order, image, identifying your ways with his" (1969b, p. 55).

The way to achieve this is to construct one's acts so that they are at least not dissimilar to the one that is being addressed and to use agencies that are recognizable by the other and present attitudes and purposes that are congruent, to various extents, to those of the other. In other words, stick to the grammar of motives and its manifestation in the constitution of identities to successfully persuade the other.

Anecdote X – Race and Identity: Hitler Speaks

Hitler delivered this speech in a public scene and with a series of acts that defined his identity as both a German patriot and the savior of the German people by claiming a distinction between himself, the German people as such – the real Germanic people – and the alien Jews, as documented by the Yad Vashem (n.d.).

> For hundreds of years Germany was good enough to receive these elements, although they possessed nothing except infectious political and physical diseases. What they possess today, they have by a very large extent gained at the cost of the less astute German nation by the most reprehensible manipulations.
>
> Today we are merely paying this people [back] what it deserves. … Above all, German culture … is German and not Jewish, and therefore its management and care will be entrusted to members of our own nation … Europe cannot settle down until the Jewish question is cleared up … we must once and for all get rid of the opinion that the Jewish race was only created by God for the purpose of being in a certain percentage a parasite living on the body and the productive work of other nations. … Today I will once more be a prophet: If the international Jewish financiers in and outside Europe should succeed in plunging the nations once more into a world war, then the result will not be the Bolshevization of the earth, and thus the victory of Jewry, but the annihilation of the Jewish race in Europe.

His fundamental strategy was to set up a series of contrasts as his agency: the German people and the alien Jews – the German people, some of whom were "less astute" and allowed these aliens, who were possessed of "infectious political and physical diseases" and who used "reprehensible manipulations" to influence "German culture." Every agency Hitler chose to use displayed attitudes: contempt and hatred for these aliens and reverence for the German culture. His purpose was to project himself as the savior of the German people as well to build his political career. Indeed, scapegoating the other is almost a universal agency with which agents define their respective identities and build a political career. Hitler used this grammar of identification throughout his career as a politician with great success and became a hero to many, not only in Germany but in other parts of the world as well.[4]

CONCLUSION

Insofar as identity is not merely a state of being but essentially a way of doing, agents typically must choose, or find themselves, in varying situations in which they must process and present an identity. In other words, agents typically come to a crossroads or a junction and must take one road and often, in retrospective reflection, may wonder whether they did take chose the fruitful and propitious one. Robert Frost expressed this in his wonderful poem, "The Road Not Taken," and I have tried to put this in a more prosaic form, with some anecdotal examples. In these anecdotes, individuals are shown to be putting into effect what Kenneth Burke called the "grammar of motives." They become, to one extent or another, agents of their own acts which they perform in accordance with defined scenes and situations in which they find themselves and display various attitudes and emotions in order to fulfill various purposes by choosing to use various agencies or instrumentations.

NOTES

1. See V. J. McGill and W. T. Parry (1948) for an excellent examination of this issue and its history in philosophical studies. Kenneth Burke and James Zappen (2006) touched on this issue in an article entitled "On Persuasion, Identification, and Dialectical Symmetry."
2. For an application of Burke's grammar to the process of marketing, see Manlow and Ferree (2021).
3. On the concept of "representative anecdote" and its uses, see Kenneth Burke (1969a, p. 59). He wrote, "Dramatism suggests a procedure to be followed in the development of a given calculus, or terminology. It involves the search for a 'representative anecdote', to be used as a form in conformity with which the vocabulary is constructed." In other words, one can find that a particular assembly of words can be taken as representing other similar phenomena. In simpler terms, a representative anecdote is comparable to what is known as a "case study" in other disciplines, where one instance of a phenomenon is taken to illustrate or define a larger phenomenon (see Cash, 2015). For its place in the dramatist perspective, see the essay by Bryan Crable (2000) for an interesting analysis of Burke's work on this topic. I have deliberately selected mundane events, except in a couple of instances, as illustrative cases to indicate that the use of the grammar of identity is essentially commonplace.
4. Burke wrote an insightful analysis on Hitler's rhetorical strategies in his work "The Rhetoric of Hitler's Battle" (1941/1971). However, this was written before he worked on the grammar of motives and did not use it explicitly.

REFERENCES

Askinasi, R., & Teh, C. (2022, December 25). 10 South Korean tourists were stranded in a blizzard near Buffalo. They spent 2 nights in a stranger's home, cooking and watching football. *Yahoo! Sport*. https://uk.sports.yahoo.com/news/10-south-korean-tourists-were-030651951.html

Bilefsky, D. (2017, May 24). They Went to Manchester Arena as homeless men. They left as heroes. *New York Times*. https://www.nytimes.com/2017/05/24/world/europe/homeless-hero-manchester.html

Blumenthal, R. (1990, March 26). Fire in the Bronx; 87 die in Blaze at illegal club; police arrest ejected patron; Worst New York Fire since 1911. *New York Times*. https://www.nytimes.com/1990/03/26/nyregion/fire-bronx-87-die-blaze-illegal-club-police-arrest-ejected-patron-worst-new-york.html.

Burke, K. (1941/1971). *The rhetoric of Hitler's 'Battle'. The philosophy of literary form*. University of California Press.

Burke, K. (1945/1969a). *A grammar of motives*. University of California Press.

Burke, K. (1968). Dramatism. In D. Sills (Ed.), *The international encyclopedia of the social sciences* (pp. 445–452). Macmillan.

Burke, K. (1969b). *A rhetoric of motives*. University of California Press.

Burke, K. (1978). Questions and answers about the pentad. *College Composition & Communication*, *29*(4), 330–335. http://openlab.citytech.cuny.edu/firstyearwriting/files/2013/11/FYW.Burke_.Rhetoric.Composition.pdf

Burke, K., & Zappen, J. (2006). On persuasion, identification, and dialectical symmetry. *Philosophy and Rhetoric*, *39*(4), 332–338.

Cash, J. (2015). The case study as representative anecdote. In *Case studies and the dissemination of knowledge* (pp. 31–48). Routledge.

Crable, B. (2000). Burke's perspective on perspectives: Grounding dramatism in the representative anecdote. *Quarterly Journal of Speech*, *86*(3), 318–333.

Denver Catholic staff. (2015, February 9). *Each garment a sign, a statement, a reminder*. Denver Catholic. https://denvercatholic.org/garment-sign-statement-reminder/

Foote, N. (1951). Identification as the basis for a theory of motivation. *American Sociological Review*, *16*(1), 14–21.

King, E. V. I. I. I. (1936). Abdication address. American rhetoric online speech bank. https://www.americanrhetoric.com/speeches/kingedwardVIIIabdication.htm

Los Angeles Country Club. (n.d.). Guest information. https://www.thelacc.org/guest-info

Manlow, V., & Ferree, C. (2021). Rhetorical processes in the sales relationship in luxury retail. In N. K. Denzin, J. Salvo, & S.-L. S. Chen (Eds.), *Radical interactionism and critiques of contemporary culture. Studies in symbolic interaction* (Vol. 52, pp. 221–235). Emerald Publishing Limited.

McGill, V. J., & Parry, W. T. (1948). The unity of opposites: A dialectical principle. *Science & Society*, *12*(4), 416–444.

Mead, G. H.. (1934). The self and the organism. In C. W. Morris (Eds.), *Mind, self, and society from the standpoint of a social behaviorist* (pp. 135–144). University of Chicago.

Nixon Tapes transcript: Cancer on the presidency. (1973, March 21). totse.com. https://newtotse.com/oldtotse/en/politics/nixon/165572.html

Perinbanayagam, R. (2023). *Dialogues, dramas, and emotions: Essays in interactionist sociology*. Lexington Books.

Seckman, M., & Couch, C. (1989). Jocularity, Sarcasm, and relationships: An empirical study. *Journal of Contemporary Ethnography*, *18*(3), 327–344. https://doi.org/10.1177/089124189018003004

Stone, G. (1970). Appearance and the self. In A. M. Rose (Ed.), *Human behavior and social processes: An interactionist approach* (pp. 86–118). Houghton Mifflin.

United States Conference of Catholic Bishops. (n.d.). Act of Contrition. https://www.usccb.org/prayers/act-contrition

Wikipedia. (n.d.a) 2019 El Paso Shooting. https://en.wikipedia.org/wiki/2019_El_Paso_shooting#Aftermath

Wikipedia. (n.d.b) Happy Land fire. https://en.wikipedia.org/wiki/Happy_Land_fire

Wikipedia. (n.d.c) *Puja* (Hinduism). https://en.wikipedia.org/wiki/Puja_(Hinduism)#cite_note-ssde-3

Wikipedia. (n.d.d). Murder of George Floyd. https://en.wikipedia.org/wiki/Murder_of_George_Floyd#cite_note-14

Yad Vashem. (n.d.). *Extract from the speech by Adolf Hitler, January 30, 1939. Yad Vashem*. The World Holocaust Remembrance Center. https://www.yadvashem.org/docs/extract-from-hitler-speech.html

THE PROMISE OF CRITICAL INTERACTIONISM

Douglas P. Schrock

Florida State University, USA

ABSTRACT

In this paper, the author advocates recognizing, developing, and promoting "critical interactionism" as a legitimate and pragmatically useful scholarly project. The author argues that critical interactionism includes different interactionist traditions, critical approaches, methodological styles, and sensitizing concepts – as long as they tell us something about how power and inequality operate. I review two fundamental elements of this project that constitute its past and likely future: (1) theoretical interventions that excavate critical insights, diversify founders, integrate critical theories, and promote interactionism's usefulness for critical inquiry and (2) empirically grounded conceptual interventions that shed light on generic processes of inequality reproduction. Although the larger discipline of sociology continues to marginalize interactionism yet selectively adopt its principles, critical interactionism has the potential to break through what David Maines called the fault line of consciousness. The promise of critical interactionism is that it can simultaneously make interactionism more relevant to our discipline and make our discipline more relevant to the social world.

Keywords: Critical interactionism; theory; power; inequality; the fault line of consciousness

In the introduction to *Critical and Cultural Interactionism*, Michael Hviid Jacobsen (2020, p. 1) noted being surprised by how many interactionists invoked "critical interactionism" in passing without clarifying what they meant. Count me among the guilty. Over the past 20 years, I have at times used the phrase "critical interactionism" to describe my approach to empirical and conceptual work – whether in my published scholarship or communication with colleagues, students, or administrators. Occasionally, I offer a simple definition of what critical interactionism means to me:

Essential Issues in Symbolic Interaction
Studies in Symbolic Interaction, Volume 59, 145–164

Published under exclusive licence by Emerald Publishing Limited
ISSN: 0163-2396/doi:10.1108/S0163-239620240000059008

I'm interested in how interactionism can help us understand how inequality is reproduced and challenged.

Although I've worried others might think "critical interactionism" implies engagement with the Frankfurt School's "Critical Theory," I join others in defining it more broadly (see, e.g., Jacobsen, 2019). I include interactionist work that engages with or is informed by feminism, humanism, intersectionality, critical race theory, queer theory, critical theory, etc. In addition, scholarship that reveals how interactionist concepts can be used to shed light on social processes that constitute or justify/promote inequality falls within critical interactionism, whether or not it explicitly engages with the aforementioned theories. I see the term "interactionist" here as inclusive of what is sometimes considered distinct traditions such as symbolic interactionism, dramaturgy, and ethnomethodology (see also, e.g. vom Lehn et al., 2021). Rather than viewing critical interactionism as a perspective with clearly defined parameters – as Lonnie Athens (2013) has done with "radical interactionism" – I view critical interactionism as a broader scholarly project that includes Athens and other approaches. I also see the value of highlighting work that sheds light on inequality processes even if the authors did not explicitly frame their work as interactionism or critical interactionism.

Critical interactionism is, in some ways, analogous to "critical criminology." In *The Handbook of Critical Criminology*, DeKeseredy and Dragiewicz (2018) explain that critical criminology refers broadly to work that takes into account the state, capitalism, racism, and/or sexism to analyze and make sense of crime and punishment. Although critical interactionism is similarly inclusive, instead of focusing on one general topic, it can be incorporated into virtually any substantive topic or research area (e.g. crime, organizations, sexuality and social movements). DeKeseredy and Dragiewicz furthermore describe critical criminology as a self-conscious *project* or a movement that developed in the 1970s, faced backlash from some criminologists and administrators, yet has become the largest section of the American Society of Criminology and has expanded internationally.[1] Critical interactionism, in contrast, doesn't seem to be widely recognized as a program and its practitioners may not even identify or be identified as critical interactionists. Critical interactionists or those doing such work may have experienced some backlash and marginalization, but they've only had limited success in creating a community, collective identity, or organizational presence.[2,3]

In this paper, I address how we might think about critical interactionism as a program of scholarship with an often-unnamed history and how naming the approach may aid in revitalizing interactionism and, more generally, benefit sociology and related disciplines. This paper is also aspirational in that I recognize our collective shortcomings in developing critical interactionism, yet I believe limitations are always opportunities. I have spent about 25 years studying, teaching, and writing about some key elements of what I now think of as critical interactionism, and I admit to overemphasizing my interests here. I offer this paper as a sketch of critical interactionism, showing how it has long existed in practice and has explored many theoretical and research paths. I also argue that if we develop critical interactionism into a self-conscious project, we might revitalize interactionism and break through what David Maines (2003) called the "fault line of consciousness."

My discipline, sociology, still adopts interactionist principles or concepts yet tends to avoid acknowledging or engaging with interactionism (see Fine, 1993). Maines (2003) argued that there seems to be a fault line or boundary between much of sociology and interactionism, which keeps most sociologists from being conscious of how their work may resonate with interactionism. This "fault line of consciousness," as Maines pointed out, marginalizes interactionism as irrelevant to most sociology and is in large part due to a disciplinary myth that stigmatizes interactionism as unable to address power and inequality. Interactionists' strong arguments to the contrary over the past half century – as addressed below – have largely been ignored by the larger discipline. I suggest that having a clear label that asserts that interactionism can and does address such matters – critical interactionism – can help us bridge the fault line. Critical interactionism as a scholarly program can be a resource for bringing interactionism explicitly into various subfields' critical conversations. Similarly, critical interactionism can also provide those whose work in some ways reflects but typically does not acknowledge interactionism an opportunity to see its value and explore its usefulness.

SKETCHING CRITICAL INTERACTIONISM

Critical interactionism is multifaceted, and its advocates – regardless of whether they adopt the term – have contributed to the perspective in many ways. In this section, I provide a high-level sketch of critical interactionism and a review of some relevant scholarship. I'll first address various theoretical interventions, which range from highlighting oft-forgotten insights from "founders," diversifying who should be considered founders, integrating interactionism and critical theories, defending interactionism against accusations of being astructural, and applying or expanding sensitizing concepts to address inequality processes. I then discuss methodological approaches and research findings that represent a sample of empirically grounded conceptual processes that critical interactionism has produced and can build upon.

Theoretical Interventions

An essential type of theoretical work that has developed critical interactionism focuses on what some of the "founders" of interactionism can teach us about inequalities and power. For example, Neeley and Deegan (2005) unearthed G.H. Mead's (1918) critique of the punitive "justice" system, including its pathologizing of the criminal and its capitalist ideology. Lonnie Athens (2007, 2009) published a series of papers examining how Mead, Blumer, and Park all allow for the examination of power. He also argued that replacing Mead's foundational notion of "sociality" with Park's notion of "domination" essentially radicalizes interactionism and reorients it to examine hierarchy and oppression. Focusing on race, Lyman (1984) unpacked how Blumer's theorizing of race as constructed, hierarchical, and embedded in large-scale processes like industrialization departed from Park's focus on assimilation. Similarly, Maines and Morrione (1991) resurrected Blumer's critical analysis of industrialization, showing how interactionism can help us understand historical processes, capitalism, and institutional actors and networks. West and Zimmerman's (1987) classic essay on Garfinkel's (1967) analysis of gender as an accomplishment and the promotion of the influential "doing gender" perspective in the sociology of gender is a notable example from ethnomethodology. And there have been numerous explorations of how Erving Goffman's analyses provide insights surrounding the operation of power (see, e.g. Jaworski, 2023).

Theorists have also worked to expand who should be considered vital figures of interactionism and/or the pragmatist tradition to include historically marginalized yet notably critical scholars. Mary Jo Deegan exemplifies this approach and has pointed to the often-forgotten women pragmatists of the late 1800s and early 1900s, including Katharine Bement Davis (Deegan, 2003), Caroline Bartlet Crane (Rynbrandt & Deegan, 2002), Dorothy Swaine Thomas (Deegan, 1994), and Jane Addams (Deegan, 2010). Deegan (2002, pp. 16, 18) examines the importance of Chicago's Hull House, where these women developed a "feminist pragmatism" focused more on women and the disenfranchised, emotions, critique, and "direct intervention."

In addition, scholars have explored how W.E.B. Du Bois' work (e.g. 1903, 1920) resonated with pragmatist philosophy, how he studied with William James, and how he was influenced by Pierce, Dewey, and Adams (Muller, 1992; Taylor, 2004). Although he did not claim the label 'pragmatist' in his writings, Natalia Ruiz-Junco and Salvador Vidal-Ortiz (2023) argue for recognizing Du Bois' contributions – especially his use of autoethnography and his conceptualization of double consciousness – as interactionist.[4] Du Bois' critical insight about race as a social construction became central to the sociology of race and critical race theory (Morris, 2015) and resonates with how interactionists conceptualize and study racial identities (e.g., Schrock et al., 2022).

Another intervention explores how interactionist theorizing can be integrated with other critical theories. T.R. Young (see, e.g. Young, 1990; Young & Massey, 1978) developed what he termed "critical dramaturgy," much of which involved integrating Goffman's conceptualization of impression management with critical theorizing on capitalism. Norman Denzin explored how interactionism could become more critical by integrating feminism, postmodernism, and critical theories of race (e.g. Denzin, 1989, 1992, 2002). Anne Rawls (2000) brought Goffman, Marx, Mead, DuBois, Sacks, and Garfinkel into conversation with one another to theorize the interaction order as racialized. Others have explored how dramaturgy, or symbolic interactionism may be integrated or at least in conversation with the Frankfort School (Joas, 1992; Langman, 2019; Shalin, 1992; Welsh, 1984).[5] Sherryl Kleinman and colleagues (Kleinman, 2007; Kleinman & Cabaniss, 2019) have developed feminist interactionism by showing how interactionist notions of language, emotions, and agency can be incorporated into understanding patriarchy. And Celia Kitzinger (2000) has advanced feminist conversational analysis (CA), arguing that some feminists have unfortunately written off CA, and some CA practitioners have unfortunately written off feminist and critical approaches.

Since at least the 1970s, interactionism has been accused of being unable to address social structure (see, e.g. Reynolds & Janice, 1973) – and this myth has been reproduced in textbooks for years (Dennis & Martin, 2005). Reacting against this charge, interactionists have long theorized how structure can be analyzed. Maines (1977, p. 253) notably showed how interactionists address social organization and social structure through the negotiated order perspective, which not only draws attention to how people interact within a given social context but also helps us understand how social contexts are "intersecting" and embedded in "successively larger overreaching contexts" (see also Fine, 1984; Strauss, 1978). As Katovich (2023) recently pointed out, Maines left us many insights into how to analyze *structurally situated action* and ground such insights in pragmatist theory.

Others have similarly shown how interactionism can address social networks and meanings (Fine & Kleinman, 1983), "historical, political, biographical, and sociocultural contexts" (Low & Thomson, 2021, p. 108), and how interaction order rules, identity stakes, and nets of accountability across settings sustain capitalism (Schwalbe, 2016, 2019b). Interactionists have also developed the concept of "mesostructure" (e.g., Maines, 1982), which can be thought of as a "hinge" that connects individuals and social structures (Fine, 2021). These and other notable examples (see, e.g. Dennis & Martin, 2007; Hall, 2003; Katovich, 2003; McGinty, 2014; Strauss, 1993) belie the accusation that interactionism can't address social structure and avoids reification by emphasizing the social processes that constitute it.

Interactionists have also theorized power as constituted by what people do together, how such actions shape what happens elsewhere, and the consequences for hierarchal and unequal relations. For example, interactionists have long seen power as a "collective transaction" (Luckenbill, 1979, p. 98) and focused on interpersonal processes – such as fostering loyalty, targeting vulnerability, and discrediting difference – through which some people exercise control over others (Prus, 1999; see also Hall, 1985). Peter Hall (1997, p. 398) theorizes an interactionist approach to "meta-power," which refers to the "creation and control of distal situations." Drawing on Mead and Blumer, Schwalbe and Mischke (2021) define power as "the exercise of capacities to modify the external world, or some part of it, to satisfy needs and desires." They argue power is accomplished through securing cooperation, which can involve controlling situational definitions and frames, emotions and self-presentation, invoking cultural and interactional norms, and using nets of accountability or relationships with those outside the social situation who can hold those within it accountable. And Watson and Goulet (1998, p. 110) explain that "For ethnomethodologists, power is something achieved through work done by participants; it is work that ethnomethodologists undertake to explicate." These approaches share the view that power isn't an abstract concept but involves people doing things together, which may have traceable consequences for what others do together somewhere else at a later time.

Finally, theorists have developed critical interactionism by engaging in critical reviews of research literature so as to distill lessons surrounding inequality. Michael Schwalbe and coauthors' (2000) interactionist analysis of published qualitative research, for example, distilled four generic processes of inequality reproduction: othering, subordinate adaptation, boundary maintenance, and emotion management. Elsewhere, I have worked with Schwalbe (Schrock & Schwalbe, 2009) to review and reframe the literature on "masculinity" in critical interactionist terms, which involved critiquing the dominant multiple masculinities approach and advocating for a manhood acts perspective. I have also worked with colleagues to distill interactionist (and other) lessons about heteronormativity by critically reviewing the history of sexuality scholarship (Schrock et al., 2015). Key to such work involves interrogating critical scholarship that resonates with but is not framed as interactionist, as well as explicitly interactionist work that was not framed as critical inquiry, and synthesizing and generating insights that are recast within a critical interactionist framework.

Empirically-Grounded Conceptual Interventions

In addition to the aforementioned theoretical pursuits, a key part of the critical interactionist project involves engaging in empirically grounded analyses of how inequality is reproduced or challenged. Such work, of course, should be grounded in interactionist assumptions and use or develop interactionist concepts that fit the empirical patterns being examined. As such, traditional methods of data collection, such as fieldwork, interviewing, collecting documents or cultural products, audio/video recordings, etc., are clearly important (e.g. Lareau, 2021; Lofland & Lofland, 1984; Weiss, 1994). Similarly, critical interactionists can employ standard techniques of qualitative analysis, including grounded theory (Charmaz, 2006), abductive analysis (Tavory & Timmermans, 2014), and other "tricks of the trade" (Becker, 1998). Such methods are, of course, standard for qualitative research and do not necessarily lead to developing insights about power and inequality or framing findings in interactionist terms.

Although it is possible that standard analysis techniques will develop into critical analyses, it depends not only on what exists in the empirical world but also on our interpretations (see, e.g. Denzin, 1989, 2019). The questions the analyst brings to bear on the empirical patterns during all stages of analysis are key to developing critical interpretations. Sheryl Kleinman's (2007) *Feminist Fieldwork Analysis* is a useful guide for bringing critical questions about how we talk, feel, and interact may reproduce inequalities surrounding gender, race, sexuality, authority, etc. Bringing critical questions to the data is key, but as Kathy Charmaz (2017) suggests, integrating constructivist grounded theory techniques with critical inquiry enables us to stay grounded in the empirical world. Adele Clarke's (2003, 2019) situational analysis additionally encourages us to develop questions surrounding the connection between personal, organizational, cultural, and political contexts. Broadly, critical interactionists build on Blumer's methodology (1969) by examining how meaning reflects or reinforces power and inequality (see, e.g. Schwalbe, 2019a). If the data aren't there, we can't see it, of course – but we have to ask the right questions in order to see how power and inequality operate in the real world.

Critical interactionism often employs, develops, or integrates interactionist concepts through empirical analyses. One key concept is language, which interactionists view as enabling the construction of meaning about situations, selves, organizations, ideologies, etc., in ways that often reflect and reinforce inequalities. Studying men who exert power over women, for example, can reveal how they use culturally supported accounts (Anderson & Umberson, 2001; Scully & Marolla, 1984) and narratives (Schrock et al., 2018) to justify their violence or use linguistic tactics to gaslight and control victims (Sweet, 2019). In addition, many have examined how gendered power operates via conversational control and interruptions (e.g. Zimmerman & West, 1975) and how common gendered labels such as "bitch" derogate women (Kleinman et al., 2009) or "you guys" makes them invisible (Kleinman, 2002).

Critical interactionism also employs and develops insights surrounding identity work or the construction of identity. Grounded in Goffman's (1959) notion of self-presentation, identity work refers broadly to individual and collective processes through which people construct or project virtual selves (e.g. Schwalbe & Mason-Schrock, 1996). Research has examined how members of subordinated groups such as homeless men (Snow & Anderson, 1987) and the racially marginalized (Browne et al., 2021) salvage worthiness via identity work. Identity work can also involve signifying categories of personhood that systems of categorical inequality are based upon; for example, people may use embodied practices, narratives, and emotions to signify gender identity (Schrock et al., 2005; Schrock & Reid, 2006; Vaccaro et al., 2011) or the lack thereof (Barbee & Schrock, 2019). Such analyses can also focus on intersectional identity work, as exemplified by research on Black collegiate men (Wilkins, 2012), gay Christians (McQueeney, 2009), and southern rock musicians (Eastman & Schrock, 2008). And, of course, much research addresses how people construct others to justify or reinforce inequalities, such as how some women rugby players degrade queer women (Ezzell, 2009), some gay men reinforce community hierarchies by putting down "unattractive" community members (Green, 2011), or how some voters degrade women political candidates as "bitches" (Erichsen et al., 2020).

Interactionists have engaged in emotions research in a variety of ways that reveal lessons about reproducing inequalities. Building on Hochschild's (1983) groundbreaking development of the concept of emotional labor when studying women flight attendants, much work has focused on how women manage emotions as part of their subordination at work (Kang, 2003) or home (Elliott & Umberson, 2008). Candace Clark (1990) revealed how emotional micropolitics is central to reproducing hierarchies of status and power (see also Cahill & Eggleston (1994) on wheelchair users' interactions with walking people). Drawing on Cahill's (1999) notion of emotional capital, Froyum (2010) examines how Black girls are socialized to develop a form of emotional deference to authority that hinders racial pride and prepares them for a life of gendered and racialized subordination. People within organizations have also been found to construct emotion norms that reproduce heteronormativity in middle school (Simon et al., 1992) or racial hierarchies in the corporate world (Wingfield, 2010). Studies of emotional discourse have also shown how leaders can use a group's dominant emotional discourse to manage dissent (Holden & Schrock, 2007) or how some women use the *language* of emotion work to preserve their self-worth and justify having engaged in unwanted sex with men (Kitzinger & Frith, 1999). Interactionists' diversity of insights and approaches to emotions and inequalities can be usefully applied to research about virtually any social context and developed in infinite ways. And, of course, focusing on emotion, identity, and language just scratches the surface of the kinds of social processes that critical interactionists study.

TRANSCENDING THE FAULT LINE

Thirty years ago, Gary Alan Fine (1993) argued that as an academic discipline, mainstream sociology paradoxically incorporated many interactionist concepts yet simultaneously seemed less likely to explicitly frame such work as interactionist. If the goal, he suggested, is to "develop a pragmatic approach to social life," interactionism has "triumphed gloriously" (Fine, 1993, p. 81). About a decade later, David Maines (2001, p. 241) documented a "fairly profound drift toward pragmatism/interactionism" among sociologists who nonetheless seemed oblivious to using interactionist concepts principles. This is problematic not only because they avoid crediting interactionists or they falsely claim to have "discovered" the importance of interactionist concepts like meaning or interaction, but because these "unaware interactionists," as Maines called them, would produce better analyses if they more fully and consistently grounded themselves in interactionism. In other words, sociology as a discipline would be better served if it came to grips with its too-often implicit or hidden interactionism.

I have witnessed this trend in the past 25 years in several subfields that I've explored. Although early sexuality scholarship was grounded in or connected to interactionism, as the field developed, scholars often emphasized explicitly critical approaches like queer or feminist theory and left their interactionist proclivities in the closet (Schrock et al., 2015). Although the "doing gender" approach (West & Zimmerman, 1987) rose to dominate gender scholarship, scholars framing findings as "doing gender" haven't typically acknowledged or engaged with ethnomethodology. Sociologists of race have increasingly examined racial discourse, emotions, and identity (see, e.g. Bonilla-Silva, 2003, 2019), yet rarely overtly or substantially ground their work in interactionism. Many social movement scholars have incorporated interactionist concepts, including identity, framing, emotion, and narrative (see, e.g. Jasper, 2011; Polletta & Jasper, 2001; Taylor & Bernstein, 2019), yet they also typically avoid engaging with interactionism per se. Influential scholars in other subfields similarly extol the importance of studying social interaction or meaning without seeming to realize that interactionists might have something useful to say about these processes (see, e.g. Roscigno (2007) on organizations or Eliasoph & Lichterman (2003) on culture). I respect and often use such work in my research and teaching, but I am often perplexed by the lack of engagement with interactionism.

Within this discursive context – where sociological subfields and leading scholars ignore or downplay how their work resonates with interactionism – the fault line is reproduced. Scholars seeking recognition in an academic community understandably try to place their work within existing conversations. But if interactionism does not explicitly exist in an area's universe of discourse, there are no clearly marked or well-worn entry points for inserting interactionism. This is not just an individual scholar's "choice" but a collective process. Most journal editors and reviewers presumably do not imagine it is useful or necessary to encourage authors to engage with interactionism even if authors' work resonates with interactionist principles or uses interactionist concepts (or perhaps they just don't know when they see it). I imagine the stereotype that interactionism is "narrow…in the sense of limited utility, of being rather deficient, and of being tangential to 'real' sociology" (Maines, 2003, p. 9) is still commonplace in many circles. Under such conditions, scholars may very well view emphasizing interactionism in their work as a liability.

Publishing work in respected general and specialty journals, of course, helps sociologists gain enough disciplinary or institutional respect to secure or maintain employment in research-oriented departments. We should also acknowledge that there is real pressure to claim one is saying something "new" and appear cutting edge, which can be quite difficult in a 130+ year discipline. Strategically forgetting (or never learning about) pragmatist principles and interactionist theory appear to be useful in this regard. Regardless, the "successful" sociologists publishing in prestigious places that don't seem to require people to explicitly engage interactionism, regardless of how interactionist their work seems to be, may also have little incentive or expertise to teach graduate students the virtues of interactionism. As departments respond to administrative pressure to hire scholars in well-funded research areas, even qualified applicants who identify with interactionism may choose to downplay it – especially if they are aware of the aforementioned stigma.

When I examined the American Sociological Association's job listings during the fall of 2023, none included "interactionist" or "interactionism" in the description. This is not necessarily surprising, as advertisements typically focus on substantive areas of research and teaching and sometimes mention methodological expertise and the ability to secure research funding. If one lands that job and the tenure clock starts ticking, even if one's sociological imagination was sparked by interactionism, they may sweep it under the rug if that is what the substantive area they were hired to teach or research in has already done. Of course, I only have anecdotal evidence of such a process. Regardless, it is easy to see the outlines of how biographical and organizational processes coalesce in ways that have the consequence – despite anyone's intentions – of reinforcing the fault line of consciousness and marginalization of interactionism.

There are exceptions, of course, most commonly in departments and journals emphasizing social psychology. As Maines pointed out (2001), interactionism often gets narrowly framed as social psychology or microsociology, which means that interactionism can – at least hypothetically – exist more explicitly in such programs and publishing outlets. When I was first hired as an assistant professor over 20 years ago, I was encouraged to create a graduate-level interactionist course that fit into our department's then-developing but now-defunct social psychology concentration. I know from personal experience that, on the one hand, social psychology often welcomes interactionism, and I myself have often felt at home in this community. On the other hand, framing social psychology as the right place for interactionism to exist in the discipline, regardless of intentions, reinforces the disciplinary myth that interactionism is of little use for the rest of sociology. Even when publishing outlets or research-centered departments are welcoming to interactionists under the guise of social psychology, it can nonetheless reinforce the fault line that typically excludes explicit interactionism from other sociological arenas.

Some may think I'm overstating things. *Symbolic Interaction* and *Studies in Symbolic Interaction* clearly support explicit interactionism. And, of course, there are still some interactionist promoters around who work at top departments, teach interactionist classes, and publish overtly interactionist articles in prestigious "non-interactionist" journals as well as books at well-respected academic presses. As grounded theorists might point out, however, the existence of negative cases or exceptions does not necessarily negate the larger pattern. Although the visibility of some interactionists publishing and working in prestigious departments could help us overcome the fault line, if the discipline tokenizes them as unique exceptions, then they may not be able to disrupt disciplinary discourse. Regardless, stigma can be rather sticky; a senior colleague once asked me, "Why do interactionists ghettoize themselves by publishing in qualitative journals?"

David Maines (2001) suggested that overcoming the fault line is not just good for interactionists but for the discipline as a whole, and he reflected on how this might happen. He said it would be helpful if sociologists accepted the fact that all social science is constructionist, that "unaware interactionists better frame their work in terms of the interactionism they in fact produce," and self-identified interactionists "look harder and more generously for the interactionist ideas in scholarship they ordinarily would regard as non-interactionist" (Maines, 2001, p. 278). He added that interactionists should dispose of the myth that we can't publish explicitly interactionist articles in top general and specialty journals.

All of these suggestions make sense to me, but under what conditions might the unaware and the identified interactionists collectively accomplish this? I argue that developing, articulating, and promoting critical interactionism as a scholarly project may be an effective intervention. Why? If the fault line of consciousness is largely based on misperceptions that interactionism is unable to address important sociological issues like power and inequality, we need a simple and clear symbolic frame that can both be a warrant and a resource to bring interactionism into scholarly conversations that are not typically or explicitly grounded in interactionism. To those who believe the myth that interactionism is inherently unable to contribute to understanding inequality, "critical interactionism" may seem like an oxymoron – and that's the point. "Critical interactionism" clearly asserts that one engages in critical inquiry via interactionism.

As Gary Fine and Iddo Tavory (2019, p. 464) argued in a recent paper about interactionism in the 21st century, it is important to "think about interactionism in new ways" to better theorize and analyze oppression and privilege. As a label for such a scholarly project, "critical interactionism" conveys to uninformed outsiders and unmoved insiders that we are indeed making sense of power and inequality in "new ways" – even if we draw on our long history of doing so. Interactionists have long crafted compelling arguments against accusations of being astructural or unable to deal with power, but they seem to have disappeared into the ether. Should we spend another 50 years trying to deflect the accusations? Should we spend the next few decades trying to figure out how we might best ask permission to bring interactionism into important critical conversations in our discipline? We need a symbolic onramp into those conversations, which ideally is also an offramp for "non-interactionists" to better understand and explore interactionism. Critical interactionism can be a bridge that transcends the fault line of consciousness.

I don't see critical interactionism as only a bridge or useful symbolic resource. Critical interactionism can be an interpretive wedge that enables us to contribute to and possibly transform scholarly conversations. The interactionist traditions in which we ground our work have assumptions and concepts surrounding how social worlds work. Such assumptions and concepts may, in some ways, align with and, in other ways, diverge from the assumptions or sensemaking practices of a particular community of inquiry. When we find some overlap between our particular interactionist perspective and the scholarly community's or subfield's discourse (regardless of whether it is acknowledged as interactionist), we can bring interactionism into the conversation with the intention of inviting readers to see how what they already understand and accept is in fact interactionist. And if we can find specific ways that an influential scholar's or the field's theorizing only partially or inconsistently employs an interactionist approach – even if just implicitly – we can then point that out and show how bringing interactionism in a more consistent manner enables us to say something new or useful about the topic. In addition, when a community of scholars implicitly or explicitly invoke a concept in noninteractionist ways (e.g. a psychoanalytic approach to emotion), we can explain not only how interactionists approach the concept differently but also demonstrate how taking an interactionist approach enables us to generate new understandings of the social processes or contexts they are invested in understanding. Using interactionism as a wedge in conceptual interventions is key to the critical interactionist project, but it can also be useful in bringing interactionism into virtually any substantive area where interactionism has gone underground or been forgotten, regardless if it focuses on power and inequality.

The aforementioned "wedge" strategy is precisely what my colleagues and I did in our recent paper analyzing how Trump supporters constructed aggrieved white selves (Schrock et al., 2022). We first positioned ourselves as interactionists grounded in Goffman's dramaturgy and pointed out how key scholars sometimes selectively appropriated interactionist concepts in inconsistent ways or otherwise conceptualized processes in noninteractionist ways. For example, Bonilla-Silva (2003) and other race scholars have selectively invoked the notion of self-presentation or identity work to frame interviewees' words that were inconsistent with their theorizing of racial discourse rather than consistently applying an identity work framework to make sense of the full range of interviewees' stories. Similarly, we showed how both critical race scholars and political scientists typically frame emotions as authentic internal experiences, contrary to a dramaturgical approach that often frames emotional expressions and discourse as resources for self-presentation. We also explained how interactionism sheds light on a key pillar of critical race theory – namely, that race is a social construct – and shared research on racial identity work. We then presented our analysis of Trump supporters' race talk – which typically othered African Americans and immigrants and signified fear, anger, and superiority – conceptualizing it as signifying aggrieved white selves. We also explained how such identity work resonated with what other critical race theorists call the politics of aggrieved whiteness, made the case that signifying aggrieved white selves is a generic process that could be examined among other groups, and adapted a classic Mead adage to make the point that racial selves and society are two sides of the same coin. Overall, we not only used interactionism as an interpretative wedge to contribute to critical race scholars' and political scientists' conversations but also showed how interactionism is a powerful analytic perspective that deserves a place in their scholarly communities.[6]

The point of such work is not just to promote interactionism or find one's way into print. Instead, it is useful – at least for me – to believe that such work is a service to members of a subfield and the larger discipline. By *showing* others what critical interactionism can contribute rather than trying to convince ourselves and others that interactionism *should* be considered relevant, we can hopefully get on with the sociological work that the world needs. Part of the promise of critical interactionism, as I see it, is wielding it to carry out such discursive interventions. Doing so necessarily involves engaging with what "unaware" or "non" interactionists are talking about and being explicit about how interactionism enables us to contribute. Accomplishing this also provides an invitation to others – who may have forgotten or denied their own interactionist proclivities – to join in. Of course, it's not just about "them" – those on the other side of the fault line; it is about the "us" who identify with and engage with interactionism. If interactionists themselves are not open to the existence of critical interactionism, the fault line may very well expand and ossify until the walling in of interactionism is complete.

DISCUSSION

I am not the first to offer up "critical interactionism" as a frame or label (see, e.g. Jacobsen, 2019), but I add here that we should consider critical interactionism a broad scholarly project akin to critical criminology. In contrast to critical criminology or other projects labeled for the topics they focus on (critical gender studies, critical race theory, etc.), critical interactionism has the potential to transcend subfields. We should consider critical interactionism a "big tent" that includes research and theorizing grounded in diverse interactionist approaches that address power and inequalities. I have sketched out a few types of theoretical interventions, including using critical insights from the "founders," diversifying who counts as founders, and integrating interactionism with critical theories, and research-based conceptual interventions, including analyzing how identity, emotion, and discourse are linked to the reproduction and challenging of inequalities.

If we develop, validate, and promote critical interactionism as a scholarly project, it can help us transcend the fault line of consciousness. The name of the project itself – critical interactionism – contradicts disciplinary stereotypes of interactionism as incapable of analyzing power and inequality. But critical interactionism has to be more than a label, marketing slogan, or a resource for virtue signaling. Interactionism, with its grounding in pragmatism, arguably provides us with the best conceptual tools to accurately make sense of the world as it exists. And because power and inequality exist in the social world, ignoring it because you believe you are not "that kind of sociologist" is to neglect our responsibilities as interactionists and as social scientists more generally.

I suppose some of you may worry, especially after reading that last sentence, that allowing critical interactionism to be seen as a valid scholarly project will create division among the interactionist-identified. I suppose anything is possible, but the opposite scenario worries me the most. Why? If interactionists are not inclusive enough to support critical inquiry, then it creates divisions and likely already has. If some interactionists accuse those developing critical interactionist analyses as "woke ideology," as reportedly occurred at a recent meeting, such gatekeeping fosters division. Under such conditions, scholars who are drawn to interactionism yet also want to address issues of inequality will likely just leave interactionist communities and find communities of inquiry that support their desires to ask critical questions. Interactionist communities will shrink and become more homogenous. If we instead validate and support critical interactionism, perhaps the opposite will occur: we can break down the walls, diversify interactionist communities and discourse, and reinsert explicit interactionism into our larger discipline, which has arguably increasingly welcomed critical inquiry.

Let me clarify one other point. Critical interactionism would likely not exist or be as analytically useful without interactionist research and theorizing on basic social processes surrounding temporality, embodiment, identity, framing, narratives, emotion, subcultures, organizations, etc. – regardless of whether such work focuses on inequality. Validating critical interactionism should not translate into invalidating efforts to analyze or conceptualize basic social processes, as that would amount to shooting ourselves in the foot. Just as it is not pragmatically useful to degrade those developing critical analyses as "woke," it is not useful to accuse those developing analyses of basic social processes as "asleep." It's also important to acknowledge that the social contexts or groups we study may vary widely with regard to how well they lend themselves to critical analyses. It is more important to keep our analyses grounded in the empirical world than it is to promote a critical perspective (although the two are not mutually exclusive).

On that note, I would like to explore one last question. Given the current political context, is it really wise to promote "critical interactionism?" Several state legislatures have been attacking academic freedom and working toward implementing the General Education Act. This sample legislation is designed by right-wing think tanks and aims to shrink academic departments and replace faculty with ideologues teaching new required general education courses (see, e.g. Schwalbe, 2023; Wilson, 2023). These courses, which would be approved by Governor-appointed boards that oversee state university policies, would orient students to accept – or at least not question – patriarchal, nationalist, white supremacist, heteronormative, and capitalist ideologies.

In the state where I reside, Principles of Sociology was recently removed from the list of courses that meet core general education requirements at all colleges and universities. The reason, as stated by our Commissioner of Education on social media: "Sociology has been hijacked by left-wing activists and no longer serves its intended purpose…Under @GovRonDeSantis, Florida's higher education system will focus on preparing students for high-demand, high-wage jobs, not woke ideology."[7] At the same meeting they banned the funding of positions, programs, and activities related to Diversity, Equity, and Inclusion. In addition, state law now defines "unlawful discrimination" on campus as including faculty speech that allegedly "espouses, advances, inculcates, or compels [a] student or employee to believe" eight different things surrounding "race, color, national origin, or sex" – most of which curtail thinking critically about such matters. Another law enables students to record faculty lectures and turn them in if they believe professors violate state-mandated speech codes.

Although our faculty union and others have been trying to fight many of these laws in court, another law – framed by our governor in an Orwellian fashion as protecting and empowering educators – aims to decertify faculty unions and thus nullify the protections in our labor contracts (see, e.g. Schueler, 2023). As I am writing this today, it is unclear if Florida faculty will have legally binding contracts by the time this paper is published. Regardless, state legislators have already all but eliminated tenure. In addition to our usual annual reviews, tenured faculty must now be reviewed every five years to assess not only our research, teaching, and service but also "unapproved absences," "student complaints," "any violation of" the previously mentioned speech codes, and "non-compliance with state law, Board of Governors' regulations, and university regulations and policies." The "chief academic officer" independently makes the final decision about whether tenured faculty are terminated or retained.[8]

Considering these political and bureaucratic conditions, it's reasonable to wonder if it is the right time to promote critical interactionism as a valid scholarly project. Although the current state of affairs is troubling, advocating for and employing critical interactionism amounts to exercising academic freedom. Having the freedom to ask questions, search for answers, and make sense of the information we gather is as critical for interactionists as it is for other academics and nonacademics alike. There are – and perhaps always have been and will be – actors who would like to restrict what we study, how we study it, how we make sense of what we find, and how we express it to others. Now is not the time to fall in line and retreat behind the fault line. Instead, we should develop critical interactionism as a form of inquiry that can, ideally, help us more clearly unpack the social processes that constitute such attacks and provide insights into how we might best intervene.

ACKNOWLEDGMENTS

The author thanks Hailey McGee and Madeleine Traylor for their analytic comments, bibliographic work, and editorial suggestions. The author also thanks members of the Society for Study of Symbolic Interaction and students in my graduate Social Interaction course for discussing the ideas presented in this paper.

NOTES

1. DeKersedy and Dragiewicz (2018) point out that what is now thought of as 'critical criminology' started out as "radical criminology" and focused on the links between capitalism and crime, but as critical perspectives grounded in feminism, critical race studies, postmodernism, etc. found their way into the field, its parameters became more inclusive. I see critical interactionism evolving in an analogous fashion.
2. Lonnie Athens (2013), for example, has written about his difficulties publishing and presenting his papers on radical interactionism in some traditional symbolic interactionist outlets and conferences.
3. T.R. Young wrote a series of articles and books promoting "critical dramaturgy" (see e.g., Young, 1990) and engaged in some community-building; he created the Red Feather Institute, which promoted the perspective, distributed writings and paper awards, and organized conferences with critical scholars. The critical criminology website critcrim.org still houses many of Young's Red Feather Institute's webpages. Norman Denzin, a founder of the Society for Study of Symbolic Interactionism, created a thriving organization, the International Association of Qualitative Inquiry, which promotes critical qualitative scholarship but not interactionism per se.
4. Although, as Ruiz-Junco and Vidal-Ortiz (2023, p. 316) note, DuBois did write the following in his autobiography: "William James guided me out of the sterilities of scholastic philosophies into realist pragmatism" (Du Bois, 1968/1997, p. 143).
5. These authors varied with regard to their optimism for integrating interactionism and critical theory; Langman suggested some interactionist theorizing may at best complement critical theory, whereas Welsh more optimistically explored a convergence.
6. Although we used interactionism to critique other scholarship and develop conceptualizations linked to critical race theory, we did not promote "critical interactionism" per se. In hindsight, it was a missed opportunity.
7. Manny Diaz Jr.'s tweet can be accessed here: https://twitter.com/CommMannyDiazJr/status/1733192839100568018.
8. The law, as implemented by the FL Board of Governor's regulation 10.003 Post Tenure Review, is available here: https://www.flbog.edu/wp-content/uploads/2022/11/Regulation-10.003.pdf.

REFERENCES

Anderson, K. L., & Umberson, D. (2001). Gendering violence: Masculinity and power in men's accounts of domestic violence. *Gender & Society*, *15*(3), 358–380.

Athens, L. (2007). Radical interactionism: Going beyond Mead. *Journal for the Theory of Social Behavior*, *37*(2), 137–165.

Athens, L. (2009). The roots of "radical interactionism". *Journal for the Theory of Social Behavior*, *39*(4), 387–414.

Athens, L. H. (2013). "Radical" and "symbolic" interactionism: Demarcating their borders. *Studies in Symbolic Interaction*, *41*, 1–24.
Barbee, H., & Schrock, D. (2019). Un/Gendering social selves: How nonbinary people navigate and experience a binarily gendered world. *Sociological Forum*, *34*(3), 572–593.
Becker, H. S. (1998). *Tricks of the trade: How to think about your research while you're doing it* (1st ed.). University of Chicago Press.
Blumer, H. (1969). *Symbolic interactionism: Perspective and method*. University of California Press.
Bonilla-Silva, E. (2003). *Racism without racists: Color-blind racism and the persistence of racial inequality in the United States*. Rowman & Littlefield Publishers.
Bonilla-Silva, E. (2019). Feeling race: Theorizing the racial economy of emotions. *American Sociological Review*, *84*(1), 1–25.
Browne, I., Tatum, K., & Gonzalez, B. (2021). Presumed Mexican until proven otherwise: Identity work and intersectional typicality among middle-class Dominican and Mexican immigrants. *Social Problems*, *68*(1), 80–99.
Cahill, S. E. (1999). Emotional capital and professional socialization: The case of mortuary science students (and me). *Social Psychology Quarterly*, *62*(2), 101–116.
Cahill, S. E., & Eggleston, R. (1994). Managing emotions in public: The case of wheelchair users. *Social Psychology Quarterly*, *57*(4), 300–312.
Charmaz, K. (2006). *Constructing grounded theory: A practical guide through qualitative analysis*. Sage.
Charmaz, K. (2017). The power of constructivist grounded theory for critical inquiry. *Qualitative Inquiry*, *23*(1), 34–45.
Clark, C. (1990). Emotions and micropolitics in everyday life: Some patterns and paradoxes of 'place'. In T. D. Kemper (Ed.), *Research agendas in the sociology of emotions* (pp. 305–333). State University of New York Press.
Clarke, A. E. (2003). Situational analyses: Grounded theory mapping after the postmodern turn. *Symbolic Interaction*, *26*(4), 553–576.
Clarke, A. E. (2019). Situational analysis as critical interactionist method. In *Critical and cultural interactionism: Insights from sociology and criminology* (pp. 189–209). Routledge.
Deegan, M. J. (1994). Bringing Dorothy Swaine Thomas back into "The Thomas Theorem". *Midwest Feminist Papers*, *4*, 3–7.
Deegan, M. J. (2002). The feminist pragmatism of Jane Addams (1860–1935). In M. R. Lewiston (Ed.), *Lost sociologists* (pp. 1–19). Edwin Mellen Press.
Deegan, M. J. (2003). Katharine Bement Davis (1860–1935). *Women & Criminal Justice*, *14*(2–3), 15–40.
Deegan, M. J. (2010). Jane Addams on citizenship in a democracy. *Journal of Classical Sociology*, *10*(3), 217–238.
DeKeseredy, W. S., & Dragiewicz, M. (2018). Critical criminology: Past, present, and future. In W.S. DeKeseredy & M. Dragiewicz (Eds.), *Routledge handbook of critical criminology* (2nd ed., pp. 1–12). Routledge.
Dennis, A., & Martin, P. J. (2005). Symbolic interactionism and the concept of power. *British Journal of Sociology*, *56*(2), 191–213.
Dennis, A., & Martin, P. J. (2007). Symbolic interactionism and the concept of social structure. *Sociological Focus*, *40*(3), 287–305.
Denzin, N. K. (1989). *Interpretive interactionism*. Sage.
Denzin, N. K. (1992). *Symbolic interactionism and cultural studies: The politics of interpretation*. Blackwell.
Denzin, N. K. (2002). *Screening race: Hollywood and a cinema of racial violence, 1980–1995*. Sage.
Denzin, N. K. (2019). A call to critical interpretive interactionism. In *Critical and cultural interactionism: Insights from sociology and criminology* (pp. 45–60). Routledge.
Du Bois, W. E. B. (1903). *The souls of black folk: Essays and sketches*. A.C. McClurg and Company.
Du Bois, W. E. B. (1920). *Darkwater: Voices from within the veil*. Washington Square Press.
Du Bois, W. E. B. (1968/1997). *The autobiography of W.E.B. Du Bois. A soliloquy of viewing my life from the last decade of its first century*. International Publishers.
Eastman, J. T., & Schrock, D. P. (2008). Southern rock musicians' construction of white trash. *Race, Gender, and Class*, *15*(1–2), 205–219.

Eliasoph, N., & Lichterman, P. (2003). Culture in interaction. *American Journal of Sociology*, *108*(4), 735–794.

Elliott, S., & Umberson, D. (2008). The Performance of desire: Gender and sexual negotiation in long-term marriages. *Journal of Marriage and Family*, *70*(2), 391–406.

Erichsen, K., Schrock, D., Dowd-Arrow, B., & Dignam, P. (2020). Bitchifying Hillary: Trump supporters' vilification of Clinton during the 2016 presidential election. *Social Currents*, *7*(6), 526–542.

Ezzell, M. B. (2009). "Barbie dolls" on the pitch: Identity work, defensive othering, and inequality in women's rugby. *Social Problems*, *56*(1), 111–131.

Fine, G. A. (1984). Negotiated orders and organizational cultures. *Annual Review of Sociology*, *1*, 239–262.

Fine, G. A. (1993). The sad demise, mysterious disappearance, and glorious triumph of symbolic interactionism. *Annual Review of Sociology*, *19*, 61–87.

Fine, G. A. (2021). *The hinge: Civil society, group cultures, and the power of local commitments*. University of Chicago Press.

Fine, G. A., & Kleinman, S. (1983). Network and meaning: An interactionist approach to structure. *Symbolic Interaction*, *6*(1), 97–110.

Fine, G. A., & Tavory, I. (2019). Interactionism in the twenty-first century. *Symbolic Interaction*, *42*(3), 457–467.

Froyum, C. M. (2010). The reproduction of inequalities through emotional capital: The case of socializing low-income black girls. *Qualitative Sociology*, *33*(1), 37–54.

Garfinkel, H. (1967). *Studies in ethnomethodology*. Prentice-Hall.

Goffman, E. (1959). *The presentation of self in everyday life*. Doubleday.

Green, A. (2011). Playing the (sexual) field: The interactional basis of systems of sexual stratification. *Social Psychology Quarterly*, *74*, 244–266.

Hall, P. M. (1985). Asymmetric relationships and processes of power. *Studies in Symbolic Interaction*, *1*, 309–344.

Hall, P. M. (1997). Meta-power, social organization, and the shaping of social action. *Symbolic Interaction*, *20*(4), 397–418.

Hall, P. M. (2003). Interactionism, social organization, and social processes: Looking back and moving ahead. *Symbolic Interaction*, *26*(1), 33–55.

Hochschild, A. R. (1983). *The managed heart: Commercialization of human feeling*. University of California Press.

Holden, D., & Schrock, D. (2007). "Get therapy and work on it": Managing dissent in an intentional community. *Symbolic Interaction*, *30*(2), 175–198.

Jacobsen, M. H. (2019). Introduction: The coming of critical and cultural interactionism. In *Critical and cultural interactionism: Insights from sociology and criminology* (pp. 1–9). Routledge.

Jasper, J. M. (2011). Emotions and social movements: Twenty years of theory and research. *Annual Review of Sociology*, *37*(1), 285–303.

Jaworski, G. D. (2023). *Erving Goffman and the Cold War*. Lexington Books.

Joas, H. (1992). An underestimated alternative: America and the limits of "critical theory". *Symbolic Interaction*, *15*(3), 261–275.

Kang, M. (2003). The managed hand: The commercialization of bodies and emotions in Korean immigrant-owned nail salons. *Gender & Society*, *17*(6), 820–839.

Katovich, M. A. (2003). Hall's hope and the focus next time: Let us now study social structure. *Symbolic Interaction*, *26*(1), 57–66.

Katovich, M. A. (2023). David Maines: The stranger who studied social structure. Festschrift in honor of David R. Maines. *Studies in Symbolic Interaction*, *57*, 9–20.

Kitzinger, C. (2000). Doing feminist conversation analysis. *Feminism & Psychology*, *10*(2), 163–193.

Kitzinger, C., & Frith, H. (1999). Just say no? The use of conversation analysis in developing a feminist perspective on sexual refusal. *Discourse & Society*, *10*(3), 293–316.

Kleinman, S. (2002). Why sexist language matters. *Qualitative Sociology*, *25*(2), 299–304.

Kleinman, S. (2007). *Feminist fieldwork analysis*. Sage.

Kleinman, S., & Cabaniss, E. (2019). Towards a feminist symbolic interactionism. In *Critical and cultural interactionism: Insights from sociology and criminology* (pp. 119–137). Routledge.

Kleinman, S., Ezzell, M. B., & Frost, A. C. (2009). Reclaiming critical analysis: The social harms of 'bitch'. *Sociological Analysis*, *3*(1), 46–68.

Langman, L. (2019). Symbolic interactionism and the Frankfurt School. In *Critical and cultural interactionism: Insights from sociology and criminology* (pp. 164–188). Routledge.

Lareau, A. (2021). *Listening to people: A practical guide to interviewing, participant observation, data analysis, and writing it all up*. The University of Chicago Press.

Lehn, V. D., Ruiz-Junco, N., & Gibson, W. J. (2021). *The Routledge international Handbook of interactionism* (1st ed.). Routledge.

Lofland, J., & Lofland, L. H. (1984). *Analyzing social settings: A guide to qualitative observation and analysis* (2nd ed.). Wadsworth Publishing.

Low, J., & Thomson, L. (2021). Symbolic interactionism and the myth of a structural bias: A textual defense and illustrative advice. *Canadian Journal of Sociology*, *46*(2), 97–119.

Luckenbill, D. F. (1979). Power: A conceptual framework. *Symbolic Interaction*, *2*(2), 97–114.

Lyman, S. M. (1984). Interactionism and the study of race relations at the macro sociological level: The contribution of Herbert Blumer. *Symbolic Interaction*, *7*(1), 107–120.

Maines, D. R. (1977). Social organization and social structure in symbolic interactionist thought. *Annual Review of Sociology*, *3*(1), 235–259.

Maines, D. R. (1982). In search of mesostructure: Studies in the Negotiated order. *Urban Life*, *11*(3), 267–279.

Maines, D. R. (2001). *The faultline of consciousness: A view of interactionism in sociology*. Routledge.

Maines, D. R. (2003). Interactionism's place. *Symbolic Interaction*, *26*(1), 5–18.

Maines, D. R., & Morrione, T. J. (1991). Social causation and interpretive processes: Herbert Blumer's theory of industrialization and social change. *International Journal of Politics, Culture, and Society*, *4*(4), 535–547.

McGinty, P. J. W. (2014). Divided and drifting: Interactionism and the neglect of social organizational analyses in organization studies. *Symbolic Interaction*, *37*(2), 155–186.

McQueeney, K. (2009). We are god's children, y'all:" Race, gender, and sexuality in lesbian-and gay-affirming congregations. *Social Problems*, *56*(1), 151–173.

Mead, G. H. (1918). The psychology of punitive justice. *American Journal of Sociology*, *23*(5), 577–602.

Morris, A. (2015). *The scholar denied: W. E. B. Du Bois and the birth of modern sociology*. University of California Press.

Muller, N. L. (1992). Du Boisian pragmatism and "the problem of the twentieth century". *Critique of Anthropology*, *12*(3), 319–337.

Neeley, E., & Deegan, M. J. (2005). George Herbert Mead on punitive justice: A critical analysis of contemporary practices. *Humanity & Society*, *29*(1), 71–83.

Polletta, F., & Jasper, J. M. (2001). Collective identity and social movements. *Annual Review of Sociology*, *27*(1), 283–305.

Prus, R. (1999). Beyond the power mystic: Power as intersubjective accomplishment.

Rawls, A. W. (2000). Race as an interaction order phenomena: W.E.B. DuBois's 'double consciousness' thesis revisited. *Sociological Theory*, *18*(2), 239–272.

Reynolds, L. T., & Janice, M. (1973). Interactionism, complicity, and astructural bias. *Catalyst*, *7*, 76–85.

Roscigno, V. J. (2007). *The face of discrimination how race and gender impact work and home lives*. Rowman & Littlefield Publishers.

Ruiz-Junco, N., & Vidal-Ortiz, S. (2023). W. E. B. Du Bois as Interactionist: Reflections on the canonical incorporation of a marginalized scholar. *Symbolic Interaction*, *46*(3), 332–348.

Rynbrandt, L. J., & Deegan, M. J. (2002). The ecofeminist pragmatism of Caroline Bartlett Crane, 1896–1935. *The American Sociologist*, *33*(3), 58–68.

Schrock, D., Buggs, S. G., Buyukozturk, B., Erichsen, K., & Ivey, A. (2022). Signifying aggrieved white selves: Trump supporters' racial identity work. *Sociology of Race and Ethnicity*, *8*(1), 114–128.

Schrock, D., McCabe, J., & Vaccaro, C. (2018). Narrative manhood acts: Batterer intervention program graduates' tragic relationships. *Symbolic Interaction*, *41*(3), 384–410.

Schrock, D. P., & Reid, L. L. (2006). Transsexuals' sexual stories. *Archives of Sexual Behavior*, *35*(1), 75–86.
Schrock, D., Reid, L., & Boyd, E. M. (2005). Transsexuals' embodiment of womanhood. *Gender & Society*, *19*(3), 317–335.
Schrock, D., & Schwalbe, M. (2009). Men, masculinity, and manhood acts. *Annual Review of Sociology*, *35*(1), 277–295.
Schrock, D., Sumerau, J., & Ueno, K. (2015). Sexualities. In J. McLeod, E. Lawler, & M. Schwalbe (Eds.), *The Handbook of the social psychology of inequality* (pp. 447–464). Springer.
Schueler, M. (2023). Florida Gov. Ron DeSantis signs anti-union bill into law, calling it 'paycheck protection'. *Orlando Weekly*. https://www.orlandoweekly.com/news/florida-gov-ron-desantis-signs-anti-union-bill-into-law-calling-it-paycheck-protection-34156024. Accessed on January 31, 2024.
Schwalbe, M. L. (2016). Overcoming procedural bias in the study of inequality: Parsing the capitalist interaction order. *Studies in Symbolic Interaction*, *46*, 95–122.
Schwalbe, M. L. (2019a). The spirit of Blumer's method as a guide to sociological discovery. *Symbolic Interaction*, *43*(4), 597–614.
Schwalbe, M. L. (2019b). Upscaling Goffman: Four principles of neostructural interactionism. In *Critical and cultural interactionism: Insights from sociology and criminology* (pp. 30–44). Routledge.
Schwalbe, M. L. (2023). Destroying the university to save it. *CounterPunch.Org*. https://www.counterpunch.org/2023/12/01/destroying-the-university-to-save-it/. Accessed on January 31, 2024.
Schwalbe, M., Godwin, S., Holden, D., Schrock, D., Thompson, S., & Wolkomir, M. (2000). Generic processes in the reproduction of inequality: An interactionist analysis. *Social Forces*, *79*(2), 419–452.
Schwalbe, M. L., & Mason-Schrock, D. (1996). Identity work as group process. In B. Markovsky, M. Lovaglia, & R. Simon (Eds.), *Advances in group processes* (pp. 113–147). JAI.
Schwalbe, M. L., & Mischke, K. (2021). Power and interaction. In W. H. Brekhus, T. DeGloma, & W. R. Force. (Eds.), *The Oxford handbook of symbolic interactionism* (pp. 368–385). Oxford University Press.
Scully, D., & Marolla, J. (1984). Convicted rapists' vocabulary of motive: Excuses and justifications. *Social Problems*, *31*(5), 530–544.
Shalin, D. N. (1992). Critical theory and the pragmatist challenge. *American Journal of Sociology*, *98*(2), 237–279.
Simon, R. W., Eder, D., & Evans, C. (1992). The development of feeling norms underlying romantic love among adolescent females. *Social Psychology Quarterly*, *55*(1), 29–46.
Snow, D. A., & Anderson, L. (1987). Identity work among the homeless: The verbal construction and avowal of personal identities. *American Journal of Sociology*, *92*(6), 1336–1371.
Strauss, A. L. (1978). *Negotiations: Varieties, contexts, processes, and social order*. Jossey- Bass.
Strauss, A. L. (1993). *Continual permutations of action*. Aldine de Gruyter. SUNY Press.
Sweet, P. L. (2019). The sociology of gaslighting. *American Sociological Review*, *84*(5), 851–875.
Tavory, I., & Timmermans, S. (2014). *Abductive analysis: Theorizing qualitative research*. University of Chicago Press.
Taylor, P. C. (2004). What's the use of calling Du Bois a pragmatist? *Metaphilosophy*, *35*(1–2), 99–114.
Taylor, M. J., & Bernstein, M. (2019). Denial, deflection, and distraction: Neutralizing charges of racism by the tea party movement. *Mobilization: An International Quarterly*, *24*(2), 137–156.
Vaccaro, C. A., Schrock, D. P., & McCabe, J. M. (2011). Managing emotional manhood: Fighting and fostering fear in mixed martial arts. *Social Psychology Quarterly*, *74*(4), 414–437.
vom Lehn, D., Ruiz-Junco, N., & Gibson, W. (2021). *The Routledge international handbook of interactionism*. Routledge.
Watson, G., & Goulet, J. (1998). What can ethnomethodology say about power? *Qualitative Sociology*, *4*(1), 96–113.
Weiss, R. S. (1994). *Learning from strangers: The art and method of qualitative interview studies*. Free Press.

Welsh, J. F. (1984). The presentation of self in capitalist society: Alienated consumption as a social source of impression management. *Quarterly Journal of Ideology*, *8*(2), 23–38.

West, C., & Zimmerman, D. H. (1987). Doing gender. *Gender & Society*, *1*(2), 125–151.

Wilkins, A. C. (2012). Stigma and status: Interracial intimacy and intersectional identities among black college men. *Gender & Society*, *26*(2), 165–189.

Wilson, J. K. (2023). The right-wing attack on academia, with a totalitarian twist. *Inside Higher Ed.* https://www.insidehighered.com/opinion/views/2023/11/16/new-front-right-wing-attack-academia-opinion. Accessed on January 31, 2024.

Wingfield, A. H. (2010). Are some emotions marked 'whites only'? Racialized feeling rules in professional workplaces. *Social Problems*, *57*(2), 251–268.

Young, T. R. (1990). *The drama of social life: Essays in post-modern social psychology*. Routledge.

Young, T. R., & Massey, G. (1978). The dramaturgical society: A macro-analytic approach to dramaturgical analysis. *Qualitative Sociology*, *1*(2), 78–98.

Zimmerman, D. H., & West, C. (1975). Sex roles, interruptions and silences in conversation. In *Language and sex: Difference and dominance* (pp. 105–129). Newbury House.

INTERSUBJECTIVITY AND COLLECTIVE INTENTIONALITY IN SYMBOLIC INTERACTIONISM: RECOVERING GERDA WALTHER'S COLLECTIVE TURN

Zeynep Melis Kirgil[a], Andrea Voyer[b] and Gary Alan Fine[c]

[a]*Tilburg University, Netherlands*
[b]*Stockholm University, Sweden*
[c]*Northwestern University, USA*

ABSTRACT

In this essay on new directions in symbolic interaction, the authors have two related goals. First, the authors argue for the relevance of collective intentionality for overcoming the critical divide in symbolic interaction theory between self and society. In focusing on the way in which collective intentionality allows for understanding how intersubjectivity is made part of the interaction order by group members and local communities, the mesolevel of analysis should be integrated into the interactionist perspective. In making this argument, the second goal is to uncover the important social phenomenology of the early 20th German philosopher, Gerda Walther, which raised similar issues. Perhaps because of her gender, the lack of a secure university position, the financial reserves of her family, or a personal turn to mysticism, her early work has largely been erased. Today her significance and her important 1922 work, A Contribution to the Ontology of Social Communities, *is being recovered, published last year (Walther, 2023). Here we highlight her relevance for the interactionist tradition and its approach to intersubjectivity.*

Keywords: Collective intentionality; intersubjectivity; Gerda Walther; symbolic interactionism; phenomenology

Essential Issues in Symbolic Interaction
Studies in Symbolic Interaction, Volume 59, 165–174

ISSN: 0163-2396/doi:10.1108/S0163-239620240000059009

INTRODUCTION

Most varieties of symbolic interactionism have emphasized the centrality of meaning-making and interpretation as shaping the choices of the individual social self. This has been taken as being at the heart of the theory. For this reason, symbolic interaction has typically been treated as a social psychological, microsociological approach. *Individual subjectivity*, including constructs such as self-concept, role, and identity, is central in symbolic interactionism. We argue for an extension of this epistemic individualism to incorporate the collective grounds on which the perspective rightly depends. Even given that symbolic interaction, in its Meadian roots, focuses on "Mind, Self, *and* Society," the significance of group and the community is often underdeveloped, merely treated as the background in which individuals' subjective action unfolds. However, symbolic interaction must be a group-oriented perspective (Fine & Hallett, 2022) that recognizes the salience of collectivity as an organizing principle through shared meanings that stand beyond the mind and the self and within the purview of society. The recognition that people think and plan together properly belongs in the center of the interactionist enterprise (Besbris & Fine, 2023). Indeed, impression management, negotiation, and framing are practices that depend upon the recognition and the embrace of sociality.

In this essay, we call for a collective turn that incorporates *intersubjectivity* into the analytic framework of symbolic interactionism. To this end, we argue for the value of collective intentionality, a philosophical concept that emphasizes shared cognition of social action, an approach that currently draws on a stream of contemporary philosophy reflected in the writings of Raimo Tuomela, Margaret Gilbert, John Searle, and Michael Bratman. However, as significant as the current analysis is, our attempt is to go back further, recovering for interactionist attention the social phenomenology of the early 20th century philosopher Gerda Walther, a largely forgotten student of Edmund Husserl who addressed many of the communal elements that we find important in understanding intersubjectivity. We argue that Walther's presentation of collective intentionality solves persistent theoretical puzzles in symbolic interactionism, notably the challenge of accounting for the social grounds of individual subjectivity and the challenge of accounting for a self that is developed through performance and shared routines.

Collective intentionality emphasizes the centrality of *we-thinking and we-doing* as an independent and influential domain of action. This understanding is consistent with symbolic interactionism's view that human behavior unfolds through active social processes of interpretation and meaning-making. However, collective intentionality also highlights that human behavior is not only relational, but it is also group-based and dependent on sociality, which makes it interpretable through an emphasis on the mesolevel of analysis. Shared goals, shared meanings, and collective practices dynamically evolve within groups (Kirgil & Wittek, 2023) – through we-experiences – either intentionally or not, creating a sense of the self as belonging to the group and equally as the group as belonging to the self. As a result, group practices are defined through their normativity – a tendency to act in accordance with collective meanings (Voyer, 2023) that explains how communal solidarity is built. Our fundamental argument is that individuals do not just conceptualize their world and act based on an understanding of themselves as individuals, treated as an isolated and distinct "self" in relationship to "others." In contrast, they act on the presumption of themselves as part of a meaningful and recognizable "us." The world depends on we-making. This collective intentionality lies at the heart of the creation of meaning and social action (Kirgil, 2023).

To make this argument, we emphasize the concept of collective intentionality as central to how our approach should develop its understanding of self and society. We then show how collective intentionality solves some persistent challenges of symbolic interactionism. Many interactionist theories attempt to account for the intersubjectivity of people through the internalizations of "others" (namely, Mead's "me," Cooley's "looking glass self," and Goffman's "impression management"), but each lacks a focus on the significance of "us." Collective intentionality serves as a solution to the persistent problem of presentism and contextualism, recognizing its synergy with contemporary symbolic interactionist research. We conclude by charting a path forward for symbolic interactionism considering a collective turn, drawing on the neglected and largely unknown social phenomenology of Gerda Walther.

GERDA WALTHER AND THE SALIENCE OF COLLECTIVE INTENTIONALITY

Collective intentionality has fascinated scholars across multiple disciplines as it sheds light on action and solidarity (Kirgil, 2023), describing "the power of minds to be jointly directed at objects, matters of fact, states of affairs, goals, or values" (Schweikard & Schmid, 2013, p. 1). Put differently, this means engaging in *we-thinking* and *we-acting* while identifying with the collective. Although collective intentionality can be said to have originated in Durkheim's (1895/1960) sociological concept of collective consciousness, it subsequently was expanded within the domain of philosophical phenomenology through the insightful, if unexplored, writing of Gerda Walther (1922; Parker, 2017). Walther, like many early female philosophers, has been marginalized and largely forgotten, but our goal in this essay is to demonstrate her significance – and that of collective intentionality – for symbolic interaction theory.

Who was Gerda Walther? Gerda Walther (1897–1977) was born to an important German lung specialist, Otto Walther, in Nordrach in Schwarzwald, Germany, and raised as an atheist (Walther, 1922). The writings of Marx and Engels, among others, sparked Walther's (1922) interest in social phenomena and the analysis of individuals within communities early on in her life. From 1915 to 1917, Walther (1922) pursued her academic interests and studied economics, economic history, constitutional law, philosophy, and psychology at the Ludwig Maximilian University of Munich where she attended lectures with Max Weber, among others. In Munich, she became interested in the writings of the prominent phenomenologist Edmund Husserl, and in 1917 moved to Albert Ludwigs-University in Freiburg to hear his lectures, along with those of Martin Heidegger and other influential philosophers. In Freiburg, she became deeply involved in the phenomenological community and presented the inaugural lecture at the Freiburger Phänomenologische Gesellschaft in 1918. Returning to Munich to finish her studies, Walther began to focus on the phenomenology of social communities, a creative approach that she developed largely on her own and where she received her PhD summa cum laude. She then moved to Heidelburg to study with Karl Jaspers, but a collapse in her family finances in the hyperinflation in Germany in the early 1920s prevented the continuation of her studies. She continued to write, often on topics of parapsychology from a phenomenological perspective.[1]

Despite her role in the development of phenomenology, Gerda Walther's work on collective intentionality and social community has been largely forgotten. Perhaps this is because of her gender or perhaps because later in her career she moved from core philosophical topics to embrace a phenomenological mysticism. In the meantime, a rich research tradition in philosophy over the past three decades has developed the concept of collective intentionality (Elder-Vass, 2015) by mostly addressing the dualistic nature of action by examining how and when collective intentions differ from aggregations of individual intentions (Zahavi, 2023). The theoretical analysis of John Searle (1990, 1995), Michael Bratman (1999), Margaret Gilbert (1989, 2014), and Raimo Tuomela (2007, 2013), and a body of contemporary writing in philosophy has focused on action-oriented collective intentions (Zahavi, 2023). In contrast, Walther's focus on collective intentionality as we-experiences in the community has received little attention.

While there is much to say about this more recent philosophical tradition, in this brief essay our goal is to recover Gerda Walther's phenomenological work on communal engagement. Our aim is to show how a persistent theoretical puzzle in symbolic interactionism – the challenge of accounting for the social grounds of individual subjectivity – can be addressed through the concept of collective intentionality.

GERDA WALTHER: COLLECTIVE INTENTIONALITY AND SOCIAL COMMUNITY

Gerda Walther's (1922) most significant potential contribution to symbolic interaction theory was her development of a phenomenological account of collective intentionality, seeing what is often treated as an internal phenomenon as being truly social and group based (Kirgil, 2023). In her doctoral dissertation "Ein Beitrag zur Ontologie der sozialen Gemeinschaft," Walther (1922) argues that collective intentionality – "the living experience of a profound similarity and unity of mind with another" (Calcagno, 2012, p. 91) or, in other words, the consciousness as mental state of shared oneness among community members (*Einigung*; Walther, 1922, p. 132) – provides for we-experiences and social community.

The Noetic Quality of (I-)experiences

Walther's (1922) phenomenological work begins with an analytical distinction between two dimensions that run parallel to each other: the *noetic dimension* with a focus on individual experiences and the *noematic dimension* focusing on collective experiences. These are concepts that we bring into symbolic interactionist theorizing. A noetic dimension describes individuals' *subjective* experiences, addressing the experiential elements of lived experiences (*how I experience or feel*; Walther, 1922, p. 10). The noetic analysis focuses both on the study of (i) individual experiences currently experienced by the individual (*aktuelle noetliche Analyse*) and (ii) experiences that are expressed through emotions (*noetliche Hintergrundsanalyse*; Walther, 1922, p. 11). Following Walther (1922), the noetic analysis is concerned with all matters related to the individual experience. Moreover, an individual's consciousness is constituted by the three elements of the (i) experiential I-center (*erlebendes Ichzentrum*), (ii) self (*Selbst*), and (iii) basic essence (*Grundwesen*; Walther, 1922, p. 56). The experiential I-center presents the center stage of experiences (*Vordergrundwissen*), describing the pure awareness of an individual who consciously experiences her current surroundings (Walther, 1922, p. 11). The I-center is embedded within the self, which is operating in the background or in the subconscious (*Hintergrundbewusstsein*) and is concerned with inner perception and sensations (Walther, 1922, p. 15). For example, the self can describe an individual's identity, history, or memory (Calcagno, 2012). In contrast to the I-center and the self, the basic essence refers to the metaphysical nature of individuals, an overarching "sense or meaning of what is it to be a subject that is an I-center as well as a self" (Calcagno, 2012, p. 94). To illustrate, Walther (1922) compares the different elements of an individual's consciousness with the process of generating light (*I-center*), which is either achieved through the wires (*self*) or another source of power (*basic essence*; Walther, 1922, p. 71). The self in this model stands outside the "I-center" but is necessary for the inner perceptions of the experiential I-center. In general, I-experiences can be assessed through their noetic quality (Walther, 1922, p. 16). For example, through a noetic analysis, I-experiences can be perceived differently by the different elements of the individual consciousness. The I-center can capture the quality of the light or its warmth (i.e. I-experiences through the I-center) while the basic essence perceives experiences through pure intuition on how certain experience relate to its metaphysical nature (Walther, 1922, p. 16). Individuals' experiences can be both intentional (i.e. active) and nonintentional (i.e. passive): Active through the recognition of intentional consciousness and passive through the reverberation of one's habitus. However, for we-experiences and communal life to emerge, individuals must be in an intentional state of consciousness. In other words, the individual's consciousness is the basis for the development of a collective consciousness.

The Noematic Object of (We-)experiences

Besides the noetic analysis of I-experiences and individual consciousness, a noematic dimension refers to we-experiences that are *directed at a shared object* (Walther, 1922). In other words, experiences that are grounded in a shared image that is held by group members. This is the core of how Walther contributes to solving the interactionist project. These experiences represent the *communal conscious* or *oneness* (Walther, 1922, p. 10), recognizing that although we each have individual perceptions, we-experiences are fundamentally collective and group based in nature that can be joined through common culture, socialization and habitus. From a noematic perspective, the object of a shared intentional consciousness can either be an idea of the community itself or the objects that members of a community share (Calcagno, 2012, p. 93). For instance, it constitutes "what 'we' as a community either intend about ourselves or what we do, think, believe, feel, doubt etc." (Calcagno, 2012, p. 94). In her formulation, communal or community consciousness emerges through the interaction between two connected individuals or group members (*Wechselwirkung*) when individuals' consciousness are directed at a shared intentional object held by the community (Walther, 1922, p. 132). To illustrate, Walther (1922) compares the interaction process (*Wechselwirkung*) between two individuals with the fusion of two lamps through the wires (the self) into the shared new light (the experiential I-center). This example emphasizes the interaction process of we-experiences as a distinct social fact. Although we-experiences are inevitably situated in individual intentions, we-experiences do not comprise a simple reflection or extension of I-experiences originating from the self and the I-center nor are they simply an additive summation of experiences through a shared I-center (Walther, 1922, p. 70). Instead, experiences arise in the self and then are translated into the I-center (Walther, 1922). For we-experiences to emerge, the self cannot merely describe "me as myself" but requires the *intentional internalization* of others into the self and the I-center, which comprise a feeling of oneness (Walther, 1922, p. 71).

In sum, Walther conceptually distinguishes communal from individual consciousness as two dimensions, with an emphasis on the former as the basis of her phenomenological approach. This highlights the parallel qualities of the noetic and noematic analysis of experiences. For *we-experiences* and *community life* to emerge, a set of social and group-based premises are required: that is, both parties' experiences must be focused on a shared intentional object in which A must empathize with B's experience and vice versa. Furthermore, there must be a mutual sense of oneness in considering each other's expectations and experiences (Kirgil, 2023, p. 6; Walther, 1922, p. 85). With her phenomenological analysis of we-experiences and community life, Walther has proposed a groundbreaking theoretical framework of collective intentionality that moves beyond the action-oriented duality of individual and collective intentions, highlighting the importance of the symbolic meaning and group boundaries of the imagined "we." Her phenomenological account of collective intentions and community life both enhances existing theories in philosophy and advances symbolic interactionism.

INTERSUBJECTIVITY AND THE INTERNALIZATION OF "OTHERS"

A central element in interactionist theory attempts to account for the intersubjectivity of people through internalizations of "others." Returning to our earlier point, we see this in Mead's "me," Cooley's "looking glass self," and Goffman's "impression management." However, these influential constructs downplay a recognition of the salience of "us." They are largely rooted in the individual actor who gazes at the world judging its effects on selfhood, even considering how that self will be seen and engaged with but ignoring the importance of communities together. The challenge for interactionist sociologists is to find a way to move beyond subjectivity. To achieve this, "others" must always play a consequential and shaping role in symbolic interactionism. In fact, Mead opposed grounding social explanation in the other worldliness of reason and instead prioritizes the social over the individual, a point that is especially clear in his examination of the past ("the past is what must have been before it is present in experience as a past") (Mead, 1929, p. 238). However much we might wish to claim that the past is constructed by subjective assertions alone, there is an obdurate reality in which the presence of events shapes the present. The same might be said of the self, that like the past is constrained by events that led to its development. Both self and society necessarily begin with interaction, given that behavior is generated by how it is observed and understood by others, that is, how it relates to communal meaning with language playing a crucial part. The transformation of the biologic individual into the thinking individual occurs through symbolic systems of signification. Through interactions with others, the individual becomes self-aware. The self develops continuously through interactions and the accumulation of experience over time, as awareness and reflection lead the self to become an "object to itself" (Mead (1934, p. 18), supporting the possibility of collective intentionality. The individual reads the situation as both self and other and responds after considering both roles. Mead brings the social context into the self through the development of this implicit objectivity:

> The individual possesses a self only in relation to the selves of the other members of his social group; and the structure of his self expresses or reflects the general behavior pattern of this social group to which he belongs, just as does the structure of the self of every other individual belonging to this social group. (Mead, 1934, p. 164)

For Mead, the individual self remains the locus of action and intention, and the group or community influences the individual by shaping the self, instead of by providing an alternative collective "structure" of perception and intention. The self from the perspective of both Mead and Walther is linked to temporal processes in which the past channels a present self as well as a future one. This constitutes an ongoing process of development dependent on shared agreements.

Cooley's (1902) concept of the "looking-glass self" makes social interactions with others crucial to the development of the individual self and to individual action as well. In close parallel with the analysis of Mead, the looking-glass self consists of how individuals envision and interpret the ways that they are seen by others, with these imaginings becoming the basis for self-evaluations and self-perception. These imaginings must have a basis in reality, deriving from experience as filtered through individual subjectivity. However, while the looking-glass self considers the collective evaluations and judgments of a particular social group or society, there is no place in the theory for intrasubjectivity: the collective others remain others, not part of "we." Such an emphasis has potential parallels with the work of Walther, developed during the same period, even if the idea of "we-ness" is not fully developed.

Despite the significance of others and their social context, symbolic interaction has largely been shaped by a persistent self/other duality. As such, symbolic interactionism does not explicitly propose a concept of we-thinking that is similar to collective intentionality. Instead, the perspective has focused on the microlevel interactions between individuals and how they construct meaning through the symbolic interpretation of social interactions. While the interactionist perspective accounts for collectivity by recognizing the role of shared meanings and understandings of social groups that are able to influence individuals, this does not incorporate a sense of we-ness, crucial to the development of shared intentions (Wohl & Fine, 2015). Furthermore, as noted, individuals engage in social interactions and communicate through shared symbols, such as language, gestures, and other forms of nonverbal communication, which depend on this belief in we-ness and carry baseline collective commitments that shape action (Voyer, 2023). Through these interactions, individuals negotiate worlds of meaning that shape their thoughts and interpretations of the interactional surround. However – and crucially – these shared meanings are not necessarily indicative of we-thinking in the sense of a unified, cohesive intentionality constituted at the level of the group. From the limited interactionist view, individuals interpret and assign meaning to symbols based on their own personal subjective experiences, social contexts, and the interactions in which they engage. Therefore, according to the symbolic interactionist perspective while individuals within a group share some common identities, understandings, and interpretations, it is ultimately their unique experiences and individual agency that determine their behavior. However, as we have pointed out, this limits the recognition of how a collective sensibility develops. To overcome the self/other duality, drawing on Walther's social phenomenology, we have proposed emphasizing the importance of collective intentionality for symbolic interactionist research.

CONCLUSION

Incorporating Walther's analysis of communal consciousness and we-experiences through oneness helps to overcome the epistemic individualism in symbolic interactionism and brings *intersubjectivity* into its analytical framework. This view emphasizes the importance of recognizing oneself as part of a community, finding that participating in a group culture solidifies the linkage between self and society, perhaps altering Mead's title to Self, Group, and Society. It is the recognition of collective belonging that provides the hinge between the individual and the institution through shared commitments, operating on the local level (Fine, 2021). Ultimately, sociology is a discipline in which action must be central, and the centrality of action arising from the recognition of an interaction order (Goffman, 1983) reminds us that those core elements of the sociological discipline such as power, status, role, change, and organization depend on people doing things together (Becker, 1986) and figuring out how that collaboration becomes possible. When it comes to understanding action, the contribution of we-thinking and we-doing relative to the contribution if I-thinking and doing is an empirical question. The answer – or at least part of it – relies on Walther's insight that one's understanding of the enveloping world is never one's alone but is possible because we respond to that surround as a place in which we's operate. This insight helps to resolve symbolic interaction's self/other problem, even if it comes a century after Gerda Walther pointed the way.

NOTE

1. Data for this biographical section primarily come from the website: https://historyofwomenphilosophers.org/project/directory-of-women-philosophers/walther-gerda-1897-1977/

REFERENCES

Becker, H. (1986). *Doing things together*. Northwestern University Press.

Besbris, M., & Fine, G. A. (2023). Planning as social practice: The formation and blockage of competitive futures in tournament chess, homebuying, and political organizing. *Theory and Society*, *52*(6), 1125–1148.

Bratman, M. (1999). *Faces of intention*. Cambridge University Press.

Calcagno, A. (2012). Gerda Walther: On the possibility of a passive sense of community and the inner time consciousness of community. *Symposium*, *16*(2), 89–105.

Cooley, C. H. (1902). *Human nature and the social order*. Charles Scribner's.

Durkheim, É. (1960). *The division of labor in society* (Trans. George Simpson). Free Press.

Elder-Vass, D. (2015). Collective intentionality and causal powers. *Journal of Social Ontology*, *1*(2), 251–269.

Fine, G. A. (2021). *The Hinge: Civil society, group cultures, and the power of local commitments*. University of Chicago Press.

Fine, G. A., & Hallett, T. (2022). *Group life: An invitation to local sociology*. Polity.

Gilbert, M. (1989). *On social facts*. Routledge.

Gilbert, M. (2014). *Joint commitment: How we make the social world*. Oxford University Press.

Goffman, E. (1983). The interaction order. *American Sociological Review*, *48*(1), 1–17.

Kirgil, Z. M. (2023). *Collective intentionality and solidarity: A multi-methodological investigation of how collective intentionality shapes solidarity on different levels of analysis*. PhD diss., Department of Sociology. Stockholm University. https://www.diva-portal.org/smash/record.jsf?pid=diva2%3A1756035&dswid=-3318

Kirgil, Z. M., & Wittek, R. (2023). Cooperation sustainability in small groups: Exogenous and endogenous dynamics of the sustainability of cooperation. *Rationality and Society*. https://doi.org/10.1177/10434631231209832

Mead, G. H. (1929). The nature of the past. In J. Coss (Ed.), *Essays in Honor of John Dewey* (pp. 235–242). Henry Holt.

Mead, G. H. (1934). *Mind, self, and society from the standpoint of a social behaviorist*. University of Chicago Press.

Parker, R. (2017). Gerda Walther and the phenomenological community. *Acta Mexicana de Fenomenologia: Revista de Investigacion Filosofica y Cientifica*, *2*, 43–64.

Schweikard, D. P., & Schmid, H. B. (2013). Collective intentionality. In E. N. Zalta (Ed.), *The Stanford encyclopedia of philosophy*. Stanford University Press.

Searle, J. (1990). Collective intentions and actions. In P. Cohen, J. Morgan, & M. Pollack (Eds.), *Intentions in communication*. MIT Press.

Searle, J. (1995). *The construction of social reality*. Free Press.

Tuomela, R. (2007). *The philosophy of sociality. The shared point of view*. Oxford University Press.

Tuomela, R. (2013). *Social ontology: Collective intentionality and group agents*. Oxford University Press.

Voyer, A. (2023). Culture, cognition, and the normativity of meaning. *SocArXiv*. https://osf.io/preprints/socarxiv/qe895

Walther, G. (1922). Zur Ontologie der Sozialen Gemeinschaften. *Jahrbuch für Philosophie und Phänomenologische Forschung*, *6*, 1–158.

Walther, G. (2023). *Toward an Ontology of social communities*. De Gruyter.

Wohl, H., & Fine, G. A. (2015). The art of together: Social coordination as dyadic achievement. In E. Lawler, S. Thye, & J. Yoon (Eds.), *Order on the edge of chaos: Social psychology and the problem of social order* (pp. 248–267). Cambridge University Press.

Zahavi, D. (2023). I, you, and we: Beyond individualism and collectivism. *Australasian Philosophical Review*, 1–18.

INDEX

Printed and bound by CPI Group (UK) Ltd, Croydon, CR0 4YY

28/11/2024

14601924-0001